Finding Facts

Finding Facts

Interviewing, Observing, Using Reference Sources

William L. Rivers
Stanford University

Prentice-Hall, Inc., Englewood Cliffs, New Jersey

Library of Congress Cataloging in Publication Data

RIVERS, WILLIAM L

Finding facts.

Includes bibliographical references and index.

1. Authorship—Handbooks, manuals, etc. 2. Research—Handbooks, manuals, etc. I. Title.

PN146.58 808′.02 74-23991

ISBN 0-13-316372-5

ISBN 0-13-316364-4 pbk.

10 9 8 7 6 5 4

Printed in the United States of America

Prentice-Hall International, Inc., *London*
Prentice-Hall of Australia, Pty. Ltd., *Sydney*
Prentice-Hall of Canada, Ltd., *Toronto*
Prentice-Hall of India Private Limited, *New Delhi*
Prentice-Hall of Japan, Inc., *Tokyo*

FOR WILBUR SCHRAMM
with respect, admiration, and affection

Contents

Preface

When I first taught Freshman English twenty years ago, I assigned my students to write about what they had read and thought and what they were then reading. The assignments were similar to those I had received as a freshman: write about something out of your memory or something out of a book. Although I never descended to requiring themes such as "What I Did Last Summer," the topics were not much more imaginative.

While teaching Freshman English so badly, I taught a course in journalism a bit more adeptly. At least I sent these students out to interview interesting people, to observe important events, and to write about both. But that was far from good teaching. Although I had worked as a journalist and was thus able to offer scraps of useful advice, my instructions added up to little more than: I have related some of my experiences; go and do likewise.

All this astonishes me now. While teaching those courses, I was completing a Ph.D. in political science by spending each summer in Washington, D.C., working on a dissertation titled "The Washington Correspondents and Government Information" (which later became a book, *The Opinionmakers*). In observing the interplay of journalists and public officials and in interviewing members of both groups for my dissertation, I used the research methods of journalists and political scientists. I mixed them because journalistic methods seemed lively and penetrating but somewhat haphazard, political science methods more careful and systematic but a bit sterile. I tried to combine the better parts of the methods of both in my research—and somehow never thought of encouraging my students to do the same.

Why, I have wondered, did I restrict the students in the English course to themes they could explore only in their memories and in the library? Why did I not tell the journalism students how to do careful research—and assign them to read books in the library that could tell them more—instead of sending them out armed only with anecdotes and ignorance?

The fault was mine, but it followed in a long tradition. Unfortunately, research methods then seemed to divide the world of learning. Students of English and history assessed the human condition primarily by reading. Students of journalism and the social sciences, in quite different ways, assessed it by observing human actions.

Finding Facts tries to heal that division by indicating how much researchers in the humanities and social sciences can learn from one another and how much journalists can learn from and can teach both groups of researchers. In fact, this book tries to synthesize the experiences and insights of people in all fields who pursue and weigh facts, interview, observe, and use reference books. The last chapter deals with some ways to report the findings and thoughts that result from this research and study.

One book alone is not likely to persuade students in different disciplines that they must learn one another's methods. Fortunately, it need not. Seeking education that they thought was "relevant," many students went out from the libraries and the classrooms recently to learn from the world—and many of them came right back in to try to understand what they had seen and done. They have learned—and have taught some of their teachers—that educated men and women need both books *and* experience. The more thoughtful ones have also learned that "What I Did Last Summer" would not be a bad topic if they were equipped to use something besides their emotions to assess their experiences.

Fortunately, great teachers have been demonstrating how researchers can make rich assessments by synthesizing several methods. It is not surprising that one of them is my former colleague Wilbur Schramm. After beginning his working life as a journalist, Schramm earned a Ph.D. in English and won the O. Henry Memorial Award for fiction, then became a social scientist whose research has brought him international renown.

This book owes much to Schramm's advice as well as his example. And like all my recent books, it was steadily improved in manuscript by the critiques of Charlene Brown of Indiana University. It has become one of my chief goals in writing anything to try to reduce the degree of her horror as she reads each succeeding draft. William Allan of Stanford University Libraries worked painstakingly and intelligently to teach me about the vast reference apparatus. Will Rogers, formerly a Stanford librarian, and Sally Drew, chief reference librarian of the Redwood City, California, Public Library, added valuable information for chapters 5 and 6. Don Dodson and Donald Roberts, both of Stanford, David Grey of San Jose State, and Leonard Sellers of the University of Wisconsin-Milwaukee helped greatly by commenting on early drafts of several chapters. I am indebted, too, to Carolyn Nelson, Janet Collom, Gwen Yamashiro, and my daughter Gail, all of whom provided patient and expert editorial assistance. If this volume is informative and persuasive, all of them deserve the reader's gratitude. They have mine.

A companion to this book, *Writing: Craft and Art,* is also published by Prentice-Hall. The last chapter of this book sketches methods of reporting research—in effect answering the question, What do I do with the facts I find?—but much more needs to be said about writing. *Writing: Craft and Art* covers in detail the principles of effective writing. I hope that it will be used as a close companion to *Finding Facts.*

Finding Facts

Pursuing and Interpreting Facts

1

In 1913, Frank Maloy Anderson, a professor of history, began one of the most painstaking pursuits of a single fact in the annals of research. Historians had puzzled for years over the authorship of "The Diary of a Public Man," which had been published, unsigned, in four installments in the prestigious *North American Review* in 1879. They had reason for concern. As the only source of a detailed picture of President Lincoln's actions from December 28, 1860, to March 15, 1861—the important winter of Secession—the diary had been mined for information, much of which was used in many volumes of history. Historians could not resist the diarist's richly detailed notes, which included close descriptions like this one of Lincoln's Inauguration: "A miserable little rickety table had been provided for the President, on which he could hardly find room for his hat, and Senator Douglas, reaching forward, took it with a smile and held it during the delivery of the address. It was a trifling act, but a symbolic one, and not to be forgotten, and it attracted much attention all around me."

Was this anecdote authentic, or was it an ingratiating bit of color in a narrative that was pure hoax? Identifying its source seemed crucial. Professor Anderson started down a trail of identification that was to wind through thirty-five years of research.

His first efforts were discouraging. The editor of *North American Review* had refused to name the author when the diary was published in 1879. Professor Anderson searched the files of fifty leading newspapers and magazines of the period to determine whether they had tried to identify the diarist. Nothing.

Then he began to analyze the diary. He found that the entry for February 20, 1861, had been written in New York. But the author described himself as a man of "long experience in Washington." A senator? A representative? Professor Anderson combed the *Congressional Globe* to determine which members of Congress had not participated in congressional proceedings on February 20. None of the absent senators had been long in Washington, and fifty-four absent representatives were eliminated for one reason or another. The representatives were unlikely possibilities in any case, because no entry in the diary referred to proceedings in the House.

But Professor Anderson's analysis of the diary drew a clear picture of the writer:

> He had prestige. His advice was sought by people who conferred with Lincoln.
>
> He was tall. Lincoln had once asked him whether he had ever matched backs with towering Charles Sumner.
>
> He was a deft writer who knew French.
>
> He was urbane. He had been amused that Lincoln wore black gloves to the opera.
>
> He had many influential friends.
>
> He was devoted to the Union, but he knew the South well.
>
> He had met Lincoln twice, once in 1848 and again in 1861.
>
> He was especially interested in tariff, patent, and postal issues and problems.
>
> He often attended Senate sessions.
>
> He was a friend of William Seward and Stephen Douglas.
>
> He was an intimate of several leading citizens of New York and knew the city well.
>
> He was in New York on February 20 and in Washington on twenty other days during the period covered by the diary.

Using this picture to reduce a long list of possibilities, Professor Anderson settled on Amos Kendall (who had been so influential a member of Andrew Jackson's "Kitchen Cabinet" that one congressman had declared: "He was the President's thinking machine, his writing machine, aye, and his lying machine"). To the delight of the researcher, Kendall was a perfect fit for every detail of the picture—with one possible exception. Had he been in New York on February 20? The search for this elusive clue demonstrated Professor Anderson's passion for certainty.

Returning to the newspaper files, he searched the lists of hotel arrivals in vain. When he learned that Kendall usually stayed at the Astor House during trips to New York, he tried to trace the hotel register, which was then more than fifty years old. A woman who worked in the Morgan Library was related to the last manager of the Astor. Professor Anderson tracked him down only to learn that the man had no idea whether the registers still existed. Then Anderson remembered hearing years earlier that hotel journals had been published in nearly every large city. He located the files of the New York journal, *The Transcript*, and found in the issue for February 20, 1861, the name of a guest at the Astor who had apparently registered as "J. Kendall." Had this actually been "A. Kendall" in some indecipherable script in the register? Professor Anderson was never able to determine.

To establish beyond doubt that Amos Kendall could have been the diarist, Professor Anderson next tried to ascertain that Kendall had been in Washington during each of the twenty days when diary entries had been written there. This investigation dissolved his theory. On two of the days, news accounts made clear, Kendall could not have been in Washington.

This information was not quite as disappointing as it might have been, for the longer Professor Anderson studied the diary, the more he doubted its authenticity. He did not consider it pure fiction for only one reason: writers of pseudo-fact commonly make at least one statement that is demonstrably false, but the diarist had not.

Professor Anderson decided that the diary was a combination of fact and fiction, a skeleton of fact that had been fleshed out with fancy. It was suspicious, for example, that the prose was polished, unlike the fuzzy sentence structure in most diaries, and was vague on exactly the points a diarist might be expected to describe precisely. Also, for such a short period, the diary seemed to carry entirely too many revealing anecdotes about Lincoln and pungent remarks by him. Moreover, the diarist seemed to be judging the leading men of the time with uncommon insight, causing Anderson to suspect that the man was recalling an earlier period and judging with hindsight rather than writing his impressions of events at the time they occurred. For these and similarly persuasive reasons, Professor Anderson concluded that he was seeking a fabricator, not an authentic diarist.

This description only sketches Anderson's dedication; he wrote a 256-page book [1] that traces all his labors. Although few researchers are so dedicated to single projects, Professor Anderson's work illustrates strikingly how a painstaking researcher attacks a complex problem.

His work also demonstrates that pursuing facts is almost always inseparable from interpreting them. The diarist's prestige, height, and urbanity, for example, are interpretations that Anderson drew from the diary. On the basis of probable facts and reasonable interpretations, Anderson then pursued the facts he needed: was Kendall at the Astor House on February 20, 1861? The information he collected led to the interpretation that the diary combined fact and fiction. This interpretation was based on facts that could not have been substantiated without previous interpretations based on other facts.

The link between fact and interpretation is even broader. *The American Heritage Dictionary* defines *fact* as "1. Something known with certainty. 2. Something asserted as certain." It is a fact that Mickey Rooney is short. But this is actually an interpretation derived from comparison. To a Pygmy in the Ituri Forest of Zaire, Rooney would be a towering figure. So it is with most facts—the "data" of the historian or the social scientist as well as the experience of daily life. They are relative and must be interpreted in the light of other facts. In short, there is seldom a real distinction between gathering facts and expressing ideas. As someone once said, "most of the facts we gather come dripping with ideas."

There are, of course, facts that delight the collector of trivia but that have neither purpose nor meaning, including some that were reported from Vietnam during the long years of American action there. Desperate to report something new in periods when one action seemed much like another, American correspondents joked among themselves about "the left-handed battalion commander syndrome." The effort to develop a "first," or "most," or "least" in the lead of a newspaper article caused them to surmise that "for the first time" a left-handed commander led a battalion into battle. Although this observation would be a fact based on interpretation, identifying one commander by comparison with others, such trivia suggests why Claude Bernard has said that a mere fact is "nothing. It is only useful for the idea attached to it, or for the proof that it furnishes."

James Brussel, a psychiatrist who is Assistant Commissioner of the New York State Department of Mental Hygiene, has related in *Casebook of a Crime Psychiatrist*[2] the fascinating details of how he brought together isolated facts to describe criminals long sought by the police. In one case, New Yorkers had been endangered for sixteen years by homemade bombs left in various spots around the city, often planted in the slashed underside of theatre seats. Some failed to explode, although examination proved they were carefully made. (Police suspected the bomber intentionally constructed duds in some cases.) The unexploded bombs and a series of neatly printed notes in which the bomber vaguely but bitterly blamed his poor physical condition on the Consolidated Edison Company were the only clues. Unable to develop an idea of how to identify the bomber, detectives asked Dr. Brussel to try. In a few hours, he produced this word portrait:

> A single man between 40 and 50 years old who is neither fat nor skinny. High school graduate. Not interested in women, but part of his problem is sexual. An introvert, unsocial but not antisocial. Contemptuous of others. Feels superior to critics. Resentful of criticism of his work but probably conceals a resentment that keeps growing. A skilled mechanic who is neat with tools and egotistical of his mechanical skill. Expert in civil or military ordnance. Moral. Honest. Religious; probably Roman Catholic. Probably foreign-born; Slav. Present or former Consolidated Edison worker. Probably a case of progressive paranoia. Wears double-breasted suits and keeps the jacket buttoned.

Dr. Brussel was not *certain* of this description, but the facts he gleaned from the detectives combined with the facts he knew about paranoia enabled him to be reasonably certain. Largely because of Brussel's work, the man was apprehended. Virtually all of Dr. Brussel's description was found to be accurate. The bomber, George Metesky, was arrested at midnight while he was wearing pajamas. He dressed for the trip to the police station in a double-breasted suit. It was buttoned.

A few examples show both the ultimate simplicity of the process and the need for facts that help to make the process simple. Although Metesky's first bomb had been planted at Consolidated Edison, the more recent bombings had been random, as though he thought he had been wronged by the world in general. Obviously, he was suffering from paranoia. Because paranoids commonly share many traits, including obsessive neatness, Dr. Brussel could make further assumptions. Paranoia develops slowly, not usually erupting before one is about thirty-five, and the bombings had taken place over sixteen years; therefore Dr. Brussel reasoned that the man was at least middle-aged. The man was probably neither fat nor skinny because a study of 10,000 paranoids had revealed that 85 percent had an "athletic" body type. In his notes about the bombings, Metesky had always referred to "the Con Ed" even though New Yorkers had been referring to "Con Ed" for years. In addition, a stilted tone ("dastardly deeds" was an often-used expression) and a lack of slang or colloquialisms suggested that the bomber was foreign-born or had been living with those of foreign extraction; the notes seemed to be those of an educated man, but one whose ear was attuned to a different pattern of speech. Because a paranoid is neat and proper, he is not likely to adopt new styles until custom has made them conservative. Hence, in 1956, when Dr. Brussel stepped into the case, a paranoid would probably wear a double-breasted suit, neatly buttoned.

Many similar examples in other fields could be related, but they would not persuade mystics, intuitionists, or poets of the ultimate value of facts. The great French writer Pascal argued against logic and for a spirit of subtlety and finesse—*esprit de finesse* over *esprit géométrique*—

holding that the heart as well as the mind has its reasons. T. S. Eliot made a similar point in his pageant play *The Rock:*

> Where is the wisdom we have lost
>   in knowledge?
> Where is the knowledge we have lost
>   in information? [3]

Let us grant that the heart's surmise and the poet's wisdom live in another realm—and perhaps a greater one—that cannot be reached by the methods described here. But wisdom—understanding what is true, right, and lasting—is not reserved only for poets, sages, and prophets, and information is not to be disdained. Information (or facts) interpreted judiciously becomes knowledge, and that is the foundation of wisdom.

Nevertheless, scholars who pursue and interpret facts seldom think in such grandiose terms. They think first of building theory, but not *theory* as the term is used colloquially to describe a vague notion. Natural scientists and behavioral scientists consider theory a system of laws or a coherent body of general propositions that explain relationships and events. A body of theory enables a researcher to hypothesize, to offer possible explanations of certain relationships, then to test them to determine whether they should be added to, or substituted for, existing theory, which is always tentative. A hypothesis directs the search for order among facts. Ideally, one tests hypotheses not to "prove" them, but to refute them. Careful scientists accept hypotheses only after vigorous attempts to refute them have failed.

Historians and literary researchers have become more accustomed recently to working in terms of theory and hypothesis. But journalists have not—at least not consciously. One of the most thoughtful journalists, Ben Bagdikian, tells of a social scientist who, after dealing with journalists in Washington for a time, excitedly announced a discovery: "You guys don't have any hypotheses!" As Bagdikian points out, the journalist must not have a hypothesis—or must appear not to have one. Although the good journalist actually *has* hypotheses, of varying strengths in varying situations, as to how things work, he has a professional prejudice against them. Ideally, he tries to report verifiable fact and to avoid presuppositions.

Pursuing and interpreting fact is not a single process. Indeed, even Professor Anderson's long and involved research illustrates only part of a single approach—and there are many. It is not necessary to explore all of them. The range can be indicated by examining the approaches of historians, literary researchers, natural scientists, social scientists, and journalists.

The Historian's Approach

The speech, "Everyman His Own Historian," [4] delivered by the late Carl Becker when he was president of the American Historical Association, argues persuasively that because history is no more than "the memory of things said and done," everyone finds it necessary to work as a historian:

> Mr. Everyman can not do what he needs or desires to do without recalling past events; he can not recall past events without in some subtle fashion relating them to what he needs or desires to do. This is the natural function of history, of history reduced to its lowest terms, of history conceived of things said and done: memory of things said and done (whether in our immediate yesterdays or in the long past of mankind), running hand in hand with the anticipation of things to be said and done, enables us, each to the extent of his knowledge and imagination, to be intelligent, to push back the narrow confines of the fleeting present moment so that what we are doing may be judged in the light of what we have done and what we hope to do.

Becker provided a homely example, showing that in the course of paying a fuel bill one may recall incurring the debt, consult personal records, call upon the creditor who in turn consults records—all these actions a miniature of historical research.

Becker hinted at Everyman's limits by pointing out that the layman remembers that the Declaration of Independence "was signed by the members of the Continental Congress on the Fourth of July. It is a vivid and sufficient image which Mr. Everyman may hold to the end of his days without incurring penalties. Neither Brown nor Smith has any interest in setting him right; nor will any court ever send him a summons for failing to recall that the Declaration, 'being engrossed and compared at the table, was signed by the members' on the second of August."

This observation indicates the essential difference between the layman and the professional historian. Although a layman may develop either a personal or a professional interest in some aspect of the past—and may then study it thoroughly and become an authority—the historian's work consists entirely of analyzing the past. Because the past can be examined only through its traces, the historian devotes himself to them: coins, stamps, art objects, buildings, and especially documents.

How the historian examines the past is indicated in part by the sketch of Professor Anderson's work at the beginning of this chapter. We can discover that a particular detail in a document is false by comparing that detail to facts established in other studies. Those facts, in turn, were first examined to determine whether they corresponded to other facts that had previously been established by careful examination. It is thus not oversimplifying to say that the writing of history is based on correspondences—on the degree to which purported fact corresponds to established fact. Essentially, historians assert *probabilities*, although many are so little in doubt that their factual basis is unquestioned. We cannot *know* in the sense of experience and observation, for example, that the members of the Continental Congress signed the Declaration of Independence on the second of August, but the other facts that make this one probable are so well established that it is not to be doubted. Many "facts" asserted by some historians are less certain because they have been challenged by other historians. In recent years, revisionist historians—known variously as "new historians," "radical historians," and "leftist historians"—have been challenging beliefs that have become widespread because they are found in standard histories. Professor Jesse Lemisch of Roosevelt University in Chicago holds that the belief that the town meetings in colonial New England were democratic is a fiction. He and others have conducted studies that show that powerful figures in New England towns commonly used devices to control the meetings, such as exile of "political, ideological, and social deviants, as well as many of the poor. Thus, the apparent consensus within the town meeting reflects the exclusion from the town of those who didn't fit the consensus." [5]

It is always disturbing to find that the "facts" historians have long used are actually myths, but historians are accustomed to seeing cherished probabilities destroyed by examinations of the past that put forth findings that are more probable. Even the publication of a book like David Hackett Fischer's *Historians' Fallacies*,[6] which is one great, and highly readable, catalog of error, does no more than persuade the historian that his method must be refined. Fischer's book, which is subtitled *Toward a Logic of Historical Thought*, is a major step toward that refinement.

Literary Researchers

The work of most literary researchers is so often like that of the historian that it can be considered briefly. Research in literature is also based on traces of the past, and it differs primarily in emphasis: It focuses on man as creator of literary art. In recent years, more and more literary researchers have invaded the field of history to place the work of the artist in the context of his intellectual, social, and artistic milieu. They have also begun to lean more heavily on the findings of psychologists in an attempt to probe the artist's temperament, motivations, and prejudices. Like most historians, most literary researchers analyze written documents intuitively, shunning the scientists' leaning toward quantifying.

In *The Scholar Adventurers,* James Altick points out that the literary scholar must have a lively imagination as well as a devotion to truth because he confronts a vast jigsaw puzzle made up of countless fragments of fact, but some pieces are missing and others are fitted into the wrong places. He must tidy up his sector of the puzzle, finding new pieces as well as rearranging old ones.

> To interpret the significance of this material in terms of literary art, he must recreate in his mind, in as minute and faithful detail as possible the social, intellectual and literary conditions of a past age, and make himself, as well, an intimate spectator of the inner life of a great artist. A Chaucerian must train himself to think according to medieval patterns of thought; a specialist in Hawthorne must recapture Hawthorne's special mood and outlook upon life.[7]

The Natural Scientist's Approach

Like historians and literary researchers, natural scientists are not dismayed (except in a limited and particular sense) when they discover that the "fact" they once respected can no longer be considered valid. Indeed, replacing one fact, or theory, with another often calls for rejoicing. New facts and theories that can be trusted depend on a foundation that can be trusted; researchers must work on solid ground instead of quicksand. Just as the proof that "The Diary of a Public Man" was a suspect source enabled historians to learn what to lean on and what to avoid, so the discovery that an atom is not a solid substance but a miniature solar system with relatively huge electrons orbiting around an almost inconceivably small sun enabled physicists to proceed from the true rather than the spurious.

In a central sense, however, the methods of the scientist and the historian are not at all alike. The scientist is ever seeking to systematize knowledge by stating general laws; some may be amended by discoveries, but the substance of science is a body of general propositions rather than the particular truths of the historian. The scientist is interested in the particular as an instance of a universal principle. He aims to write sentences that begin with "Whenever," "If ever," "Any," "No," and "All." Many historians and other scholars have vainly attempted to assert and prove "laws." Scientists alone have succeeded. They alone can *predict*—should we say "with certainty"? Perhaps not, for scientists themselves hold that no proposition is so well supported by evidence that other evidence may not increase or decrease its probability. But scientific prediction is reasonably certain.

How do scientists work? So many volumes would be required to describe all the individual methods that we must be content with a brief sketch gleaned by James Bryant Conant from many statements by scientists:

> (1) a problem is recognized and an objective formulated; (2) all the relevant information is collected; (3) a working hypothesis is formulated; (4) deductions from the hypothesis are drawn; (5) the deductions are tested by actual trial; (6) depending on the outcome, the working hypothesis is accepted, modified, or discarded.[8]

This process may seem no more complicated than Everyman's method of meeting everyday problems, and indeed one who tries to solve common problems carefully and logically with mechanical devices may follow this pattern. Like the character in Molière's comedy who remarked wonderingly that he had been speaking prose all his life without knowing it, one without scientific pretensions might decide from this description that he had always been an unwitting scientist. But the professional scientist differs in at least this respect: He can select all the relevant information, test his deductions, and evaluate the result in the light of the many facts and general propositions that bear upon it. Only when we take account of what the scientist knows as he begins his research can we appreciate, without oversimplifying, the remark of P. W. Bridgman that "the scientist has no other method than doing his damndest."

The depth and range of the knowledge that a scientist may bring to a problem is suggested by Henri Poincare:

> Suppose we have before us any machine; the initial wheel work and the final wheel work alone are visible, but the transmission, the intermediary machinery by which the movement is communicated from one to the other, is hidden in the interior and escapes our view; we do not know whether the communication is made by gearing or by belts, by connecting rods or by other contrivances. Do we say that it is impossible for us to understand this machine because we are not permitted to take it to pieces? You know well that we do not, and that the principle of conservation of energy suffices to determine for us the most interesting point. We easily ascertain that the final wheel turns ten times less quickly than the initial wheel, since these two wheels are visible; we are able thence to conclude that a couple applied to the one will be balanced by a couple ten times greater applied to the other. For that there is no need to penetrate the mechanism of this equilibrium and to know how the forces compensate each other in the interior of the machine.[9]

On a much higher level, this kind of reasoning about hidden mechanisms led to the theory of gravity, the theory of organic evolution, and the theory of relativity.

The Social Scientist's Approach

Sketching the approach of the social scientist follows naturally the approaches of historians and natural scientists, for fact-finding in the social sciences is riven by leanings in both directions. Some sociologists, anthropologists, psychologists, political scientists, and communication specialists are drawn to the research techniques of the historian, some to the methods of the scientist (and a few historians are beginning to apply scientific methods). Given the rapid growth of the leaning toward science, however, it seems obvious that those who think of themselves as social *scientists* are winning the day—or at least the most attention. They can be distinguished from the others by the title *behavioral scientists.*

The behavioral scientist seeking to construct methods like those used by natural scientists faces a critical problem: If the distinguishing feature of science is the ability to state general propositions—Galileo's laws of falling objects, for example—how is he to state the *laws* of human action? Kenneth Colby tells an apocryphal story of an object that reaches Earth from outer space and defies the efforts of physicists and astronomers to analyze its composition, structure, or function. At last, a social scientist asks, "What's your name?" and the object answers, "Ralph." The fable is designed to suggest that the nature of the behavioral scientist's work allows him research techniques denied to natural scientists. But, of course, the techniques create infinite problems.

The mission of all social scientists is to examine mankind, and not only have they found it impossible to establish a universal proposition, or law, for any human behavior, the prospect for establishing one is nowhere in sight.

From time to time, a behavioral scientist will claim to have established a universal, as when Clark Hull published in *The Scientific Monthly* an article titled "A Primary Social Science Law." [10] It states that human responses to stimuli, physical and verbal, diminish with increasing distance from the point of stimulation. For example, if an aunt lives with or near a mother and assists the mother in caring for a child, the child will regard the aunt as a mother, and less so—or not so at all—if the aunt lives at a distance. Like the other "laws" of human action that are occasionally set forth, this one has not been accepted by behavioral scientists.

It is not true, however, that behavioral scientists have no real mission, because human behavior is not always individual and particular, with every human reacting differently and unpredictably. Although universals that will enable us to predict all human action are neither established nor in prospect, it is obviously absurd to argue that there are no patterns of human behavior. The various findings that Dr. Brussel used to describe the paranoid bomber indicate that useful, if not certain, predictions are possible. Nor are reasonable predictions limited to paranoid personalities. It is certainly simpler to predict the actions of those who suffer from a defect that drives them along reasonably predictable paths, but that may mean only that we can speak more confidently of the actions of particular kinds of people than of people in general. Mail a dollar bill in an envelope with no return address to an American, and he is almost certain to spend it. Mail a dollar under the same conditions to an Australian aborigine; he may convert it to money that he can use, discard it, or burn it.

The behavioral scientist cannot begin his sentences "Whenever," "If ever," "Any," "No," and "All," but he can sometimes assert with confidence that in given circumstances most people will usually react in a predictable way. In some instances, the behavioral scientist can also explain why most of the others react differently.

It is no more possible to explore in a short space all the methods through which the behavioral scientist makes judgments than it is to treat adequately the methods of the historian, the literary researcher, or the natural scientist. Increasingly, some behavioral scientists are using content analysis, a research technique that enables them to study written works systematically and quantitatively. For example, psychologists Richard Donley and David Winter, both of Wesleyan University, analyzed the inaugural addresses of twelve United States presidents to try to measure the need for power versus the need for achievement of each president. The researchers considered words indicating strong action, aggression, persuasion, and argument as showing need for power. Words such as "good," "better," "excellent," and "high quality" were analyzed as showing a need for achievement. Theodore Roosevelt and John F. Kennedy were judged to have the strongest need for power. The inaugural addresses of each contained 8.3 power images per 1,000 words. Only three presidents were judged to have a greater need for achievement than for power: Herbert Hoover, Lyndon Johnson, and Richard Nixon. (A few historians and literary researchers occasionally use this kind of content analysis, but most continue to rely on intuition, which is usually better suited to most of the questions they try to answer by analyzing documents.)

Most behavioral investigation, however, has long been based on two methods, *survey research* (commonly referred to as polling, which is based on interviews, questionnaires, or both) and *experiments*, and on two techniques, *asking questions* and *observing actions*. Both methods are so common in *all* research involving humans that they are treated in detail in this and the next three chapters. Many researchers prefer laboratory experiments because of the many problems of "field work." (Some experiments are conducted in the field; most survey research is.) Leonard Sellers describes the field work problems he and his colleagues experienced in conducting a survey when he was a graduate student:

> We randomly pulled some 300 names from the mailing lists of the two local Sierra Club chapters. This was for a survey of "eco-activists"—defined as any members of a conservation group—to find where they got environmental information.
>
> First, we had to word the introduction very carefully to convince people that we weren't selling something. This worked for most people, but we still had to spend time with some assuring them that we were not selling magazines.
>
> Second, the demographics of our population—high education and income—caused some problems. There was a high percentage of unlisted telephone numbers and, with M.D.'s, answering services. Additionally, because of the high education, some respondents were very hip to what we were doing. We were asked astute questions about our sampling procedure, questionnaire construction, and intended method of data analysis. The range of "experts," from biologists to statisticians, was wide and more than a little unsettling. To have your questionnaire critiqued while in the process of administering it is unnerving.
>
> Because of the mixture of demographics and the survey area, which included Palo Alto and Berkeley, we also had a strange but rare problem. Graduate students administering the survey would sometimes find themselves dealing with "academic giants." At least one student completely blew a questionnaire because the respondent turned out to be the man who had written the main textbooks in his undergraduate major; the student was so rattled by personally talking to the man that the survey was worthless.

This is only one aspect of the range of problems in field work that runs from irritations to injuries. Perhaps the greatest obstacles researchers encounter are that survey findings cannot establish causality and that all field work is so little subject to control that it seldom yields findings in which they can place complete confidence. As one put it, "The real world is a messy place."

By contrast, a researcher *can* control human subjects in a laboratory experiment, but in controlling them he takes them out of the real-life situations:

> As long as we test a [broadcast] program in the laboratory we always find that it has great effect on the attitudes and interests of the experimental subjects. But when we put the program on as a regular broadcast, we then note that the people who are most influenced in the laboratory tests are those who, in a realistic situation, do not listen to the program. The controlled experiment always greatly overrates effects, as compared with those that really occur, because of the self-selection of audiences.[11]

Another example of how experimental work can lead to misinterpreting facts is the Hawthorne effect, which took its name from a classic study of the effect of various working conditions on rate of output at the Hawthorne plant of Western Electric Company. The experimenters varied the number of rest periods and lengths of rest periods and working days over several weeks for six women, expecting that this would determine which kinds of conditions promoted work and which interfered with it. Regardless of conditions, however, the women worked harder and more efficiently with each succeeding experimental period. The most important reason was their feeling that, having been chosen for an experiment, they were special people and should perform exceptionally.

In experiments, the researcher tries to control and manipulate some factors, called "variables," so that he can focus on the effect of one factor (or a few). But this increases the probability that he will find an effect for the factor he has isolated; it does not share influence with other factors in the same way that it does in life.

There are other problems with laboratory experiments, and although researchers have devised ingenious methods of discounting them or allowing for them, a few always exist to a degree that mars the findings.

The problems that spring from studying people who are aware that they are being studied—in the field as well as in the laboratory—have led some behavioral scientists to devise techniques that allow unobtrusive investigation. The best summary of them is a readable book entitled *Unobtrusive Measures* [12] by Eugene J. Webb and three colleagues. To ask visitors to the Museum of Science and Industry in Chicago which exhibit they prefer, for example, would undoubtedly cause many to name one that might confer distinction on them (just as unbelievable numbers of respondents in surveys claim to read prestigious but not widely read magazines like *Harper's* and *The Atlantic*). A research committee that was formed to set up a psychological exhibit at the museum learned, however, that vinyl tiles around the exhibit containing live, hatching chicks had to be replaced every six weeks or so; tiles in other areas of the museum went for years without replacement. The conclusion is obvious.

Unobtrusive Measures carries hundreds of other examples of studies that avoid the most evident difficulty in human research: The act of measuring may change the measurement. Such methods are valuable but somewhat limited. The behavioral scientist must continue to refine his methods of studying the subjects who are all about him.

The Journalist's Approach

More often than any other serious researcher, the journalist pursues facts for their own sake, many of them amounting to information that may have neither value nor significance. This is an inevitable result of the work of journalists—at least those who face daily deadlines. A reporter can seldom know as he sets out to cover an event whether it will be banal or significant, nor can he always judge its value in the hot moment of occurrence. Indeed, the value of many of the events the journalist reports can be judged only by specialists. At least occasionally, the reporter relates events whose significance he will never know. Some are certain to be insignificant. The criteria of newsworthiness include that which will interest or titillate some large portion of the public for a passing moment, and thus much of the journalistic mission comes to little.

But if most journalism produces a mass of information, much of it *mere* information, the immensity of that mass coupled with the fact that journalists pursue significances as well as trivialities indicate that their reports can be mined profitably. It would be odd if this were not true, for the journalist has entrée to great events and to decision-makers ("a right to butt in," one has called it) seldom granted to any other researcher.

Because journalists are so often eyewitnesses to history, most of us are forced to depend on the mass media for current information. Newspapers and magazines, radio and television tell us most of what we know about public figures and public affairs. We are always subject to journalism and incapable of doing much about it because we can see too little for ourselves. Days are too short and the world is too big and complex for anyone to be sure of much about the web of government. What most of us think we know is not known at all in the sense of experience and observation.

We get only occasional first-hand glimpses of government by catching sight for a moment of a presidential candidate in the flesh, by shaking hands with a senator (or talking with one while he absently shakes hands with someone else), by doing business with the field offices of federal agencies, by dickering with the Internal Revenue Service—all the little bits and pieces of contact with officialdom that are described, too grandly, as "citizen participation in government."

We learn more at second hand—from friends, acquaintances, and lecturers on hurried tours, especially those who have just come from Washington or the state capital and are eager to impart what they consider, perhaps erroneously, to be the real story of what is going on there.

Yet this is sketchy stuff, and it adds only patches of color to the mosaic. Most of our knowledge of public affairs comes from the mass media. There simply are no practical alternatives to living in a synthetic world.

A distinguished political scientist, Harold Lasswell, has urged that his colleagues collaborate with journalists, rather than merely use their reports, because a journalist is often stationed at a vantage point that allows him to provide a first-hand account of the birth of a new elite or the demise of an old regime:

> Attuned to the immediate, he is impatient of delay. Accustomed to coping with tacticians of deceit, he is a sophisticated assessor of false witness. A journalist is also aware of who knows what, since his dramatizing imagination often perceives the relationship of every participant to the central action, recognizing potential informants who would otherwise be overlooked.[13]

Like the social scientist, the journalist most often pursues fact by interviewing and observing, processes that are treated in detail in other chapters. Here, we should focus on an important aspect of journalism: how raw, unevaluated facts are reported for the sake of timeliness.

The assassination of President Kennedy in 1963 is an excellent case. Dozens of reporters were in the motorcade with the president when he was shot. Hundreds of others had descended on Dallas a few hours after the shooting. In the inevitable confusion, the accounts varied alarmingly.

Item. The rifle from which the bullets came was found by the window on the second floor of the Texas Schoolbook Depository Building. Or it was found in the fifth-floor staircase. Or it was hidden behind boxes and cases on the second floor. Ultimately, all reports agreed that it had been found on the sixth floor.

Item. The rifle was first reported to be a .30 caliber Enfield. Then it was a 7.65mm Mauser. But it was also an Army or Japanese rifle of .25 caliber. Finally, it became an Italian-made 6.5mm rifle with a telescopic sight.

Item. There were three shots. But some reports mentioned four bullets: one found on the floor of the president's car, one found in the president's stretcher, a third removed from Governor Connally's left thigh, and a fourth removed from the president's body. There was even one report of a fifth bullet, which was said to have been found in the grass near the side of the street where the president was hit. Finally, there was general agreement that there were only three bullets.

Item. The first reports of the president's wounds described a "bullet wound in the throat, just below the Adam's apple" and "a massive, gaping wound in the back and on the right side of the head." The position of the president's car at the time of the shooting, seventy-five to one hundred yards beyond the Texas Schoolbook Depository Building, explains the head wound. But how does one account for a bullet in the throat?

Item. The shots were reported to have been fired between 12:30 and 12:31 P.M., Dallas time. It was also reported that Lee Oswald, who was accused of the shooting, dashed into the house at Oak Cliff where he was renting a room "at about 12:45 P.M." Between the time of the assassination and the time of his arrival at the rooming house, Oswald reportedly (1) hid the rifle, (2) made his way from the sixth floor to the second floor of the building, (3) bought and sipped a Coke (lingering long enough to be seen by the building manager and a policeman), (4) walked four blocks to Lamar Street and boarded a bus, (5) descended from the bus and hailed a taxi, and (6) rode four miles to Oak Cliff. How did he accomplish all this in fourteen minutes?

The confusing array of misleading reports is easily explained. *Reporters* did not say on their own authority that a bullet had entered the president's throat; they quoted Drs. Malcolm Perry and Kemp Clark of the Parkland Memorial Hospital in Dallas, who turned out to have been wrong. The Dallas police first identified the rifle as a .30 caliber Enfield and a 7.65mm Mauser. A Secret Service agent said he thought the weapon was a .25 caliber Army or Japanese rifle. The housekeeper at the Oak Cliff rooming house said that Oswald had come dashing in at about 12:45. And so on.

The most that one can charge the journalists with is haste, which gave equal status to everything posing as fact. Some errors were inevitable. Texas Governor John Connally said that the president's car had just made the turn at Elm and Houston Streets when the firing began. Mrs. Connally said that the car was nearing the underpass—220 yards beyond the turn. Both cannot be right. In fact, the consensus of other observers indicates that both were wrong; the car was about midway between these points.

Such discrepancies mar the work of the reporter who is on a deadline. He observes what he can and relies on authorities, or purported authorities, for the rest. The nature of journalism makes it obvious that although such methods cannot be supplanted, they can be refined to yield closer approximations of fact—for example, by choosing authorities more wisely.

Increasingly, another kind of journalism seeks to go beyond reporting random facts. More and more journalists are linking, combining, and interpreting facts to paint coherent pictures. Although they cannot have the long perspective that is available to most historical writers, the effect and value of their work is much like that of the historian. In a few cases, journalists employ the methods of survey research developed by behavioral scientists. Again, systematic research enables the journalist to pursue and report relevant information.

To set forth briefly some of the similarities and differences among research approaches:

1. Historians and literary researchers analyze traces, usually written documents, and they usually pursue particular truths. They try to establish probable truth by determining how the facts they find correspond with

other facts that have been established. They work by accretion, adding a bit here and a piece there. They ordinarily analyze facts that cannot be empirically verified.

2. Natural scientists are chiefly concerned with stating general laws. They work from theory and hypothesis and are usually able to control their experiments.
3. Some social scientists use methods that are more like those of historians and literary researchers than they are like the methods of scientists. Behavioral scientists, however, adapt the methods of natural scientists. But they are unable to assert laws with assurance, and analyzing human behavior makes it more difficult for them to control experiments. They often try to analyze behavior by interviewing and observing.
4. The journalist usually pursues facts that may not be part of a large and coherent design. Although he tries to select interview subjects judiciously, in reporting what they say he asserts *that it was stated,* not necessarily that the statement is true. The journalist does assert the truth of his reports of actions that he observes.

At no point have I spoken of *the* method of research, nor even of *the* scientific method, a familiar phrase. As Abraham Kaplan points out in his useful book *The Conduct of Inquiry,* "there is no one thing to be defined."[14] Speaking of the method of research is like speaking of the method of baseball. There are ways of pitching, hitting, running bases, catching and throwing the ball, devising strategy, and developing myriad skills and tactics. All vary. One can state a kind of method succinctly: to score runs if you are batting and to prevent them if you are not. But that is only a sketchy and unsatisfying description of the goals.

I have touched upon some of the many methods used in various disciplines to pursue facts that can be translated into knowledge and theory. Succeeding chapters will cover strategies for weighing and assessing facts and prescribe ways of recognizing and avoiding pitfalls in researching human behavior.

Evaluating Facts

2 Brit Hume, a young reporter who once worked for columnist Jack Anderson, had an experience early in 1972 that illustrates the central problem in researching human behavior, evaluating facts. Hume had acquired a two-page memorandum that he described as "the single most incriminating piece of paper I had ever seen." [1] The memo had been written by Dita Beard, a lobbyist for the International Telephone and Telegraph Company (ITT) and was addressed to W. R. Merriam, the head of the Washington office of ITT, one of the largest conglomerates in the world. In it, Mrs. Beard urged Merriam to use more discretion in discussing the company's pledge of $400,000 to underwrite the 1972 Republican National Convention, which was then scheduled for San Diego. Dated June 25, 1971, the memo made it clear that the pledge was helping the company negotiate mergers that had once seemed in doubt. The Antitrust Division of the U.S. Department of Justice had brought three landmark suits against the ITT mergers. The suits had been settled in July, 1971, a few weeks after Mrs. Beard had written her memo, in a way that allowed the largest merger in corporate history. Soon after, Richard McLaren, chief of the Antitrust Division, was given a federal judgeship in Chicago. The memo implicated, among others, President Nixon and Attorney General John Mitchell.

When Hume confronted Mrs. Beard, she admitted writing the memo and even confessed that she herself had worked out with Attorney

General Mitchell the agreement by which ITT got most of what it wanted. But she denied the main point of her own memo: that the ITT pledge to underwrite the Convention helped the company win a favorable settlement.

All the principals in the case, government officials as well as company executives, denied that point. But as Hume and other reporters broadened their investigations, questioning an ever-widening circle of officials, executives, and other sources, officials unwittingly contradicted other officials, executives unwittingly contradicted other executives, and both parties contradicted each other.

The effort to discount the memo eventually brought into the case Richard Kleindienst, the Assistant Attorney General who had been nominated to succeed Mitchell as Attorney General. Hume had called Felix Rohatyn, a director of ITT, to ask about the memo. In his eagerness to prove that it was valueless, Rohatyn said that he had met with Kleindienst half a dozen times to handle "some of the negotiations and presentations." This did not square with another document Hume turned up. When the chairman of the Democratic National Committee became suspicious about the settlement of the ITT case in 1971 and inquired at the Department of Justice about it, Kleindienst had written him a letter saying that the settlement was "handled and negotiated exclusively" by McLaren and his Antitrust Division staff. Hume read that letter. The Anderson column then accused Kleindienst of an "outright lie."

Testifying before the Senate Judiciary Committee, Kleindienst admitted meeting with Rohatyn but denied that he had "influenced the settlement of government antitrust litigation for partisan political reasons." For his part, Rohatyn told the Senate that he had not actually negotiated anything in his meetings with Kleindienst, that he was merely making an economic case for the mergers.

Hume and Anderson published column after column reporting their findings and accusing ITT and the Republican administration of making a mutually beneficial deal. But the Senate confirmed Kleindienst as Attorney General, 64 to 19. Many of the senators who voted to confirm were Democrats. Some probably believed Kleindienst's statement at the Senate hearing, others undoubtedly had other reasons.

But the votes to confirm are less important to our present examination than the dozens of questions that might be asked about this case, all of them springing from the basic questions that haunt anyone who investigates human action: What should I believe? How should I evaluate facts?

For example: There is no doubt that a memo exists, but was it accurate in saying that the ITT pledge of money was helping with the antitrust merger cases, or was this little more than a subtle argument by Mrs. Beard that her own work for the company was effective? Lobbyists often claim to do more than they have done. Was her subsequent denial of a connection between the pledge and the settlement accurate?

There is no doubt that Kleindienst wrote a letter saying that he took no part in the negotiations. But was Rohatyn's statement that he had handled "some of the negotiations" with Kleindienst accurate, or did he misstate the nature of those meetings to persuade Hume that *his* work was effective and Mrs. Beard's memo was inaccurate? Did Rohatyn's quite different testimony to the Senate committee accurately describe the meetings with Kleindienst?

Such questions can be multiplied, but a hundred questions would not show how complicated the central problem, evaluation, really is. The true complexity is suggested by asking whether anyone should believe the account of the case sketched above. Some of the principals would surely argue that it is not accurate, or at least that it misleads, and that the account should have included other bits of evidence.

And what would be the effect on the reader if, instead of "columnist Jack Anderson," "muckraking columnist Jack Anderson" had been used in the first paragraph of this chapter? What if, instead of presenting only one investigation by Anderson and his staff, this account had cast doubt on Anderson's credibility by pointing up one of his grievous errors, as when in 1972 he erroneously reported that Senator Thomas Eagleton, who was then the Democratic nominee for vice-president, had been arrested for drunken driving? Introducing such a fact would certainly cause at least a few readers to evaluate this case quite differently.

To evaluate all the relevant facts in this case, you must first weigh the probable truth in the oral and written testimony of the principals, government officials and company executives; then the probable truth in the accounts of that testimony published by Hume and Anderson; then the probable truth in the account published in this book; finally and not least, you must try to weigh the degree to which your judgments of probable truth were affected by your *own* whims, idiosyncrasies, leanings, biases, and prejudices. For this much is certain: Whether you are Democrat or Republican, liberal or conservative, a cynic about the processes of representative democracy or one who values the political system, what you are affects your judgment. If you have no political leanings or beliefs because you consider politics a dirty business, *that* may be pivotal. If you consider politics a bore—not even worth your attention—the attitudes toward Nixon, or Anderson, or congressional hearings expressed by someone you respect are likely to shape your judgment. In short, no one brings an *open* mind to anything that interests him. Evaluation is personal.

The Impossible Objective

If any results of human action might be considered pure, without taint or error, they would seem to be the findings of the physicist. He works not with the fragilities and imperfections of men, but with the forces of nature, whose "certainties" are open to discovery by a dedicated, dispassionate scientist. But in 1927, a German physicist named Werner Heisenberg proved the uncertainty principle, which showed that every attempt to describe nature was marred by an irremovable uncertainty. The more accurately one measures the position of a particle, the less able he is to measure its velocity at the same time, and vice versa. According to Heisenberg's principle, every intervention in nature affects it unpredictably. This is, of course, much like the Hawthorne effect that distorts the study of humans, described in chapter 1.

Moreover, even when natural scientists devise methods of measuring nature without intervening in its processes, and when behavioral scientists develop unobtrusive measures for human behavior, the inescapable fact is that the scientists are human. Not only is a man's work shaped to some degree by human desires—to win a Nobel Prize, to publish a learned paper or an admired article, to earn a promotion, or simply to make a point—at bottom, it is impossible by definition for a human to be objective, to be like a machine or other object which can have neither concepts nor beliefs.

Journalists (like historians, natural scientists, social scientists, and other professionals) have long worked to develop formulas that will assure objective reports. Because, unlike most other professionals, many journalists often pursue unadorned facts, attempting to report rather than evaluate events, and because journalists often have no stake or interest in the events they report, it might seem that the journalism known as "straight" or "objective" reporting is often objective. Lester Markel, the retired Sunday editor of the *New York Times*, has pointed up the error in this judgment with:

> The reporter, the most objective reporter, collects fifty facts. Out of the fifty he selects twelve to include in his story (there is such a thing as space limitation). Thus he discards thirty-eight. This is Judgment Number One.
>
> Then the reporter or editor decides which of the facts shall be the first paragraph of the story, thus emphasizing one fact above the other eleven. This is Judgment Number Two.
>
> Then the editor decides whether the story shall be placed on Page One or Page Twelve; on Page One it will command many times the attention it would on Page Twelve. This is Judgment Number Three.
> This so-called factual presentation is thus subjected to three judgments, all of them most humanly and most ungodly made.[2]

What happens is suggested by the varying news stories about a simple report on gifts to Stanford University during one fiscal year. The university-published *Campus Report* headed its story:

HIGHEST NUMBER OF DONORS
IN STANFORD HISTORY

The *San Francisco Chronicle* headline said:

STANFORD AGAIN RAISES
$29 MILLION IN GIFTS

The *Palo Alto Times* story was headed:

DONATIONS TO STANFORD
LOWEST IN FOUR YEARS

The student-published *Stanford Daily* announced:

ALUMNI DONATIONS DECLINE:
BIG DROP FROM FOUNDATIONS

These headlines accurately reflected the stories they surmounted—which were also accurate. Stanford did have more donors than ever, as the *Campus Report* story said. It did raise more than $29 million for the fourth consecutive year, as the *Chronicle* said. Donations were the lowest in the past four years, as the *Palo Alto Times* reported. The total was lower than in the preceding year and it included less foundation money, as the *Stanford Daily* said.

But if we cannot be objective in the ultimate sense, this does not mean that we should simply throw up our hands and surrender to subjectivity, following wherever it leads. It leads too many toward the rationale expressed by Ray Mungo in his book *Famous Long Ago:*

> *Facts* are less important than *truth* and the two are far from equivalent, you see, for cold facts are nearly always boring and may even distort the truth, but Truth is the highest achievement of human expression. . . . Now let's pick up a 1967 copy of the Boston *Avatar,* and under the headline "Report from Vietnam, by Alexander Sorenson" read a painfully graphic account of Sorenson's encounter with medieval torture in a Vietnam village. Later because we know Brian Keating, who wrote the piece, we discover that Alexander Sorenson doesn't exist and the incident described in *Avatar,* which moved thousands, never in fact happened. But because it has happened in man's history, and because we know we are responsible for its happening today, and because the story is unvarnished and plain and human, we know it is *true,* truer than any facts you may have picked up in the *New Republic.*[3]

No "truth" can spring from fiction *disguised* as fact (although great fiction presents truths about the human condition). Instead of throwing up our hands, we must analyze our human failings and allow for them to the high degree that is now possible so that our evaluations of fact lead to the best that we can attain: probable truth.

Who Am I?

A great English scholar, Sir John Clapham, once observed: "Thirty years ago I read and marked Arthur Young's *Travels in France*, and taught from the marked passages. Five years ago I went through it again, to find that whenever Young spoke of a wretched Frenchman I had marked him, but that many of his references to happy or prosperous Frenchmen remained unmarked." [4]

An honest man who seeks truth can balance some of his biases by cold self-examination. Note that Clapham discovered his own distortion. What if, as he began reading *Travels in France* the first time, Clapham had sought to analyze his biases? He might then have placed a proper focus on the happy Frenchmen.

Trying to balance one's biases begins with becoming aware of the selective processes: exposure, perception, and retention. We tend to expose ourselves to information with which we agree. Thus, Republicans tend to hear and read more information they perceive as favorable to Republicans than to Democrats (and vice versa), businessmen tend to read articles they perceive as favorable to businessmen, doctors tend to read articles they perceive as favorable to doctors, and so on. It is not possible, of course, to avoid all information that opposes our beliefs; a Democrat is certain to be exposed, at least occasionally, to the views of President Ford, and a doctor who dislikes the policies of the American Medical Association (AMA) is nonetheless exposed to them. But there is another protection for our biases: When we are exposed to information with which we disagree, we tend to perceive elements in it that will not disturb our established attitudes and beliefs. Thus, the partisan Democrat may sneer at a Republican president's statement regarding love of country as pietistic flag-waving (while the partisan Republican applauds it as evidence of fervent patriotism), and the idealistic doctor is likely to focus on that aspect of AMA policy that seems to prove that Establishment doctors place money above service to humanity. Finally, we tend to remember that which will leave us in uninjured possession of our prejudices: the Republican statement that had a false ring rather than the one with which the Democrat might agree, the AMA policy that benefits doctors financially rather than the one that represents sacrifice.

One who makes himself aware of these processes and tries to gauge their effect takes a long step toward countering them. He can take a second step by imagining that the information with which he disagrees came from a source he approves. If the partisan Democrat will try to imagine for a moment that the statement made by the Republican was made by a Democrat, and the idealistic doctor will try to imagine that the policy announced by the AMA was put forth by his own group, Doctors for Society, they can determine whether the statement and the policy or their authors are the focus of disagreement. If either imagining yields nonsense —if a Democrat could not have made the statement, if Doctors for Society could not have enunciated the policy—*that* is significant.

There is a lesson in the actions of a Californian who was outraged upon reading a report of a peace march on Washington written by Robert Donovan of the *Los Angeles Times*. The reader telephoned Donovan to complain that the report surely lent encouragement to the young dissidents. But when the reader learned that Donovan was fifty-seven years old, had served in the infantry in World War II, and had a son who was about to be commissioned by the Army through ROTC, his attitude changed. If readers only knew, the man said, that Donovan was neither young nor unpatriotic, they would read his reports quite differently. The reporting, then, mattered less than the reader's assumptions about the author.[5]

One must thus counter the forces that injure accurate evaluation by recognizing the forces, then working to correct them by seeking information that challenges personal opinions. The conservative might subscribe to *The New Republic*, the liberal to *National Review*. (The middle-aged might even listen to rock music, the young to the songs of the forties and fifties.) Mere exposure can have results, but, of course, a conscious effort to appreciate another viewpoint is more effective. The aim is not to change one's opinions—*that*, as many studies show, is far too complicated a process to put the devout in much danger of losing their beliefs.

The actions prescribed here do not require that we deny our humanity or that we analyze ourselves into negating individuality. Instead, these prescriptions suggest how to combat our own ignorance. When the Puritans settled Massachusetts, the Narraganset Indians reasoned that the English must have burned all the firewood in their homeland; that would have been one of the Indians' principal reasons for moving to a new home.[6] Similarly, if we judge only from the base of our own understandings, our evaluations will remain narrow and personal.

Who Is He? Who Are They?

In judging the evaluations offered by others, we must know who the others are. When a speaker warned in 1972 that the pressures of the clean-environment movement endanger the economic health of the nation by requiring too much of industry, it was naturally important to know that the speaker was an industrialist. This is not conclusive; one may suspect self-interest, but the speech may have been accurate. The speaker cited U.S. Department of Commerce figures that "show that 210 plants last year were forced to shut down primarily because of economic pressures." The Department of Commerce, which is directed by former businessmen, has a certain affinity for the business viewpoint; its findings, too, may be suspect. But Gladwin Hill of the *New York Times* reported that the speaker's words "were untrue," that Commerce records show no such thing.[7]

The next question, of course, is whether Gladwin Hill and the *Times* are suspect sources. Any newspaper is basically a human institution, and humans err, even those who work for an institution as august as the *Times*. But we always seek probable truth, and the weight of probability is that the *Times* report should be trusted. Either the speaker or the reporter treated the truth casually, and the evidence points to the speaker. He had a strong self-interest (one that led him to err unintentionally), and the likelihood was slender that anyone in the college audience he addressed would know the Department of Commerce data. Gladwin Hill, on the other hand, had no apparent self-interest, and he had to take greater care than the speaker; many *Times* readers are armed with accurate information about the effects of pollution control.

In addition, because the *Times is* a business, its reporting of information that injures business might be considered a strong indication of probable truth: an argument against self-interest.

This example illustrates one of the central concerns in deciding whether to accept an evaluation: Who says so? In many cases, it is not possible to learn everything we need to know about individuals (although chapter 5 provides a guide to reference books that will help). More often, one must judge the individual by the groups to which he belongs. It is not certain that a man will share group values in all things, and everyone belongs to many groups. But the group process has been studied rigorously, and nearly everything we know about it indicates that a member of a group is usually lured into sharing the opinions of the other members, both because it is usually in his self-interest and because he wants them to like him, accept him, and respect him. Were the speaker's words automatically suspect because he was an industrialist? No, but they needed to be examined by one who did not share that group's values.

It would be misleading to leave the impression that groups are no more than propaganda machines with little other purpose than promoting their own interests. Understanding other aspects is important.

Groups have standards, and as the late H. L. Mencken observed, a man wants the approval of his colleagues, those who know what he is doing and are expertly equipped to judge his work. It follows that knowing the standards helps to gauge the worth of an evaluation.

Consider the leading scholarly journals listed in chapter 6, such as *The American Political Science Review* and *The American Historical Review*. Almost all are published by associations of specialists who reach their conclusions on the basis of generally accepted standards of research. The articles are published, as a rule, only after they have been reviewed and criticized by other specialists. This does not mean that the specialists agree with the conclusions; the range of opinion is wide. And some articles are published to test ideas, to put them in the marketplace of expert opinion for debate and refinement. It is also true that some members of almost any scholarly association consider most of its publications inconsequential. The point is not that scholarly publications carry ultimate truth but that they do not publish random observations.

One must be aware of dubious standards as well. When a politician is nominated for the U.S. presidency and announces that he has selected as his vice-presidential running mate the man most capable of succeeding him, no one who is politically astute believes that. Richard Nixon chose Spiro Agnew in 1968, claiming that Agnew was the best successor, but Agnew was selected primarily because he was governor of a border state, Maryland, and might be able to draw votes from border states and the South. The discrepancy between the claim and the actuality was hardly worth pointing up by the Democrats, who also tried to balance *their* ticket. The standard of political discourse is to claim the ideal. That is understood in politics, and it should be understood by anyone who tries to interpret political action.

Group standards may be set forth in a code of ethics, but that code sometimes has no meaning. Item 7 in "The Code of Professional Standards for the Practice of Public Relations" rules that "A member shall not intentionally disseminate false or misleading information and is obligated to use care to avoid dissemination of false or misleading information." But members of the Public Relations Society of America, which framed the code, often set up front organizations for their clients to make it seem that persuasive information comes from those who have no vested interest, and they are neither reprimanded nor expelled. In such cases, a group rarely honors with leadership positions or awards members who are unethical—except a group in which devious practice is itself a kind of ethic.

One can, of course, share the attitudes of one group for a time, then share the quite different attitudes of another group. There was not much doubt, for example, that Professor Theodore N. Beckman of the College of Commerce and Administration of Ohio State University had changed his consumer-group attitudes after he appeared before a Senate committee to oppose truth-in-lending legislation as a consultant for the National Retail Merchants Association.

"At no time," Professor Beckman said, "have I been motivated solely or primarily by pecuniary considerations on matters of this kind because all of my adult life has been devoted to teaching and research at the university level, and thus in a constant search for truth." But Senator Paul Douglas of Illinois placed in the hearing record excerpts from Professor Beckman's book *Principles of Marketing,* which supports truth-in-lending by noting that "few consumers know just how to determine the rates paid by them on a per annum basis, and yet such knowledge is indispensable in making intelligent comparisons with respect to alternative methods of financing."

Beckman hastily explained that he was preparing a new edition of the book: "In that edition, I am treating the subject with greater maturity, with much more knowledge, a great deal more sophistication, and you will not find me making statements of that character." [8]

Fearing that sharp practices may bring public condemnation or government regulation, or both, some groups, like doctors and lawyers, that cannot exclude applicants or expel members, publicize standards or tests that may have similar effects. When the American Association for Public Opinion Research (AAPOR) set up the National Council on Polls to issue guidelines for examining poll results, the effect was to stigmatize pollsters, including some AAPOR members, whose work could not stand that kind of examination.

When a specialist (scholar, politician, industrialist, plumber, or whoever) communicates with a general audience, any one of three influences is likely to distort his presentation—sometimes all three. First, he may distort in his own interest, or in the interest of his group. Second, he may distort through oversimplification because he is convinced that his audience cannot grasp the fine points. Finally, he may distort because he does not believe that anyone in his audience can catch him out.

Ideal conditions are so seldom available that one can sometimes only wish for them. The ideal condition for learning what people really believe often requires hearing or reading the communications within a group: a presidential candidate consulting with party leaders about a suitable vice-presidential candidate, industrialists discussing among themselves the probable effects of pollution control, scholars talking or writing to other scholars.

A layman seldom has the time or the entrée for first-hand observation or access to documents and must usually rely on publications. Some are comprehensible to anyone with intelligence, but many are not because specialists are communicating among themselves. They share a fund of knowledge and experience that confounds the layman, and they speak and write a language that may seem to resemble English only because it uses an occasional familiar connective. It is small consolation to be told that the jargon is both concise and precise. A social psychologist who says, "That was because of the Hawthorne effect," has communicated long paragraphs of information, but only to those who know the language.

In such circumstances, the layman who is not sufficiently interested to devote the time to becoming a knowledgeable amateur must usually rely on journalists, many of whom make a mission of translating specialties into everyday English.

Journalists also usually have a vantage point, or can arrange one, that is denied to most others. When American troops in Vietnam invaded Cambodia in 1970, Governor Raymond P. Shafer of Pennsylvania was a member of a team of dignitaries who visited the troops at a site called Shakey's Hill. He climbed atop a sandbagged bunker manned by three soldiers and asked, "What do you feel the attitude is of our men with reference to coming into Cambodia?"

Knowing the answer he wanted, the soldiers squirmed and glanced nervously at one another. Then one said, "They feel it might help end the war, so they came, you know."

"Well, I've been talking to men everywhere and I find they think it should have been done sooner," the governor said. "Is that your attitude too?"

"Yes, sir," said the first soldier. "That's what I think too."

"Do you all agree to that?" the governor asked the others.

"That's right, sir. Yes, sir." They nodded emphatically.

"That's good," the governor said. "I think Americans sometimes get a distorted picture, and I'm here to find out the real facts."

The governor then strode off to join the other fact-finders. An Associated Press reporter stayed at the bunker long enough to hear the first soldier breathe deeply and say, "Jeez, I hope none of the guys heard us." [9]

Samples—and Samplers

One who sips a cup of coffee and decides that it is good or bad is, in effect, conducting a survey. If the taste is bitter, he does not think merely that the *sip* is bitter; he judges all the coffee in the cup, and probably that in the pot as well. He need not drink it all to prove the point. A sample is enough.

No one questions this technique to interpret such everyday facts. But using sampling to describe the behavior of living things invites questions. An apocryphal story is told of a scientist who published an astonishing generalization about the behavior of rats. When a colleague asked to see the records of the experiments on which the judgment was based, the scientist pulled a notebook from a pile of papers and said, "Here they are." He pointed to a cage in the corner and added, "There's the rat."

Nearly everyone thoughtlessly generalizes from samples that are too small. Anyone who has had two or three bad experiences with car salesmen is likely to decide that all of them are crooks. But we tend to suspect the conclusions of those who make a profession of sampling human behavior and generalizing about it, since most of us feel that men are much too individual and erratic for safe prediction. It is right to be suspicious, but necessary to be suspicious for the right reasons. Instead of questioning whether there are patterns in human behavior that are sufficiently sharp and distinctive for investigation—which is quite clearly true—one should question the methods and conclusions of the investigators.

A classic example of shoddy sampling was the effort of the now-defunct *Literary Digest* to forecast the 1936 presidential election. The sample was large: more than ten million ballots were mailed, more than two million were returned. The returns led the *Digest* to predict 370 electoral votes for the Republican, Alfred Landon, and 161 for Franklin Roosevelt. In fact, Roosevelt won 523 electoral votes, Landon only 8. The error in the *Digest*'s methods was using mailing lists derived from telephone directories, automobile registration lists, and magazine subscriptions. The pollsters may have accidentally received ballots from an adequate sample of voters with telephones, automobiles, and magazine subscriptions, but these were hardly representative of the general population in the depression year of 1936.

By the time of the presidential campaigns of 1948, the leading pollsters knew that it was essential to assure response from voters at random. Nonetheless, they wrongly predicted victory for the Republican, Thomas Dewey, over the Democrat, Harry Truman. Why? Primarily because their surveys during the early stages of the campaign showed Dewey leading so decisively that they stopped polling. Truman's campaign gathered momentum in the last days; Dewey's stagnated. (It is important to realize that no matter how close to an election one conducts a survey, it is *prior* to the election. It may show accurately how most voters are leaning at the time of the survey, but at least a few are certain to change their minds by election day.) The pollsters also learned in 1948 the importance of intense political convictions. A respondent who is certain about his preference is much more likely to vote than one who expresses a vague leaning.

The National Council on Public Polls has issued guidelines aimed at political polling that are also useful for testing other kinds of surveys.

1. *Who paid for the poll?* Obviously, if someone who has a vested interest in the results sponsored the poll, that should be known.
2. *When was the poll taken?* Changes caused by events are so common that it is important to know, for example, whether the voters favoring the 1972 Democratic presidential candidate, Senator McGovern, were asked their preference *before* it became known that the first running mate he chose, Senator Thomas Eagleton, had undergone psychiatric treatment, *immediately after* that fact became known, or *after* McGovern had chosen a new running mate.
3. *How were the interviews obtained?* Telephone interviewing is relatively inexpensive, but, as George Gallup has pointed out, it has a built-in bias toward middle- and upper-income groups and older people. In mail surveys, it is important to know how many letters were mailed and how many were returned. If the percentage of return was small, the sample may be heavily biased.
4. *How were the questions worded?* Questioning his constituents by mail, one congressman asked, "I publicly proposed an extra tax credit for parents of college students. Are you in favor of such a tax exemption as presently gaining bipartisan support in Congress?" The answer the congressman wanted, and toward which he steered his constituents, is obvious. (Precise wording is considered in detail in chapter 3.)
5. *Who was interviewed?* A front-page story on the Vietnam War in the *New York Times* was headlined 54 PER CENT IN OHIO POLL ASSERT U.S. ROLE IN WAR IS MISTAKE. Readers who went no further were misled. As the story made clear, Congressman Charles Mosher had sent a mail questionnaire to constituents in his 13th Ohio District, not to the entire state. It is important to know not only the area sampled but also the demographic breakdown of the sample.
6. *How large was the sample?* The response to Congressman Mosher's questionnaire was 3.5 percent. Because Gallup, whose work is widely respected, uses a sample of only 1,500 in his monthly opinion index (some pollsters use only 1,200 in national surveys), and more than 1,500 responded to Mosher's questionnaire, it might seem that Mosher was safe in generalizing. Size is important; a survey of thirty-six voters in a city of 300,000 is too small. But random distribution is vital. Certainly, those in the 13th Ohio District who respond to congressional surveys are not randomly distributed. In fact, many mail surveys are biased because those who have the ability, the confidence, and the inclination to respond are seldom representative. (Those with little education may have the ability to respond to a simple mail survey, but many are not accustomed to writing and lack the confidence to respond.)
7. *What was the base of the data if it is based on part of a total sample?* One of the subtlest tricks in polling is to use partial data as though it represented the entire sample. For example, if a politician surveys 1,500 people and reports that among Jewish voters he is nine time as popular

as his opponent, the reader of the report is likely to believe that 1,500 Jewish voters were surveyed. In fact, only forty Jews might be in the sample.

Stephen Isaacs of the *Washington Post*, who devised the "Jewish voter" example above, has written:

> Many other points can be useful in evaluating a poll. These include whether interviewers had any discretion as to whom they interviewed (in a pure probability survey, they have no choice—each respondent is chosen mathematically); what time of day interviews were conducted (most professional men, obviously, aren't home at 2 in the afternoon); how the interviewers were supervised and whether their work was "validated"—checked to determine whether they actually did the interviews they reported and whether they reported the interviews truthfully; whether any "weighting" was done to bring the actual interviewees into line with the demographic makeup of the electorate, and so forth.[10]

Much survey research hinges on interviewing, the subject of the next chapter. Interviewing is also important in other kinds of social science research, in researching recent history, and especially in journalistic reporting.

3 Interviewing

To be properly warned about the pitfalls of interviewing, consider the gloomiest judgments. Psychologists David Weiss and Rene Dawis have written that "it is indefensible to assume the validity of purportedly factual data obtained by interviews." [1] A journalist, Thomas Morgan, has said of the conflicting goals of an interviewer and his subjects: "*I* want the truth; *they* want to be beautiful." Irving Wallace, who has written many magazine articles and several best-selling novels based on extensive interviewing, said that anyone attempting to depict Wallace himself would fail because, "You wouldn't really know what goes on in my head and heart, because I wouldn't tell you, even if *I* understood. We all have protective devices out of necessity, because a living man must possess a private self, for without it he is only half alive." [2]

There is much support for these judgments. Researchers have found that mothers report childrearing practices that are different from what they actually did, homeowners report incorrectly on household repairs, hospitalized patients report their preoperative anxieties incorrectly —the list of discrepancies increases with nearly every careful investigation by social scientists.[3] Using less methodical techniques, journalists also find, again and again, that what they are told often differs from the truth. Some of them probably reflect ruefully on a judgment published in *The Nation* in 1869, when formal interviewing was not common in journalism: "The 'interview,' as at present managed, is generally the joint product of some humbug of a hack politician and another humbug of a reporter." [4]

If the interview is so error-prone, why use it? The primary answer is suggested by the title of an excellent monograph by two social psychologists, Eugene J. Webb and Jerry R. Salancik, *The Interview, or The Only Wheel in Town.*[5] The title comes from an anecdote familiar to gamblers:

FIRST GAMBLER, *arriving in town:* Any action around?
SECOND GAMBLER: Roulette.
FIRST GAMBLER: You play?
SECOND GAMBLER: Yes.
FIRST GAMBLER: Is the wheel straight?
SECOND GAMBLER: No.
FIRST GAMBLER: Why do you play?
SECOND GAMBLER: It's the only wheel in town.

As Webb and Salancik point out, the interview is not really the only wheel for those who investigate and describe human behavior, but it has become an important one for understandable reasons. We rely on sight for direct observation of events and for reading documents.* But what we can see and read is limited. How absurd not to use speech! And if we can usually rely on questions and answers in informal fact-finding—"Is it too warm? Shall I turn down the thermostat?"—the questioning that is the foundation of formal interviewing follows naturally.

There is also a basic defense for interviewing, one that tempers the gloomy judgments: The more we learn about the inaccuracies that crop up frequently in interviews, the more we know about what kinds of questions are likely to be answered inaccurately—and what kinds we can trust. Threatening experiences are often repressed: Mothers whose infants have difficulties immediately after delivery frequently forget this quite rapidly, but they remember accurately other events surrounding the delivery.

Significantly, as we learn more about the inaccuracies of interview findings, we are better able to devise techniques to counter them.

The Single-Interview Error

A single brief interview may be enough to establish a particular fact that does not involve the interviewee's self-interest, but it is usually absurd to expect to picture a person or to relate his purposes or policies adequately

* We also rely on sight in interviewing. Nonverbal communication is covered in detail in the chapter on observing. The fact that we observe during interviews emphasizes the close relationship of interviewing and observing.

by talking to him briefly. Interviewing the same subject again and again is helpful, for the same reason that a lengthy interview is usually better than a short one. Ricardo Diaz, a documentary film-maker, tells of interviewing a young American race-car driver who sought the world's land speed record, which was then held by a foreigner. When Diaz asked him, early in the interview, why he was in such a dangerous occupation, the young man spoke grandly of the challenge of speed and the need to bring the world's record home to the United States. Much later, when they had covered many other subjects and were less formal with each other, Diaz asked him again why he drove for a world record. The driver then admitted that, as one with little education and a taste for splendor, he saw no other path for himself. Perhaps the real answer combined elements of the first and second—and more. But the pitfalls of the single brief interview are obvious.

Nor can interviewing to depict a person or to explain his policies and purposes be limited to the subject. To do so is to invite imprisonment in the subject's perspective. "The reporter has to talk to enough people so that he can reduce the degree to which he is misled," Joseph and Stewart Alsop have written.[6] Stewart Alsop vividly relates Lyndon Johnson's prime technique, which was to overwhelm the reporter. While Johnson was Senate Majority Leader, Alsop reported: "As for Johnson, his record on defense has been good. But he is obviously open to the charge that he only summoned his Preparedness Subcommittee to make a serious inquiry into preparedness after the issue had been dramatized by the Sputniks." Alsop later reported on Johnson's reaction, referring to himself as "the reporter":

> On the day the article appeared, the reporter was summoned to the Majority Leader's small, ornate, oddly impressive office in the Capitol. Treatment A started quietly. The Majority Leader was, it seemed, in a relaxed, friendly, and reminiscent mood. Nostalgically he recalled how he had come to Washington in 1937, a mere freshman Congressman, and how Franklin D. Roosevelt had prevailed on the chairman of the Naval Affairs Committee to put "young Lyndon Johnson" on his powerful committee. That was, it seemed, the beginning of Johnson's interest in the national defense, which had continued ever since.
>
> By gradual stages the relaxed, friendly and reminiscent mood gave way to something rather like a human hurricane. Johnson was up, striding about his office, talking without pause, occasionally leaning over, his nose almost touching the mesmerized reporter's, to shake the reporter's shoulder or grab his knee. Secretaries were rung for. Memoranda appeared and then more memoranda, as well as letters, newspaper articles and unidentifiable scraps of paper, which were proffered in quick succession and then snatched away. Appeals were

> made, to the Almighty, to the shades of the departed great, to the reporter's finer instincts and better nature, while the reporter, unable to get a word in edgewise, sat collapsed upon a leather sofa, eyes glazed, mouth half open. Treatment A ended a full two hours later, when the Majority Leader, a friendly arm around the shoulder of the dazed journalist, ushered him into the outer office. It was not until some days later that the reporter was able to recall that, excellent as Johnson's record on national defense undoubtedly is, the two sentences he had written had been demonstrably true.[7]

One must counter such techniques by learning more than the subject relates. Additional interviewing and careful research in documents enables the reporter to triangulate: Here is what he says, here is what others say, here is what the record seems to show. The probable truth is more likely to emerge from this process than from a single interview.

The truth will not always emerge neatly. A reporter once wrote an article on Congressman John J. Rooney of New York, who was the chairman of a congressional committee that was pivotal in deciding the budget for the U.S. Department of State. Year after year, he would present his committee's budget recommendations to the House of Representatives and verbally attack the State Department at the same time. He consistently called "representation allowances," money which enabled United States missions to make small expenditures for entertaining, "booze money for those striped-pants cookie-pushers." The allowances for such major embassies as those in England and France were always too small for the entertaining that had long been traditional. As a result, only wealthy men who could pay entertainment bills out of their own pockets could afford to represent the United States there. But a high official of the State Department assured the reporter that Congressman Rooney was actually the best friend the Department had. He explained that most congressmen were contemptuous of the State Department. By attacking it, Congressman Rooney seemed to be their ally, when in fact he always presented a budget that was larger than Congress would have approved had Rooney not attacked. Given the known attitude toward the State Department of many congressmen, this theory seemed plausible. But checking budget records over several years and conducting other interviews—especially with retired State Department officials who no longer had anything to gain or lose from Congressman Rooney's actions—persuaded the reporter that it was not true. The weight of all the evidence caused him to judge that the congressman's attacks were sincere—but the possibility that the State Department official was right led the reporter to report that theory as well.

Social scientists and historians and biographers who interview have also learned that they cannot rely on a single source. Many social scientists ask questions that can be checked against records ("Do you have a library card?"—and because using a library lends status, many who do not have cards report that they do) and ask questions of friends and relatives of the interview subject. Any competent historian or biographer uses much the same techniques for checking accuracy.

Standardized Questions and Pretesting

Many who have learned to enhance accuracy by questioning widely give too little attention to standardizing: asking exactly the same questions of each respondent in exactly the same way. The result of varying the questioning slightly is illustrated by the differing responses to these similar questions:

"Do you think anything *should* be done to make it easier for people to pay doctor or hospital bills?"

"Do you think anything *could* be done to make it easier for people to pay doctor or hospital *bills?*"

"Do you think anything *might* be done to make it easier for people to pay doctor or hospital bills?"

The difference in the answers is instructive: 82 percent said something *should* be done, 77 percent said something *could* be done, and 63 percent said something *might* be done.[8]

Survey researchers who have studied such effects extensively have much to teach other researchers about the value of standardizing (although many social scientists use unstandardized interviews at least occasionally). It is true that social scientists usually have methods and purposes—using many interviewers to ask hundreds of people for their opinions or experiences regarding one subject, for example—that other researchers seldom share. But the standardizing that social scientists have found essential in survey research is worth considering at length.

In a valuable paper titled "The Interview: An Educational Research Tool," Andrew Collins of the University of Minnesota points out that most of the interview schedules used in social science research are highly standardized because "Even under the best conditions, the differences between the way one interview and another are conducted may wipe out the comparability of the respondents' answers." [9] He explains:

> In the completely standardized interview schedule, there is a list of carefully worded questions, and the interviewer is expected not to deviate from the schedule in getting the respondents' answers. In other words, every respondent is asked the same questions in the same order. This assures that the information from every respondent is obtained under approximately the same conditions.

> When the conditions are the same, you can be more sure that differences in people's answers are due to real differences in the people, and not to variations in the way the interview was conducted.[10]
>
> . . . Questions should never be explained to respondents or re-worded to make them clearer unless the interviewer has been instructed to do so. If a respondent doesn't understand the question, the interviewer can only re-state it exactly as it is written, slowly and with proper emphasis. If the respondent still doesn't understand, the interviewer should ask him to answer it according to his best understanding and note on the record that the respondent claimed not to have understood it.[11]

The interviewer has a bit of latitude to probe, Collins points out, but he must be certain to ask only for clarification. For example, "What do you mean by ————?" A respondent who uses "They say" should be asked who "they" are. A respondent who attributes something to "the government" probably should be asked whether it is local, state, or federal—or perhaps whether he means the president, Congress, or the courts.

Those who have had interviewing experience may protest that although uniformity is valuable it is too constricting: a question may be meaningful for one respondent and not for another. Social scientists try, often quite successfully, to remove that uncertainty before undertaking interviews. First, the researcher frames his questions in the context of other interviewing experiences, recalling problems that he has faced before. Next, he is likely to confer with colleagues who can provide not only a different perspective but also different survey research experiences. So far, the process differs little from that of any thoughtful group of Washington correspondents who get together informally prior to a press conference to decide exactly how to ask what questions of the president.

The social scientist's method differs in the next step, the pretest. Instead of going into the field immediately to question the prospective respondents, he arranges to try his interview schedule on a few of them, or on a few people who are *like* those he plans to interview.

The value of pretesting is indicated by an experience of Rae Goodell when she was a graduate student. Her part in a large research project that was designed to analyze mass media coverage of environmental news in the San Francisco Bay Area was to identify the "environmental reporters" (a difficult term to define) and describe their standards for environmental reporting and their opinions of its quality. She spent several weeks developing one questionnaire[12] for reporters and another for editors: devising her own questions, then checking them with professors and other graduate students. Several project workers who had other assignments asked Goodell to include questions that would yield information useful to them (a fairly common occurrence in large research projects). The questionnaires grew so long that she had to delete some items. When she was ready to pretest, the questionnaire for editors ran four pages, that for reporters ran five. Goodell has written of the results of the pretest:

> a. I had the dullest question first. Dave [the project director] wanted a definition of "environmental reporting" to come out of all this, and I had the two questions about definition first. After one of the pretests, I wrote in the margin, "Hit with a grabber first. This the dullest."
>
> b. As a once and future newspaper reporter, I had written the questions for the newspaper people, overlooking the radio and TV respondents; e.g. one question asked if the reporter had a problem getting enough "space from editors" for environmental stories; had to be changed to "space from editors or air time from directors."
>
> c. Some of the questions were hard to read—it was difficult to figure where I wanted the answer put. I typed up the final version for photocopying myself, to make sure questions were arranged clearly.
>
> d. On one question, the pretest interviewees pointed out that I would get the "ideal" answer, the answer everyone knew was "right," rather than what was really going on. The question asked, "How diverse an audience do you try to reach with environment stories," Everybody checked, and guaranteed that all survey respondents would check, "all readers or listeners." [13]

As a result, the questionnaire that Goodell ultimately used in the field was quite different from the pretest version in length, spacing, question order, and wording.

The full panoply of survey research methods is not essential, of course, in all interviewing. But all researchers can benefit from the principles that undergird standardizing and pretesting.

Conducting the Interview

Because they have relied for so long on interviews and have conducted so many, journalists and social scientists have developed a large body of useful techniques. Placing the insights of experienced journalists within a framework provided by social scientists yields lessons for almost any researcher.

Psychologists Eleanor and Nathan Maccoby point out in their chapter on interviewing in the first edition of *The Handbook of Social Psychology* that concepts of role are central: "The interviewer must occupy some role, whether he wishes it or not, and therefore the research worker must be conscious of the various roles possible . . . and attempt to establish the role which will best further the purposes of this study." [14]

This is excellent advice, and almost any researcher can adapt his role to some degree depending on circumstances—and, of course, depending on the role the interview subject establishes for himself. It is nonetheless clear that roles—or major aspects of roles—are already assigned by the occupations of the interviewers. Consider:

· Most often, the journalist is welcome and his questions answered eagerly. Because he sometimes assumes the role of adversary to those in power, especially politicians, some of the journalist's *questions* may be distasteful to the subject. But the mass media are usually considered to confer status on those whose opinions are quoted and whose experiences are related. In general, then, the natural role of the journalist is one of power because most of those he interviews want to have their views quoted in print or on the air.

· The favors that a social scientist can confer on an interview subject are seldom so immediate, so direct, or so obviously beneficial. The subjects are not likely to have their opinions or experiences publicized tomorrow or next week, and they probably will not receive *any* personal publicity; little social research singles out individuals. There is another, usually weaker, lure for the interview subject: the possibility that he is contributing in a small way to important findings. Many social scientists emphasize this contribution with satisfying results. It is also true that so few in any society are ever asked to offer their opinions or relate their experiences that many who are asked for interviews—especially by people of high status—are flattered and cooperative.

To contrast the positions: the *journalist* is often *offering* a favor when he interviews (or *seems* to be; gathering information is, of course, necessary to his professional life); the *social scientist* is often *receiving* a favor. What these generalizations say about the usual role of the different interviewers should be obvious.

· The student who interviews for campus publication or broadcast usually shares the favorable position of the professional journalist (depending, naturally, on the reputation of the newspaper or the station). The student who interviews for a project supervised by social scientists usually shares their status and can make the same appeals for cooperation. But the student who seeks interviews for, say, a term paper is usually in the unfortunate position of requesting cooperation for his own purposes. Fortunately, many who are asked for interviews by students are willing to help, usually because they were once students who needed help. (The desire to help *anyone* accomplish a task—if assisting requires little effort—is often a factor in granting interviews to journalists and social scientists.) But the role of the student is nearly always that of supplicant, which limits his ability to ask questions that his interview subject is likely to consider abrasive or embarrassing.

The Maccobys have pointed to six possible sources of error in interviewing: (1) the appearance and manner of the interviewer, (2) the way interviewers word and deliver questions, (3) the interviewer's own attitudes, (4) the interviewer's expectations of the respondent's attitudes, (5) interviewer variations in fullness of probing, and (6) interviewer variations in recording respondents' answers.[15]

Appearance and Manner of the Interviewer

Interviews are often distorted, in effect, before they begin. Studies show that the interviewer's race, religion, sex, and even age influence response. For example, one group of researchers reported:

> Negroes were more reluctant to express to white interviewers their resentments over discrimination by employers or labor unions, in the army and in public places [or] . . . to reveal to white interviewers sympathy for the CIO (possibly out of fear that the white interviewer might consider them too radical). Even on some of the factual questions such as auto ownership, reading of Negro newspapers, and CIO membership, apparently some Negroes reported differently to white interviewers than to Negro interviewers.[16]

The mass media have increased the hiring of Negroes and other minorities in recent years in an effort to control this effect. Editors ask, or in some cases order, reporters to wear beards, hair, and clothes in line with the conventional (which is often difficult: conventions have changed and are changing). Others who employ interviewers have done much the same. Most of these actions are efforts to reduce the social distance between the interviewer and his subject. In a few cases, a vast social distance is useful, as the success of journalist Tom Wolfe, whose dress is usually bizarre, has shown. Most often, a great distance causes distortion. Many respondents who think an interviewer represents a higher social class than themselves answer questions in a way that they believe the interviewer will approve. Some others resent an interviewer who seems to be of a higher class and are hostile.

The interviewer's manner may indicate social distance quite as readily as his appearance. Often, an interviewer must adapt to his subject. Saul Pett, a veteran Associated Press feature writer, has related two experiences that indicate how adaptable an interviewer must be. His most difficult interview subject was Dr. Albert Kinsey, the sex researcher, who was himself a practiced—and no-nonsense—interviewer. Kinsey met Pett for their appointment at the precisely agreed minute, pulled out a travel alarm clock, wound it, set the alarm, set a coffee table between himself and Pett, checked the clock against his wristwatch, and, finally looking up, said, "Yes." It was obviously no time for small talk.

Pett's best interview subject was a writer, Dorothy Parker. When he went to interview her shortly after her seventieth birthday, she opened the door and asked, "Are you married, my dear?" "Yes, I am," he ansewered. "Well, in that case," she said, "you won't mind zipping me up." [17]

The Way Questions are Worded and Delivered *

The classic case of confusion in question wording appeared not in an interview but in the appeal of a newspaper for its readers to participate in a survey. It was the summer of 1972, and an obnoxious young American, Bobby Fischer, was playing a Russian, Boris Spassky, for the chess championship of the world. Fischer was behaving so abominably that the editors of the *Sacramento Union* thought many of their readers might favor the Russian. So they printed a small ballot that asked: "Are you pulling for Fischer or Boris Spassky to win? Yes________. No________."

This is more than a light example. It is an extreme case of muddled thinking that shows how thoughtlessly most of us frame questions. *The Art of Asking Questions,* which was cited earlier in this chapter, is full of

* Allen Barton parodied the pollsters' careful attention to question wording and delivery in his article "Asking the Embarrassing Question" (*Public Opinion Quarterly,* Vol. 22, 1958) showing how their elaborate methods might lead them to ask respondents "Did you kill your wife?":

1 The Casual Approach:
"Do you happen to have murdered your wife?"
2. The Numbered Card:
"Would you please read off the number on this card that corresponds to what became of your wife?"
   1. Natural death.
   2. I killed her.
   3. Other (What?)
3. The Everybody Approach:
"As you know, many people have been killing their wives lately. Do you happen to have killed yours?"
4. The Other People Approach:
(a) "Do you know any people who have murdered their wives?"
(b) "How about yourself?"
5. The Sealed Ballot Technique:
In this version you explain that the survey respects people's right to anonymity in respect to their marital relations, and that they themselves are to fill out the answer to the question, seal it in an envelope, and drop it in a box conspicuously labelled "Sealed Ballot Box" carried by the interviewer.
6. The Kinsey Technique:
Stare firmly into respondent's eyes and ask in simple, clear-cut language such as that to which the respondent is accustomed, and with an air of assuming that everyone had done everything: "Did you ever kill your wife?" (pp. 67–68)

examples of loose wording. It points up many subtle effects of different word uses. "Do you think the United States should allow public speeches against democracy?" would seem to be the opposite of "Do you think the United States should forbid public speeches against democracy?" One would expect opposite percentages when matched samples of respondents are asked these questions. Instead, these were the results:

First Question	*Second Question*
Should allow 21%	Should not forbid 39%
Should not allow 62%	Should forbid 46%
No opinion 17%	No opinion 15%

Clearly there is something forbidding about "forbid." People will more readily say that an act should not be allowed than will say it should be forbidden.[18]

The primary points in wording are, first, to decide what one wants to know, then to frame a question that is both precise and simple, and, finally and crucially, to evaluate it from the viewpoint of the respondent. To try to determine whether workers think merit or seniority is more important in winning higher salaries, one would not ask, "Do you think most raises in pay are based on merit or that most raises are based on seniority?" This satisfies the first two necessities: It is addressed to the opinion sought and it seems to be precise and simple. But one need only think about the possible responses to realize that any number of workers may think *most* raises are based on favoritism, strikes, or across-the-board increases. A better question: "Which is more important in deciding whether a worker is given a raise in pay—merit or seniority?"

Although it is fairly easy to avoid loaded questions in writing interview schedules and questionnaires (constant evaluation is essential, however), it is not so easy to avoid them in free-flowing interviews. More distortions may spring from questions that lead respondents down the interviewer's path than from any other source. Note how this respondent is pulled by the interviewer:

Q: What kind of writers are left in television then?

A: Those who are still around are trained in the taboos of the business. . .

Q: Again this stems from the commercial exigencies of television, doesn't it?

A: It comes from the commercial nature. I don't want to be unfair to the businessman but. . .

Q: But all these purposes—artistic, commercial, etc.—are at war with each other.

A: Continually at war. The thing I object to is that the world of commerce is using the resources of the theatre, of all our culture, for sales purposes.

Q: On a medium that belongs to the public.

A: Yes, I think that is short-sighted and foolish. . .

Q: What can a governmental regulatory agency do in this regard? The Federal Communications Commission has been a rather toothless organization in recent years, hasn't it?

A: Until the last few months, the FCC has been an utter disaster as far as making its influence felt.[19]

Most often, the interviewer should ask questions in a way that indicates that there are no right or wrong answers. He should not show surprise at an answer, nor should he agree or disagree. Perhaps the model for the unemotional interviewer was Dr. Albert Kinsey, who undertook his research at a time when sexual behavior was seldom openly discussed. "The interviewer should not make it easy for a subject to deny his participation in any form of sexual activity," Dr. Kinsey wrote. "We always begin by asking when they first engaged in such activity." [20] When a subject admitted an unusual sex act, Kinsey would ask in a matter-of-fact tone, "How many times?"

The Interviewer's Own Attitudes

Because an interviewer's own attitudes and opinions should not be allowed to influence an interviewee, they should not be expressed. An interviewee who asks for the interviewer's opinion should usually be told that the interviewer's job is to gather opinions, not have them.

Of course, an interviewer *does* have opinions and may be challenged in such a way to express them that the interview will not continue, or will not continue satisfactorily, unless he does. In such a case, it is useful to know Benjamin Franklin's techniques in argument:

> I made it a rule to forebear all direct contradiction to the sentiments of others, and all positive assertions of my own. I even forbid myself the use of every word in the language that imported a fixed opinion, such as certainly, undoubtedly, etc., and I adopted instead of them, *I conceive, I apprehend, I imagine a thing to be so and so, or so it appears to me at the present.* When another asserted something that I thought to be an error, I denied myself the pleasure of contradicting him abruptly, and of showing immediately some absurdity in his proposition; and in answering I began by observing that in certain cases or circumstances his opinion would be right, but in the present case there appeared or seemed to me some difference, etc. I soon found the advantage of this change in my manners; the conversations I engaged in went on more pleasantly. The modest way in which I proposed my opinions procured them a readier reception and less contradiction;

I had less mortification when I was found to be in the wrong; and I more easily prevailed with others to give up their mistakes and join with me when I happened to be right.

Interviewers should avoid arguments, but Franklin's *manner* is a model when they cannot.

Journalists, especially those who report politics, often ask questions that interviewees consider challenging and abrasive. Such questions *may* grow out of a journalist's own opinions, but it is a mistake to assume that they often do. Many politicians find it useful for their own purposes to charge that reporters are, in effect, political opponents. After they retire, however, most politicians admit that asking tough questions is the job of the journalist. Former California Governor Edmund G. "Pat" Brown developed a fairly detached and philosophical perspective on questions from reporters when he was out of office. He wrote to his successor, Ronald Reagan:

There's a passage in *War and Peace* that every new Governor with a big majority should tack on his office wall. In it young Count Rostov, after weeks as the toast of elegant farewell parties, gallops off on his first cavalry charge and then finds real bullets snapping at his ears.

"Why, they're shooting at me," he says. "Me, whom everybody loves."

Nothing worse will happen to you in the next four years. Learn to live with that; the rest is easy.

As you must have noticed by now, the press fires the first real bullets at new governors.

. . . There is also not much I can tell you about the weekly news conference that you haven't already learned. You will find that while both surgeons and reporters operate with professional detachment there is only one real difference between them. Surgeons make more money for cutting you up.

But their motives are the same—to make sure everything is running properly. And in the case of the press, they operate with a proxy from the voters. For the voters, news conferences are as close to a first-hand accounting of what happened to their money as they ever get. . . .

Invest as much time preparing for these inquisitions as you can spare, but don't feel bad if you are caught off-guard. I can still hear a voice from the back of the room asking: "Governor, do you think lobbyists should be required to wear little green buttons on their lapels?" Maybe you would have a ready answer for that. I didn't.

Harrowing as they are, news conferences do provide a chance for correspondents to bore in, a practice that philosophers find a healthy thing for the democratic process. Few governors take any comfort in that.[21]

The Interviewer's Expectations of the Respondent's Attitudes

Just as the interviewer who reveals his own attitudes may influence response, the interviewer who seems to expect certain responses may receive them for that reason. In one of the earliest investigations of this kind of distortion, Stuart Rice found that welfare recipients blamed their plight on causes that they thought would square with the interviewer's values: an interviewer who identified himself as a Prohibitionist obtained three times as many answers blaming alcohol as did another interviewer who described himself as a socialist; the socialist obtained twice as many answers blaming industrial factors as did the Prohibitionist.[22]

The interviewer can indicate his expectations much more subtly, as Collins points out:

> The interviewer may use facial expressions, gestures or sounds that encourage a respondent in a particular line of comment which he might not otherwise follow. Many laboratory studies have shown that if the interviewer smiles, leans forward, or says "mm-hmm" or "good" when the respondent uses particular words or phrases, the respondent will tend to use those expressions even more often. The same things happen if these encouraging signals are given when a particular attitude is expressed; it comes to be expressed even more often and strongly.[23]

Interviewer Variations in Probing

How strongly an interviewer pursues a line of questioning, or how strongly he "probes," varies widely with purposes and situations. In the standardized technique already described, the interviewer probes gingerly, if at all. When a researcher is conducting one of many interviews in a sample, it is necessary to make the interview as much like all the others as possible. If he probes deeply and asks many kinds of questions of one interviewee that are not asked of others, the research project becomes distorted.

Interviewing one subject who is to be the focus of a study is, of course, quite different. Probing is recommended—unless the interviewee is granting a favor by submitting to an interview (and may withdraw the favor). There are dozens of other situations in which probing must be limited, or in which the interviewer must probe tactfully and with restraint, nearly all of them obvious to a sensitive interviewer.

One danger in probing should be emphasized. For example, in surveying preferences, especially among voters during presidential campaigns, so many prospective voters say they are "undecided" that interviewers are often instructed to try to determine whether each respondent really *is* undecided. Perhaps he leans toward one candidate. But the respondent may try to determine whether the interviewer approves the leaning and may look for hints as to *his* opinion. "Would you say that you lean toward Kennedy?" may be taken to mean that the respondent should lean that way. In short, probing can distort.

Whatever the danger, strong probing is often essential, especially in political journalism. Dan Rather of CBS News offered several lessons in skillful probing during an hour-long interview with President Nixon on January 2, 1972. Nixon had not then announced whether he would seek re-election. Rather asked, "May we assume you are a candidate for re-election?" Nixon answered that he would have to decide by January 14, the date for filing for the New Hampshire presidential primary: "I will be making a decision and I will be announcing it by the fourteenth."

Not satisfied, Rather posed the question another way, asking whether Attorney General John Mitchell, who had managed Nixon's 1968 campaign, would resign soon to prepare the new campaign. Nixon responded:

> Well, you're getting me right into the question that I just refused to answer, but I understand that. If I make the decision to become a candidate—and there is, of course, good reason to think that I might make the decision in that direction. . . .[24]

Rather asked two more questions relating to re-election: "Mr. President, under what circumstances would you *not* be a candidate for re-election?" and "Mr. President, can you give us assurances, categorically and unequivocally, that if you are a candidate, that you want to run again with Vice President Agnew and that he will be your running mate if you have anything to do with it?" When Nixon had answered these questions, no one needed to wait until January 14 to be aware that he would run for re-election. And no one had to wait until July, when Nixon formally announced his choice of a running mate, to be aware that he would again run with Agnew.

Interviewer Variations in Recording

No matter what method of recording is used—a tape recorder, pen and notebook, or memory—the interviewer may have trouble with the respondent and with himself. Many interview subjects are made nervous by a recorder or by an interviewer taking notes, and many become nervous when neither a recorder nor a notebook is used, reasoning that interviewers, like everyone else, have fallible memories. More will be said later in this chapter about the fears of respondents. Here, let us focus on a few of the problems the interviewer creates for himself.

Recorders are not infallible. The point is stated that way because our trust in gadgets and machines is sometimes total. More precisely: Interviewers who use recorders are not infallible. Even when they operate the recorders without error, they must interpret, selecting the telling and appropriate points from an often unwieldy mass of information. Different interviewers, of course, often interpret differently.

A properly operated recorder, however, usually yields a faithful, full record, although some researchers find that they cannot understand things on tape that they had understood in the face-to-face interview. The visual cues are missing. But no note-taking interviewer comes close to making such a full and faithful record, whether he relies on notes taken during the interview or notes written from memory after it.

Fortunately, few interviewers need an exact record of every response. More and more of those who do need one are turning to recorders, especially now that their use for many purposes is so common that they have become familiar and seem less threatening. The principal problem is that long tape-recorded interviews yield a discouraging quantity of tape. It is time-consuming to transcribe (or even to hear) all of it, and it is frustrating to know that a few valuable words are submerged somewhere in what seem to be miles of tape. For such reasons, researchers who need no more than a few direct quotations ordinarily rely on notebooks. Many political reporters use notebooks *and* a recorder, using their written notes primarily or exclusively in writing stories, the taped record in case of disputes. When a former automobile dealer, Douglas McKay, was appointed Secretary of the Interior in a Republican administration, his first words during an important speech to the Chamber of Commerce of the United States were, "Well, we're here in the saddle as an Administration representative of business and industry." An Associated Press reporter, Sterling Green, published the statement. The Democrats leaped on it, charging that the administration represented only one segment of society. McKay denied making the statement. But a taped record showed that Green's report was accurate. "In a difficult, disputatious situation," Green says, "a tape is a good thing to have going, even if you're not planning to use it at all for the purpose of writing your story." [25]

Guidelines for Interviewing

As some of the preceding points indicate, journalists have purposes and needs that often vary from those of other researchers. Most of the others can benefit, however, from journalistic experiences and perspectives.

Prepare for the Interview

An interviewer should always learn as much as possible about his subject before the appointment. Subjects who are not actually incensed by an interviewer's ignorance are likely to be uncomfortable with one who demonstrates that he has not done his homework. Doing the homework —learning at least the basic facts about the interviewee—is complimentary and encourages response. John Gunther, the late author of the famous *Inside* books, warned, "One thing is never, never, never to ask a man about his own first name, job, or title. These the interviewer should know beforehand." And, of course, much more.

The late A. J. Liebling, who was one of the most accomplished writers for the *New Yorker*, described the value of preparations, or "preps":

> One of the best preps I ever did was for a profile of Eddie Arcaro, the jockey. When I interviewed him the *first question* I asked was, "How many holes longer do you keep your left stirrup than your right?" That started him talking easily and after an hour, during which I had put in about twelve words, he said, "I can see you've been around riders a lot." [26]

The precise value of extensive preparation is shown by Dan Rather's television interview with President Nixon. Rather cited a recent Harris Poll which showed that about 50 percent of the American people "said that you had failed to inspire confidence and faith and lacked personal warmth and compassion. Why do you suppose that is?"

Nixon thought he saw an unusual opportunity and took it:

> Well, it's because people tell the pollsters that, of course. So that's what the people must believe. But on the other hand, without trying to psychoanalyze myself, because that's your job, I would simply answer the question by saying that my strong point is not rhetoric, it isn't showmanship, it isn't big promises, those things that breed the glamor and excitement that people call charisma and warmth.
>
> My strong point, if I have a strong point, is performance. I always do more than I said.

Rather was prepared not only for that response but others as well:

> . . . But the same Harris Poll indicated that only about a third of the people thought that you had kept your campaign promises. I think you'd agree that anyone in politics should be held accountable. I, as a journalist, think that anyone in politics should be given an opportunity to explain.
>
> So would you explain, obviously as briefly as possible but as fully as you

think necessary, in 1968 you said, "I pledge to redress the present economic imbalance without increasing unemployment"—direct quotation. Now, unemployment was, I believe, 3.6 when you came in; it's at or near six percent for the last several months.

PRESIDENT NIXON: Let's take that one first.

RATHER: Yes, please.

PRESIDENT NIXON: Unemployment was 3.6 when I came in, at a cost of 300 casualties a week in Vietnam. Since I've come in, we have got 400,000 people home from Vietnam; there're two million people who have been let out of defense plants and out of the Armed Services as a result of our winding up—winding down the war in Vietnam, and if those people were still in the defense plants and still in Vietnam, unemployment would still be 3.6. That's too high a cost.

RATHER: But wasn't that foreseeable, Mr. President?

PRESIDENT NIXON: That was foreseeable, but my point is—my point is that we were—what I was saying was that we should have a combination: a combination of bringing a war to an end and then moving from there to a kind of prosperity of high employment and low unemployment that we haven't had since President Eisenhower was President in this room in 1957. That was the only time it was less than five percent. In all the years of the sixties, unemployment averaged 5.8 except in the war years. Now, we can do better than that, and as we move from war to peace in the year 1972, we're going to bring the unemployment rate below that.

RATHER: Now, another—September 1968—quotation: "Seventy-four percent of farm parity is intolerable. I pledge that in my Administration, farmers will have better." Unquote. Now farm parity has been—is at or near 70 now, has not been back up to 74—even 74 percent through most of your Administration.

PRESIDENT NIXON: Well, let's look at the farm parity in terms of another factor. Farm income, which is what farmers really care about a great deal, as you know, because it was also reported on CBS just two weeks ago, came up sharply in the last month. I look for the year 1972 to be a very good year as far as the farmers are concerned, in terms of their income, and also in terms of parity, and I should point out that in this instance, here is where you're going to get one of the benefits of our new international economic policy. . . .[27]

Many of Nixon's political opponents considered his responses weak; many of his supporters considered them strong; and hundreds of viewers protested to CBS that Rather had been disrespectful. But there is no doubt that Rather did his homework well.

For lengthy and important interviews like this one, journalists customarily prepare lists of questions. But they do not feel bound to ask all of them, and they frame new questions during the interview. They argue that an interview is a human, not a bookkeeping, situation. Growth and continuity in an interview spring from conversation. Transitions should be natural: Questions should grow logically from the discussion, one answer suggesting another question. One who plans exactly what he will ask may miss the opportunity to pose a question that occurs during an interview. Some journalists believe so strongly that they must promote a free-flowing discussion that they seldom do more than jot down a few key words prior to interviewing. But even they are likely to advise beginners to write questions in a notebook and leave spaces to record answers. Attempting to move immediately into the smooth discourse of the professional interviewer leads to floundering—and to forgetting important questions.

Take Notes and/or Record

Journalists are so divided among themselves whether to take notes, use a tape recorder, or take notes *and* use a recorder that generalizing is dangerous. But this rule-of-thumb may be useful: Take notes freely or use a recorder, or do both, in interviewing those who are accustomed to speaking for publication or broadcast (politicians, civic leaders, and entertainers). There are, of course, exceptions. Vladimir Nabokov, author of *Lolita* and other acclaimed novels (and a notable punster), told an interviewer, "No, tape recorders are out. No speaking off the Nabocuff. When I see one of those machines, I start hemming and hawing . . . hemming and hawing. Hemmingwaying all over the place." [28] It may be significant that Nabokov is in his seventies. In any case, younger celebrities are more likely to be accustomed to such gadgetry.

Young or old, many of those who are not used to speaking for publication or broadcast are likely to become self-conscious in the presence of note-taking or a tape recorder. Some actually freeze, but many soon relax and forget that their words are being recorded. This is especially likely in group interviews; the interplay of conversation leads to a focus on the other individuals and away from devices. All this points up the other end of the journalist's rule-of-thumb: Be careful in introducing a notebook or a recorder into an interview with those who are not accustomed to being quoted.

W. H. Crockford of the Richmond, Virginia, *Times-Dispatch* says, "Flipping out the notebook the minute you flush the quarry has never worked too well for me. It scares some subjects. The best excuse I find for breaking out the pad is a bit of blue-eyed admiration for some happy observation they've just made. I may try, 'Say, that's good. I want to be sure I get that down just right.' And write. The notebook now spells reassurance."

As for the mechanics of note-taking, most researchers devise their own shorthand: *imp.* for *important, w/* for *with, w/o* for *without.* One journalist's technique for winning time to record an important answer without causing an awkward silence is to ask another, minor question immediately. While the subject is responding to the second, the journalist records the answer to the first.

Truman Capote, author of *In Cold Blood* and many other books, is part of the small minority that is against using notes or tape recordings:

> If you write down or tape what people say, it makes them feel inhibited and self-conscious. It makes them say what they think you *expect* them to say. . . . Long before I started *In Cold Blood,* I taught myself to be my own tape recorder. It wasn't as hard as it might sound. What I'd do was have a friend talk or read for a set length of time, tape what he was saying, and meanwhile listen to him as intently as I could. Then I'd go and write down what he had said as I remembered it, and later compare what I had with the tape. . . . Finally, when I got to be about 97 per cent accurate, I felt ready to take on this book.[29]

Encourage Response

Only when interviewing busy and abrupt people—and those who are merely suffering the interview—should one begin questions abruptly. Small talk at the beginning is usually designed to encourage the later conversation. This does not mean that the interviewer should make an all-too-obvious and awkward effort to chitchat, which requires a stumbling leap to the real subject. It simply means that the usual prelude to questioning a politician about his candidacy is not the weather, but politics in general.

William Ryan, Sterling Green, Saul Pett, and Peter Arnett, all of the Associated Press, recently discussed the value of various interview beginnings:

RYAN: . . . I like to work up gradually to major questions.

GREEN: I generally do it quite the opposite. I like to land on him with a hard one right at the start and show him that we mean business and get away from any idea that "This is a puff piece." There's considerable benefit in this because it puts him on his mettle and he begins to answer responsively from the start.

PETT: I think it depends on the kind of story. If it's a hard news spot interview, we can't really fool around too much. If it's a personality type interview, you almost have to. On an interview with Mayor Lindsay, I knew that he had a good sense of humor. So I prefaced my first question by saying, "I have something terribly serious to ask you. I hope you'll be frank in your answer." And I could see him straighten up and get ready for this tough question. And then the question was: "Would you want your daughter to marry a mayor of New York?" Well, we got along fine after that. But, I cite that only as an example of work put into questions in advance.

ARNETT: Much of my work has been in the foreign field, where I interviewed people who were not very familiar with English and used an interpreter. In that case I went right into the biggest question first. However, with others familiar with English, I prefer the small talk approach.[30]

Usually, the ideal should mark the halfway point between monologue and dialogue. If the subject talks in an endless monologue, leading points may be ignored. Most subjects must be steered. But if the interview is a real dialogue, and the interviewer is doing half the talking, he is probably showing himself off and perhaps irritating his subject. The most delicate point in journalistic interviewing may be the necessity for the interviewer to comment appropriately on an answer in developing his next question without seeming to dominate the interview. A comment is important in connection with at least a few questions, for an interviewer usually invites a full response by making it clear, modestly, that he is knowledgeable. His subject usually speaks freely, reasoning that his responses will be reported in a meaningful context. It is a cardinal error, however, for an interviewer to fail to ask questions because he fears exposing his ignorance of particular points. If he knew *everything,* there would be no reason for an interview. On some occasions, though, usually when he tries to dig up hidden information, a journalist pretends that he knows more than he actually knows. The pretense ordinarily suggests: Because I know three-quarters of the story, you might as well give me the rest so I can come out with the full story rather than a distorted version of it. This sometimes works, even if the journalist has only a vague tip.

Inevitably, there are awful occasions when a bored subject answers in monosyllables: "Yes." "No." "Who knows?" Transforming these deadly situations is difficult, but it can sometimes be accomplished with a simple question: "Why?" Although a subject can answer most direct questions with a simple positive or negative, it is quite another thing for him to explore the *why* of his answer in one syllable. The real aim, of course, is to inspire interest, to ask the interviewee to explore the depths of his own point of view. Gunther has commented: "One thing I have found out is that almost any person will talk freely—such is human frailty—if you will ask him the measure of his own accomplishment."

Respect Confidences

Anyone who conducts many interviews is certain to be asked at some point to keep information confidential. Although the request is most often made for only part of the information divulged, journalists have been surprised to be asked at the end of an interview to keep *everything* secret. This occurs most often because the source suddenly decides that he has been indiscreet. Some journalists refuse such requests, holding rightly that an agreement should have been reached at the beginning. In ideal circumstances, the interviewer and his subject stipulate at the beginning what kind of information can be reported and what kind will be disclosed only to give the journalist a broad understanding.

Agreements are now frequently made that allow disclosing all or part of an interview, but that require cloaking the name of the source. Washington correspondents and government officials have established fairly explicit ground rules for attributing information. "Off the record" means that information is disclosed only to widen the journalist's general understanding and is not to be reported in any form. "Background only" means that information may be reported, but not attributed to its source —which is why so many news reports from Washington are attributed to "congressional spokesmen," "informed sources," and "White House officials" rather than to specific persons. Journalists helped frame these rules because some information could not be obtained without protection for the source. A congressman who has information about another congressman or an administration official, or an official who has information about another official or about a congressman might not disclose it if he must be identified as the informant. Julius Frandsen, Washington Bureau Chief of United Press International, has said that "A lot of skulduggery in government would never come to light if everything had to be attributed."

Journalists must decide whether an informant is serving public purposes or his own. He usually serves both to some degree, which makes decisions difficult. Many editors and at least a few reporters are convinced that officials have learned to use the ground rules for their own advantage. This causes the periodic battles in Washington over "backgrounders," the many briefing sessions during which an official may disclose "background only" information to scores of reporters. Seldom will an official arrange or submit to such a session unless he can see *some* advantage for himself or his policies. But the journalist who does not attend a backgrounder finds it difficult to compete with those who do. And those who attend must try to analyze the degree to which they are being used in a way that does not serve the public interest.

Confidential information is thus sometimes complicated, and guidelines may be confusing. But there are two clear necessities: Ground rules must be established, and an agreement to keep confidences must be respected.

All rules and rules-of-thumb must, of course, be adapted to interview situations, and some interviewers are by nature better than others.

One who has never conducted a formal interview and knows little or nothing about techniques may in fact be a better interviewer than one who has conducted many interviews and has studied in depth the insights and experiences of professional interviewers. Interviewing has a highly personal character, and curiosity, intelligence, and warmth are extremely valuable. Anyone who studies interviewing techniques, however, can certainly improve his interviewing style.

4 Observing

In the story titled "The Red-Headed League," Sherlock Holmes remarks about a client he has met only a few minutes before, "Beyond the obvious facts that he has at some time done manual labor, that he is a freemason, that he has been in China, and that he has done a considerable amount of writing lately, I can deduce nothing." He had deduced enough, of course, to startle the impressionable Dr. Watson. Then Holmes reeled off the observations that led to his deductions. The man had once done manual labor, Holmes concluded, because his right hand was a size larger than his left. He wore a breastpin that signaled Freemasonry. A tattoo of a fish on the right wrist could only have been done in China (Holmes had contributed to the literature of tattoo marks), and besides, a Chinese coin dangled from the man's watch-chain. Because the man's right sleeve cuff was shiny for five inches, and the left exhibited a smooth patch near the elbow where it had probably been rested on the desk, Holmes concluded the man had been writing recently.

Perhaps all this evidence should have been quite elementary for anyone who observes well. Arthur Conan Doyle, author of the Sherlock Holmes stories, was a physician who patterned his detective on one of his teachers in medical school, Dr. Joseph Bell, a diagnostician with highly developed powers of observation and deduction. For most of us, though, observation seems to be the *least* developed power. In a series of experiments in Geneva, a group of students proved themselves incapable of describing the entrance hall of their own university. We need only read the work of an extraordinary observer such as Annie Dillard, author of *Pilgrim at Tinker Creek,* to become aware of how little we see. In an article in *Harper's* magazine, she wrote:

> Often I slop some creek water in a jar, and when I get home I dump it in a white china bowl. After the silt settles I return and see tracings of minute snails on the bottom, a planarian or two winding round the rim of water, roundworms shimmying frantically, and finally, when my eyes have adjusted to these dimensions, amoebae. At first the amoebae look like *muscae volitantes,* those curled moving spots you seem to see in your eyes when you stare at a distant wall. Then I see the amoebae as drops of water congealed, bluish, translucent, like chips of sky in the bowl.[1]

We are not accustomed to that kind of seeing, partly because focusing so sharply is hard work for most of us and partly because there is so *much* to see all around us that focusing on one object requires ignoring others. We thus tend to see only a vague outline of nearly everything around us. Moreover, we usually tend to see in a way that our language and culture have shaped for us.

Walter Lippmann made the point explicitly in a famous essay that explains how "stereotypes" shape our view of the world: "For the most part we do not see first, then define; we define first and then see. In the great blooming, buzzing confusion of the outer world we pick out what our culture has already defined for us, and we tend to perceive that which we have picked out in the form stereotyped."[2]

In their book *Individual in Society,* David Krech, Richard Crutchfield, and Egerton Ballachey broaden the view to show how we assign people to predefined categories:

> Because so many Americans ascribe a *stereotyped* set of personality traits to such groups as Jews, Negroes, Catholics, or Russians, judgments of individual members of these groups often show typical and stereotyped biases.
>
> Thus, many Americans . . . tend to overestimate the shrewdness of a particular Jew, or the inscrutability of a somewhat reticent Russian —because they believe Jews to be shrewd and Russians to be inscrutable. Through contrast, they tend to overestimate the intelligence of an intelligent Negro and to overestimate the liberalism of a Catholic who is liberal in some of his religious views. Again, the reason appears to be due to the stereotyped notion that Negroes are stupid and that Catholics hold extremely conservative religious beliefs.

The critical point to remember is that this bias in perceiving people is not a fault found only among the prejudiced many. It is found in all men and is due to the very nature of our perceptual processes.[3]

How our perceptual processes work is indicated by an experiment conducted by Mason Haire and Willa Grunes. They gave two groups of students two descriptions of a "certain working man":

To Group I: "Works in a factory, reads a newspaper, goes to movies, average height, cracks jokes, intelligent, strong, active." *To Group II:* "Works in a factory, reads a newspaper, goes to movies, average height, cracks jokes, strong, active."

Thus, the descriptions were identical except that the students in Group I were told that the worker was intelligent.

Then the students were asked to describe the worker in a paragraph. The typical description by students in Group II was summarized by the investigators:

Virtually every description would fit into the pattern of the typical American Joe: likable and well-liked, mildly sociable, healthy, happy, uncomplicated and well-adjusted, in a sort of earthy way; not very intelligent, but trying to keep abreast of current trends, interested in sports and finding his pleasures in simple, undistinguished activities.

Group I had trouble. The students could not reconcile their stereotype of a factory worker with "intelligent." They solved the problem in a variety of ways:

He is intelligent, but not too much so, since he works in a factory.

He is intelligent, but doesn't possess initiative to rise above the group.

The traits seem to be conflicting. . . . Most factory workers I have heard about aren't too intelligent.

Several students who were incapable of ascribing intelligence to a factory worker simply made him a foreman.[4]

It must be pointed out that many stereotypes are valuable. Knowing that someone is a factory worker, we are probably correct in assuming that he is more interested in discussing labor and management issues than in discussing foreign policy, that he probably prefers popular music to classical, that he is more likely to watch sports on television than either Shakespearean plays or soap operas. Such assumptions may be wrong. How could anyone guess, for example, that one of the most respected American poets of the twentieth century, the late Wallace Stevens, was an insurance executive? But our stereotypes of the worker *and* the executive are useful; interactions with either are likely to be smoother if we rely to some degree on what we know about most factory workers and most business executives.

Stereotypes, then, are helpful as well as injurious. As in interviewing, one should be aware of the dangers and correct distortions by recognizing those that usually afflict observers.

Common Distortions

On more than forty occasions, Gordon Allport and Leo Postman used college students, Army trainees, members of community forums, teachers, hospital patients, and police officials in experiments that analyzed the basic psychology of rumor. They began with a simple but imaginative test of observation. A slide showing a semi-dramatic picture was flashed on a screen before an audience. Six or seven subjects who had not seen the picture waited in another room. Then one of them entered and stood so that he could not see the slide. The picture was described to him in about twenty details. A second subject then entered the room and also took a position where he could not see the screen. The first subject, who was instructed to report as "accurately as possible what you have heard," attempted to describe the picture to the second. Then a third subject entered, stood with his back to the picture, and heard it described by the second. The process was repeated until all the subjects had attempted to describe the picture. The members of the audience, of course, were able to see the picture while they listened to the descriptions.

The presence of the audience helped to assure that the subjects' reports were likely to be more accurate than most rumors. A subject was certain to be more cautious in his description before an audience that knew the facts than he would be in spreading rumors. Similarly, the effect of the instructions was to maximize accuracy and induce caution. In everyday life, no critical experimenter looms over one's shoulder. The likelihood that the reports would be accurate was also enhanced by the time factor; the lapse of time between the hearing and the telling was short in the experiment, and is usually much longer in life. Most important, the subjects were struggling for absolute accuracy. Their hates, fears, and wishes were not likely to be as strongly involved in the experiment as in life.

Despite these factors, the resemblance between the pictures and the descriptions deteriorated rapidly. Deterioration began with shortening. The descriptions became more concise, more easily grasped and related. After five or six mouth-to-mouth transmissions, 70 percent of the details recounted at the beginning had been lost. As the descriptions became shorter, they also became sharper: fixed on some details to the exclusion of others. When one subject said, "There is a boy stealing and a man remonstrating with him," *all* the other subjects remembered the unusual word "remonstrating" and passed the sentence along without change.

The most important changes resulted from the subjects' attempts to square the pictures with their personal views of reality. Although one of the pictures showed a Red Cross truck loaded with explosives—and it was so described to the first subject—the repeated transmissions changed the cargo to medical supplies—which is, of course, what we have come to believe a Red Cross truck should carry. Similarly, this same picture, a battle scene, showed a black civilian. He gradually became a soldier—no doubt because most people in battle scenes are soldiers. A drugstore, quite clearly described as situated in the middle of a block, became "a corner drugstore"—we are accustomed to thinking of corner drugstores.

Other distortions were also revealing. When police officers were subjects and a picture involving police was shown, the subjects identified immediately with the pictured police to the exclusion of the other people in the picture, and the nightstick was greatly sharpened as a focus of the picture. Describing a picture that included a black person, a black subject said the man "is being maltreated" (which *may* have been the message of the picture, but an equally plausible interpretation was that he was a rioter about to be arrested). The most sobering distortion involved another picture, which showed a white man holding a razor and accosting a black man. In more than half the experiments involving white subjects, as the descriptions moved from one subject to another, the razor shifted from the hand of the white man to the hand of the black man.[5]

What does this experiment show us about the errors of observing and repeating descriptions of observed events?

First, Allport and Postman speak of the process of *leveling:* The description becomes shorter, more concise, more easily grasped and told. A companion effect is *sharpening:* the selective perception, retention, and reporting of a limited number of details from a much larger context. Then comes *assimilation:* absorbing new information in a way that will not disturb the habits, interests, and sentiments in the subject's mind. These three processes occur simultaneously and represent an effort to reduce a large amount of information to a simple and meaningful structure; Allport and Postman call this *embedding.*

Although this analysis pertains more to rumor than to observation, the effects are the same. Other experiments indicate that the three-pronged process is basic in all remembering.[6] What we bring to a visual experience helps to shape what we see.

A college teacher, H. H. Kelley, once demonstrated how an experience can be distorted by giving his students written descriptions of a guest lecturer. The descriptions were alike with one exception: one group of students read that the lecturer was "rather cold"; the other group read that the lecturer was "very warm." The students did not know that the descriptions varied.

After the lecture, the students were asked to rate the guest. Those who had read the "warm" description rated him as more considerate of others, more informed, more sociable, more popular, better natured, more humorous, and more humane than did the students who had received the "cold" description. Also, 56 percent of the students who had read the "warm" description engaged in discussion with the lecturer; only 32 percent of those who had read the "cold" description did so.[7]

The students were misled, of course, but perhaps no more than everyone is misled by public figures and their detractors. In effect, nearly all public figures act publicly in a way that they hope will show them as "very warm"; their detractors are usually trying to show them as "rather cold."

Distorted perception is also common among those who suppose that their observations are accurate because they were *there:* at a battle, a political convention, or some other event of greater or lesser magnitude. Maurice Bloch, a noted historian, has pointed up this error by imagining that a military commander is trying to describe a victory won on a battlefield of a size so limited that he has been able to see the entire conflict.

> Nevertheless, we cannot doubt that, in more than one essential episode, he will be forced to refer to the reports of his lieutenants. In acting thus as narrator, he would only be behaving as he had a few hours before in the action. Then as commander, regulating the movements of his troops to the swaying tide of battle, what sort of information shall we think to have served him best? Was it the rather confused scenes viewed through his binoculars, or the reports brought in hot haste by the couriers and aides-de-camp? Seldom can a leader of troops be his own observer.[8]

Nor, of course, can any other participant fully observe all the action.

The tendency to rely on the absolute truth of pictures leads to distortions of perception that become more common as the use of film increases. One kind of distortion is basic: the human eye takes in an angle of about 120 degrees, but a typical 50-millimeter camera lens takes in only 25, and a typical telephoto lens takes in only 5 degrees. As Karl Wieck has remarked, much that meets the eye does not meet the lens. And because lenses also foreshorten perspective, especially telephoto lenses, people who are actually standing quite far apart are made to seem a closely packed mass on film.

Subtle distortions by camera are common. It makes a difference how a cameraman who is filming a person moves his focus the length of the body. Movement from head to toe is "looking him over" and is likely to be derogatory. Movement from toe to head implies appreciation. A camera held low and pointed up lends importance to the subject; held high, the camera makes the subject insignificant.[9]

Most of the distortions of perception that are common to particular groups are predictable. Not surprisingly, researchers have found that those who strongly desire a small car see a Volkswagen as physically smaller than do those who have no such desire, and that poor children see quarters as larger than they actually are while rich children see them as smaller.

Nor should it be surprising that political partisans see larger crowds gather to hear their candidate than are actually there. "Crowdsmanship," publicizing inflated figures for political advantage, is so common that it is sometimes difficult to be sure whether the inflation is unintentional. But there is evidence that, partisan or not, almost everyone overestimates the size of a large crowd, perhaps because the sight of packed masses is so unusual as to be awesome. Herbert Jacobs, a retired professor who once worked as a journalist, and has studied such distortions, tells of an occasion when a plane carrying Richard Nixon landed at the Milwaukee Airport. A Republican Party official estimated the crowd at 12,000. The police estimate was 8,000. A reporter present said there were 5,000. Skeptical editors of the *Milwaukee Journal* enlarged a general crowd picture and counted heads. The number was 2,300.[10]

Distortions Caused by Observers

Observers can help themselves to counter distortions, too, by realizing how often and in what ways their presence distorts what they see. To fit the Heisenberg uncertainty principle to this subject: The act of observing changes what is observed. Thus, a dean who sits in on a class session to learn whether a young instructor is an effective teacher confounds his own effort to observe a typical classroom performance; his presence alters it.

It is important to be able to judge the degree to which the presence of an observer alters what he sees. The alteration varies with situations, of course. Few soldiers in action will behave much differently because a reporter is on the battle scene; the stress of combat is far too great to make the observer an important element. An actress who hopes to promote a favorable image is more likely to alter her actions to influence a movie columnist.

Moreover, there are limits to the changes that the presence of any observer *can* make. The presence of a reporter is unlikely to cause a coward to become a hero. Nor can an authoritarian teacher become an adaptable or permissive one—or not very persuasively—merely because a dean is watching. As one researcher has pointed out:

> One cannot completely set aside on a moment's notice the attitudes and patterns of social behavior which have been developed and practiced for years in favor of other, unnatural forms of behavior fancied to be more acceptable.[11]

The pivotal element in nearly all cases in which the observer makes a difference is *time*. Those who can put on a facade that covers their attitudes and behavior—or are caused to do so involuntarily by the stress of being observed—cannot maintain their pose. How long does the dean observe the teacher? How long does the reporter stay with the soldiers? How long does the columnist watch the actress? Virtually every study of the degree to which an observer's presence changes behavior emphasizes that the effect diminishes over time, and in many cases the observer is forgotten. Consciousness of being observed is strongest, then, at the beginning.

This suggests important questions that an observer must consider: How does the subject behave when he is most conscious of being observed? How does he behave later?

Guidelines for Observing

Being aware of the pitfalls of observing enables one to prepare strategies for avoiding them. Consider these guidelines:

Remember the Process of Distortion

Anyone who sets out to play the role of observer or record the memories of those who have observed should remind himself of the central human failings in observation. As Allport and Postman point out, we tend to level, sharpen, and assimilate. These processes are largely unavoidable; one *must* shorten and select because human powers are not infinite, and habits, interests, and sentiments are deeply embedded and will affect the way one takes in new information. But the process of maturing is largely learning from new experiences, and thus opening oneself to a wide variety of experiences is valuable. One experience that leads to maturity is reading attentively "The Basic Psychology of Rumor" (which is reprinted in *The Process and Effects of Mass Communication* by Wilbur Schramm, first edition). Remembering its lessons will surely enable anyone to guard against the strongest effects of the most evident kind of distortion. At the very least, the sobering experience of tracing the distortions Allport and Postman have analyzed will make one less certain of his certainties.

Recall Emotional States

An observer can also learn to question his certainties by judging his emotional state at the time they were formed. Most of us learn to discount some unfounded impressions, usually angry ones, and dismiss them with, "Well, I guess I was pretty emotional at the time." This ability is useful in trying to recall observations. What mood heightened my impression of this facet and obscured that one?

The influence of emotional states has been recognized at least since the time of Aristotle, who wrote:

> Under the influence of strong feeling we are easily deceived regarding our sensations, different persons in different ways, as e.g., the coward under the influence of fear and the lover under that of love have such illusions that the former owing to a trifling resemblance thinks he sees an enemy and the latter his beloved. And the more impressionable the person is, the less the resemblance required. Similarly, everybody is easily deceived when in anger or influenced by any strong desire, and the more subject one is to these feelings the more one is deceived.[12]

Because study after study has shown what most of us could have guessed, that memory deteriorates rapidly over time, it is clear that the most accurate observations are likely to be those recounted immediately after an event. But if the event places emotional stress on the observer, he is more subject to distortion caused by emotions. This dilemma can be resolved in many cases by recording impressions of an event immediately after it occurs in order to capture details that might be forgotten. Later, the observer can assess his first account when he is more tranquil and can evaluate his emotional state at the earlier time.

Concentrate on Significant Details

Bruce Bliven, one of the most accomplished of modern journalists, had the good fortune early in his career to work under Fremont Older, a demanding editor who, Bliven said, "had a personality so vigorous you could feel his presence through a brick wall." How Older taught young reporters to observe is illustrated by an incident. Despairing of an unobservant young reporter who wrote with little flavor, Older decided that the man would be able to write compellingly only if he immersed himself in the life of his subject. Older assigned him to spend three weeks playing and singing hymns with the Salvation Army, which was then a familiar sight on San Francisco street corners. But the reporter's effort to breathe life into his story of the Army was a failure. "Didn't you observe anything?" Older bellowed. "At night, for instance, *where did they hang the bass drum?*" The reporter did not know, and he was fired. Older recounted this incident for years to push young reporters into becoming sensitive observers. Now, fifty years after his own experiences with Older, Bliven says, "After I meet someone, I ask myself questions about his personal appearance, to make sure I really saw him."

This kind of observation requires concentration, for nearly everyone is mentally lazy. The laziness grows out of understandable habits. A man who drives a car properly does not really focus on the myriad details that are open to his view. Indeed, avoiding accidents depends on seeing only essential features: the road ahead, other cars, pedestrians, and traffic signals. Moreover, the driver ordinarily does no more than *notice;* he does not observe in a way that would enable him to recall even these features accurately. Such habits carry over into important situations. Concentration is required to bring even essential features into sharp focus.

Concentrating vision is often more difficult than concentrating hearing. Spoken words come successively, one after the other, but many visual forms appear simultaneously. Focusing on the shape, the color, the dimensions, and the movements of a single form is taxing when there are many others. The observer must decide beforehand which forms, events, or details are worth his attention. The task of the observer who attends, say, a political convention is hopeless if he does not have in mind or on paper what he expects to focus on. He should be guided, not bound, by his plans. Then he must train himself to concentrate on what is significant for him. The ability, or the will, to concentrate varies, which is the primary reason some football coaches are better than others at scouting upcoming opponents and picking out small but crucial details of interior line play while nearly everyone else in the stadium is watching the ball. But everyone with vision can train himself to concentrate it.

Remember the Distortions of Perspective

Consider a hypothetical scene on a California campus. Several students and faculty members are holding a noon rally to protest the governor's control of higher education. A reporter stands only fifteen feet from the principal speaker. He is close enough to observe the speaker's vigorous little gestures and rubs elbows with the speaker's lieutenants and chief supporters, who move about excitedly and fill the pauses in the speech with "Right on!" "On strike! Shut it down!" and similar words of response and encouragement. Twenty-five feet away, in a good position to hear every word of the speech but not close enough to feel and see the excitement among the speaker's supporters or to hear *their* words, stands another reporter. He is ringed about by the speaker's detractors and by students who have merely stopped by on their way to classes. Some of the listeners in *his* area mutter insults, others yawn. If the first reporter is persuaded by his senses to write that the rally demonstrated considerable support for the speaker, and if the second writes that the rally demonstrated little support, who can blame either? Anyone should. The situation is a simple illustration of limited perspectives. The reporter, or any other researcher, who allows himself to be limited by such narrow perspectives will never come within shouting distance of probable truth.

If the problems of perspective were no more acute than this example suggests, solving them, or at least devising methods to reduce their effects, would be simple. But perspective is much more complicated. Consider an experiment conducted by Kurt and Gladys Lang.[13] The television age had barely begun in 1951 when President Harry Truman relieved General Douglas MacArthur of his command in the Far East, and thus command during the Korean War. MacArthur came home to crowd-lined streets in many American cities. The Langs decided to study "MacArthur Day" in Chicago by stationing thirty-one observers along the parade route and using other observers to monitor the television reports of the parade. A typical account by one of the observers along the parade route ran:

> I had listened to the accounts of MacArthur's arrival in San Francisco, heard radio reports of his progress through the United States, and had heard the Washington speech as well as the radio accounts of his New York reception. . . . I had therefore expected the crowds to be much more vehement, contagious, and identified with MacArthur. I had expected to hear much political talk, especially anti-Communist and against the Truman administration.
>
> These expectations were completely unfulfilled. I was amazed that I did not once hear Truman criticized, Acheson [Secretary of State under Truman] mentioned, or as much as an allusion to the Communists. . . . I had expected roaring, excited mobs; instead, there were quiet, well ordered, dignified people. . . . The air of curiosity and casualness surprised me. Most people seemed to look on the event as simply something that might be interesting to watch.

In sharp contrast were the impressions of television viewers. One observer who was monitoring television reported:

> . . . the last buildup on TV concerning the "crowd" gave me the impression that the crowd was pressing and straining so hard that it was going to be hard to control. My first thought, "I'm glad I'm not in that" and "I hope nobody gets crushed."

No one was really in danger of being crushed, despite the television impression. A parade observer reporting from streetside on the same scene said only:

> Everybody strained but few could get a really good glimpse of him. A few seconds after he had passed most people merely turned around to shrug and to address their neighbors with such phrases: "That's all," "That was it," "Gee, he looks just like he does in the movies," "What'll we do now?"

In short, then, the camera does lie—or, in any case, those who report with cameras can manipulate them by juggling scenes in such a way that reality and reporting are quite different. Another more striking aspect of the Langs' study was that the television viewer found General MacArthur the center of attraction throughout the telecast. The camera followed MacArthur, and the viewer focused on the interplay between heroic figure and enthusiastic crowd. The cheering seemed constant, and even seemed to reach its crest as the telecast ended. Meanwhile, the reality along the streets was much less exciting. The spectators caught a brief glimpse of General MacArthur, and that was all.

How can an observer avoid the distortion caused by perspective? The most obvious and direct method is to recognize that any single perspective is necessarily limited and must be supplemented with others. A careful researcher is usually quick to realize that he must consider other perspectives when he is weighing another observer's report, but he is often not so quick to supplement his own observations. Nearly everyone is all too ready to trust the evidence he has seen. Wilbur Schramm says that whenever possible he arranges to have another researcher accompany him for observing and interviewing, especially in developing countries. He has learned that checking one impression against another often yields surprising and useful results.

Deciding whose impression to accept is not always easy, but a guideline used in courts is helpful. The law asks not only whether a witness was actually present and whether his vision was adequate, but also whether the witness was *competent*. Many scholars who study Henry James believe that some of the literary figures who talked with James and recalled that he stuttered and hemmed and hawed were probably wrong. Elizabeth Jordan, who had been trained in speech and who also spoke with James, was so entranced by his extraordinary manner of speaking that she wrote down one of his characteristic sentences. It became clear from her description that James was neither a stutterer nor a hesitant speaker but chose to repeat his words variously, "instinctively bringing out the perfect sentence the first time; repeating it more deliberately to test every word the second time; accepting it as satisfactory the third time, and triumphantly sending it forth as produced by Henry James." [14] In such cases, the judgment of an expert is usually accepted.

Seek Other Evidence

Considering perspectives of other observers is usually valuable, but even that kind of crosschecking must often yield to physical evidence. William L. Prosser, a professor of law, has observed, "There is still no man who would not accept dog tracks in the mud against the testimony of a hundred eye-witnesses that no dog had passed by." [15]

When General MacArthur visited New York in 1951, a police commissioner estimated the size of the crowd that turned out to see him at eight million—more people than lived in the entire city and suburbs. By 1960, the editors of the *New York Times* had become irritated and suspicious of the large estimates of crowds. Using official city maps and measuring sidewalk widths, they calculated that the traditional ticker-tape parade route from Battery Park to City Hall could accommodate no more than 141,436 spectators. Even allowing generously for spectators peering out of office windows and watching from side streets, the total could never be higher than 500,000 according to the *Times*.

Before he retired, Herbert Jacobs taught at the University of California at Berkeley during the period when protest rallies drew large crowds. Distressed by the varying published estimates of the sizes of crowds in Sproul Plaza, he used photographs, density counts, and blueprints of the plaza to devise a formula: If a crowd seems fairly loosely composed—if spectators can be seen moving in and out of the middle—multiply the sum of the length and width of the area they occupy by seven. If the crowd seems compact and there is little movement within it, multiply by ten. Thus, a crowd in an area that measures 100 by 150 feet—a sum of 250 feet—contains about 1,750 people if it is loosely composed, about 2,500 if compact.[16]

The authors of *Unobtrusive Measures* [17] tell how much can be learned from other kinds of physical evidence. They report on research techniques that range from judging reading habits by examining the wear and tear on library books to counting noseprints on the glass that encloses exhibits. One researcher whose work they describe estimated liquor consumption in a "dry" city by counting liquor bottles in garbage cans.

Observe Unobtrusively

Undetected observation has this great value: The subjects behave normally because they are unaware that they are being watched. But nearly all undetected observation raises a question of ethics: Should privacy be invaded? Even the actions of concealed observers who are trying to help those they observe—doctors who watch patients through one-way mirrors, for example—may be questionable, so strongly does nearly everyone value privacy.

The question of ethics becomes sharp in other cases. Sociologists' observations often help a society understand itself, but would that explanation mollify those who swapped small talk with David Riesman and Jeanne Watson when they were unobtrusively studying the interactions of guests at parties?

Riesman and Watson defended the fact that they did not inform those with whom they interacted:

> Many people come to social gatherings with more than one objective: they do not announce everything they have in mind . . . the important thing is not the presence or absence of these other objectives but the question of whether the manifest role—that of friend and partner in sociability—is misrepresented. It is exploitation if the guise of friendship is assumed for an unfriendly purpose: but if the friendly interaction is entered into in good faith, with other objectives being *in addition to* and not *instead of*, we see no serious violation of ethical standards.[18]

Others take a more stringent view, arguing that concealment is never justified unless the behavior being observed is open to public inspection. Thus, unobtrusively observing interaction at a private party would not be justified, but circulating unobtrusively through the many delegates to a national political convention to observe their behavior would be.

It is also argued that unobtrusively observing behavior at private gatherings is ethical when the report does not identify the subjects. If this is the proper standard—and most social scientists and journalists have adopted it—many observations have been justifiable, including those of two psychologists who eavesdropped on students in dormitory smoking rooms and washrooms, listened to telephone conversations, and even concealed themselves under beds.[19] Unobtrusively recording conversations at street corners, in theatre lobbies between the acts of plays, and at rock festivals has become a common method among social scientists and journalists.

Some who observe behavior have adapted the methods of Allen Funt, the producer of "Candid Camera." In one study, a young passenger with a cane on a New York subway seemed to lose his grasp, staggered a few feet, then collapsed. He lay staring at the ceiling of the subway car until a few of the other passengers helped him to a sitting position. A few days later, the same young man boarded the subway carrying not a cane but a bottle and smelling strongly of alcohol. He collapsed again. His fellow passengers were less sympathetic and helpful this time. Only when the train stopped was he helped to his feet by a student. Still later, he returned with the cane, sober, and repeated his first performance as a cripple. Then again he performed as a drunk. He repeated the act so often—sometimes as a cripple, sometimes as a drunk—that eventually more than four thousand subway riders had seen it. They did not know, of course, that he was a student, unobtrusively accompanied by another student who sometimes helped him in order to give the other subway riders the idea. Two female accomplices were always in the crowd, taking notes on the reactions of the passengers.

Ethical questions must be resolved according to a reasonable standard. It is doubtful that such a standard would rule out the kind of observation made by the students on the subway. Indeed, when those who are being observed are not personally embarrassed or injured by an experiment or a report of an experiment, ingenious research is in order.

Become a Participant—But Cautiously

The methods in participant observation are similarly numerous, but they are also likely to distort behavior. Four psychologists who wanted to study a small secret group that was preparing for the end of the world tried to avoid distortion by joining the group, not as observers but as full participants. They were rebuffed at first because the group required that its members have had a "psychic experience." The psychologists had one —or said they had—and were accepted. The method was not entirely successful, for reasons the investigators explained:

> There is little doubt that the addition of four new people to a fairly small group within ten days had an effect on the state of conviction among the existing members, especially since the four seem to have appeared when public apathy to the belief systems was great. . . . Most important of all, perhaps, is that the four observers could not be traced through any mutual friends or acquaintances to existing group members and thus the most common and expected channel of recruitment was evidently not responsible for their appearance.[20]

Obviously, this is a special case; observers have been able to participate unobtrusively in groups less sensitive to new members. Young observers have joined adolescent gangs without causing suspicion, and many social scientists and journalists have surreptitiously become ostensible residents of Skid Row, racketeers, and, especially in recent years, members of counter-culture and protest groups. The mere presence of researchers, even if they are not known as researchers, may affect a group's actions in some way, if only by adding to its numbers. (It is often said that the Communist Party in the United States seems larger than it is because so many undercover FBI agents are in the Party.) But researchers who are not detected as researchers seldom *distort* the actions of those they observe.

When one who participates is known to be an observer, the other participants usually react much as they do in the presence of an observer who is not a participant: Their initial behavior is likely to be self-conscious and even secretive. Except in unusual instances, awareness of the outsider tends to diminish in time. But it may not disappear unless the observer's actions are so compatible with those of the other participants that they come to think of him as one of them. Gerald Berreman, an anthropologist, has written of his study of a village in India: "It was six months after my arrival before animal sacrifices and attendant rituals were performed in my presence although they had been performed in my absence or without my knowledge throughout my residence in the village." [21]

The compatible observer may begin his participation already sharing the goals of the group he joins, or he may come to share them over time. This suggests a deep pitfall: To what degree is he a participant, to what degree an observer? The psychologists who joined the end-of-the-world society were clearly more observers than participants. But one who shares the goals and values of the participants may be a bad observer for that reason—or, in any case, he will not perceive as an outside observer would. What he gains by participating may be more than overbalanced by his loss of a more detached view.

This problem is especially important for the so-called New Journalists, such as Norman Mailer, whose central method is participant observation. Anyone who attempts to report from the perspective of a participant observer should first pose this question: *Why* am I a participant observer—to participate or to observe and report? Then he must evaluate the consequences of the answer and try to provide a balance between participation and observation.

When participant observation lasts for an extended period, one may be able to restore balance through discussions with outsiders during that period. While conducting research for his famous book *Street Corner Society*, William Whyte so immersed himself in the life of his subjects that he did not know how he had changed until a friend came to visit him:

> . . . When John Howard first came down from Harvard to join me in the Cornerville study, he noticed at once that I talked in Cornerville

> in a manner far different from that which I used at Harvard. This was not a matter of the use of profanity or obscenity, nor did I affect the use of ungrammatical expressions. I talked in the way that seemed natural to me, but what was natural in Cornerville was different from what was natural at Harvard. . . . When I was most deeply involved in Cornerville, I found myself rather tongue-tied in my visits to Harvard.[22]

Whyte found that when he finally left Cornerville he lost most of the manner that it had imposed on him, which suggests that participant observers should try to arrange for a lapse of time after they leave the milieu they are observing before reporting their findings.

The susceptibility of the participant observer should never be lightly regarded. Two scientific observers of audience behavior at a Billy Graham crusade in New York left their posts at the end of Graham's sermon and went to the altar to make *their* "Decision for Christ"! [23]

Study Nonverbal Communication

Albert Mehrabian of the University of California at Los Angeles has reported research indicating that what a person says in words is only 7 percent of what he communicates when he talks; 38 percent is conveyed by his manner of speech and 55 percent by his facial expressions and body movements.[24] Ray Birdwhistell of the University of Pennsylvania says that in an average two-person conversation the verbal components carry less than 35 percent of the social meaning of the situation; more than 65 percent is nonverbal.[25] These analyses are not contradictory despite the differences in percentages; Mehrabian and Birdwhistell are reporting on different speech situations. We may doubt that research of that kind can be so precise, but we receive so many *wordless* messages—from hitchhikers, sports fans brought to their feet by actions on the field, frustrated motorists kicking flat tires, students sleeping in class—that recalling them should persuade us that much (if not most) communication is nonverbal.

If reflection is not persuasive, consider the true story of a horse that was bought in Berlin in 1900 by a German named von Osten. The horse, Hans, was taught to count by tapping his front hoof. He learned fast and was taught to add, subtract, multiply, and divide. Eventually, he learned to tell time, use a calendar, and perform other feats, all of which he demonstrated by tapping his hoof. Exhibited to the public, Hans would count the crowd and the number wearing eyeglasses.

Hans became so famous that he was examined by an investigating committee made up of professors of psychology and physiology, cavalry officers, veterinarians, a director of a circus, and the director of the Berlin Zoological Garden. Von Osten was not present during the examination, but there was no change in his horse's apparent intelligence. The committee announced that Hans actually was able to perform as advertised, that no trickery had been involved.

But then a second investigating committee was established. One of the examiners told von Osten to whisper a number in one of Hans's ears while another examiner whispered another number in the other ear. Then Hans was told to add them. He could not. Similar tests revealed why he failed: Hans could see no one who knew the answer. The secret of his remarkable feats became clear. When the horse was asked a question, anyone who knew the answer unwittingly became tense and assumed an expectant posture. When Hans's hoof taps reached the right answer, the onlooker would unwittingly relax and make a slight head movement. That was the signal to Hans to stop tapping.[26]

Even though Hans did not perform feats that proved high intelligence, his feat of observation was remarkable enough. It hints at how much we say without speaking. But it is only a hint, for in recent years researchers have begun to uncover a vast field of nonverbal communication that includes body language but is not limited to it. One researcher, Mark L. Knapp, defines the field by placing the many studies in seven classes:

1. Body motion (also known as "kinesic behavior") includes gestures, movements of the body, limbs, hands, head, and feet, facial expressions, eye behavior, and posture.
2. Physical characteristics include physique or body shape, general attractiveness, body or breath odors, height, weight, hair, and skin color or tone.
3. Touching behavior includes stroking, hitting, greetings and farewells, holding, and guiding another's movements.
4. Paralanguage deals with *how* something is said rather than what is said—voice qualities and vocalizations such as laughing, crying, sighing, whispering, and heavily marked inhaling or exhaling.
5. Proxemics is the study of man's use and perception of his social and personal space—how people use and respond to small-group settings, crowds, and the like.
6. Artifacts include use and manipulation of objects such as perfume, clothes, lipstick, eyeglasses, wigs and other hairpieces, false eyelashes, and the entire repertoire of personal aids and falsifications.
7. Environmental factors are different from all the others in that they are not concerned with personal appearance and behavior. They include furniture, interior decoration, lighting conditions, smells, colors, temperatures, and added noises or music.[27]

So much has been learned about how we communicate without words—and nonverbally in conjunction with words—that it defies summarizing. A few findings seem to be no more than analyses of the obvious, such as one reporting that many attractive students use their good looks to get better grades than they deserve.[28] A few findings are presented with dubious precision, such as an analysis of the "courtship dance" of the American adolescent, which is reported as consisting of exactly twenty-four steps between the initial contact of the young male and female and the coitional act.[29] But many of the research reports are convincing, and useful to anyone who hopes to observe accurately. One of the best collections of studies is Knapp's *Nonverbal Communication in Human Interaction.*

The experience of Don Dodson of Stanford shows how body language helps us understand what people mean when they speak. Interviewing in Nigeria in 1971, he took notes and made tape recordings. He discovered when he returned to the United States that his rather sketchy notes were more valuable than the recordings. Although the tapes provided a full record of what had been said and could be used in interpreting paralanguage (*how* something is said), they were divorced from the interviewees' facial expressions, movements, gestures, general appearance, and surroundings. The notes did not include these factors either, but Dodson discovered that he had been influenced by such factors in taking his notes. In many instances, he had been able to note exactly what he needed because the notes were part of the nonverbal experience in a way that the recordings were not.

There is a danger, however, in trying consciously to apply what one has learned about nonverbal communication. Like those who read Freud's *Interpretation of Dreams* and consider themselves instant experts on dream states, many are so taken with the ideas and insights of nonverbal theory that they try too quickly to move from theory to practice, or try to interpret almost any noticeable movement, tone, facial expression or gesture as highly significant. Beginners are not alone in being over-enthusiastic about the traces of nonverbal communication they observe. In an otherwise excellent book entitled *Word Play,* Peter Farb proclaims that "Pupil performance does not depend so much upon a school's audio-visual equipment or new textbooks or enriching trips to museums as it does upon teachers whose body language communicates high expectations."[30] Farb may be right, but other theorists doubt that a teacher's body language is as important as Farb makes it seem.

A researcher can avoid much of the danger by testing his observations over time. He might focus almost exclusively on nonverbal rather than verbal language in the first of several interviews with one interviewee. Does the interviewee inhale and exhale markedly? Does he laugh nervously? Does his clothing seem to be highly individual? These or other traits are likely to seem pronounced to a researcher who looks primarily for them. In later interviews, however, the researcher is likely to find that he was misled in at least one particular *because* he was looking for traits. Such an exercise helps place observation in perspective.

No research strategy can transform a fallible human into a faultless observer. But one who is armed with knowledge of the many pitfalls and with strategies for avoiding them has taken a long step toward observing truly.

5 Using Libraries

Researchers who are limited to interviewing and observing are crippled. They bypass the vast bodies of information in libraries, or rely only on such widely known books as *Encyclopaedia Britannica, Readers' Guide to Periodical Literature,* and *Who's Who in America.* On the other hand, a researcher who can find his way in a large library can sometimes avoid interviewing and can often supplement information derived from interviewing. Neale Copple, a professor of journalism at the University of Nebraska, tells of the newspaper editor who was proud of spending $250 on telephone calls to run down the background facts for an important story. The editor had his reporters call cities all over the United States to gather figures on street-paving costs. It would have been a model of research in depth except that, as Copple observed, even better figures were available in the reference room of a library ten blocks away.

Not only do researchers waste time and money, they also often sacrifice accuracy when they bypass library research. Nearly every specialist has been asked by a researcher for information that is set down more clearly, accurately, and completely in books, articles, and reference works than he can possibly recall. In fact, even the specialist who has *himself* written definitively on a subject often wishes that interviewers would consult his works rather than asking him. No specialist can remember everything—perhaps not even the most important details in a work that he wrote years earlier.

The Incomprehensible Card Catalog

Many researchers simply do not understand how libraries work. In some cases, experienced researchers know little more about libraries than the freshman who is attempting to write his first ambitious research paper. The late Douglas Southall Freeman, a respected newspaper editor who was also the author of several distinguished volumes on George Washington, knew so well the collections of Washington documents in the Library of Congress that the librarians often consulted *him*. But Freeman became so knowledgeable about his specialty that he no longer needed to observe rudimentary principles of library research. Once when he visited the Library of Congress to seek information on another subject, he needed the help of a young librarian with little experience in order to solve a problem in using one of the keys to all libraries, the card catalog.

So it is with most of those who are undertaking library research. Perhaps in grade school or junior high, they listened to a librarian explain the card catalog system. But if the explanation went beyond first principles, it was of such little use at that age that few retained anything more than "Dewey Decimal System," "Library of Congress System," and the fact that both use letters and numbers.

Perhaps because such early experiences were of little value then, many students who seek a broad range of information sigh as they approach a card catalog. Locating *all* the needed cards seems hopeless, and they are at least dimly aware that each card is a mine of information, most of which they will find incomprehensible.

Is it possible to reduce the distaste for card catalogs? Perhaps not, but anyone who attempts to conduct research in a library should know that the card catalog symbolizes an achievement that is the center of intellectual progress. Great minds—among them Aristotle, Francis Bacon, and Thomas Jefferson—brought all their intellectual power to bear on the problem of classifying knowledge. The importance of the problem is suggested by the fact that until Linnaeus developed a classification system for botany and zoology in the eighteenth century, research in those fields was so utterly devoid of logic and method that it was almost at a standstill. In devising his system, Linnaeus enabled researchers to order and organize their own work, build upon the work of others who had made similar observations and performed similar experiments, and thus push back the frontiers of knowledge about plant and animal life.

Librarians were long faced with a similar but much larger problem: how to order and organize—*classify*—*all* recorded knowledge. The systems devised by Aristotle, Bacon, and Jefferson and others proved unworkable as knowledge expanded. Then in 1876, Melvil Dewey introduced the Dewey Decimal Classification. Although it has been revised often, the basic system has endured. It divides all knowledge into ten major groups or classes:

First, a class of general works—among them encyclopedias, and general periodicals—which contain so many different kinds of information that they do not fit into any other class

Second, Philosophy (conduct of life)

Third, Religion (nature and meaning of life)

Fourth, Social Sciences (man's relations with his fellows)

Fifth, Language (human communication)

Sixth, Pure Science (observation of man's environment)

Seventh, Technology (manipulation of man's environment)

Eighth, Arts (enrichment of life)

Ninth, Literature (thoughts about life)

Tenth, History (examination of the past)

In this scheme, each of these ten classes is further divided into ten classes for a total of one hundred, then each of the one hundred is further divided by ten for a total of one thousand. Adding decimal points and numbers after the first three digits creates thousands of other subdivisions. The major classes and principal subdivisions of the Dewey Decimal Classification are:

000 General Works

010	Bibliography
020	Library science
030	General encyclopedias
040	General collected essays
050	General periodicals
060	General societies
070	Newspaper journalism
080	Collected works
090	Manuscripts and rare books

100 Philosophy

110	Metaphysics
120	Metaphysical theories
130	Branches of psychology
140	Philosophical topics
150	General psychology
160	Logic
170	Ethics
180	Ancient and medieval
190	Modern philosophy

200 Religion

210	Natural theology
220	Bible
230	Doctrinal theology
240	Devotional and practical
250	Pastoral theology
260	Christian church
270	Christian church history
280	Christian churches and sects
290	Other religions

300 Social Sciences

310	Statistics
320	Political science
330	Economics
340	Law
350	Public administration
360	Social welfare
370	Education
380	Public services and utilities
390	Customs and folklore

400 Language

410 Comparative linguistics
420 English and Anglo-Saxon
430 Germanic languages
440 French, Provençal, Catalan
450 Italian, Rumanian
460 Spanish, Portuguese
470 Latin and other Italic
480 Classical and modern Greek
490 Other languages

500 Pure Science

510 Mathematics
520 Astronomy
530 Physics
540 Chemistry and allied sciences
550 Earth sciences
560 Paleontology
570 Anthropology and biology
580 Botanical sciences
590 Zoological sciences

600 Technology

610 Medical sciences
620 Engineering
630 Agriculture
640 Home economics
650 Business
660 Chemical technology
670 Manufactures
680 Other manufactures
690 Building construction

700 The Arts

710 Landscape and civic art
720 Architecture
730 Sculpture
740 Drawing and decorative arts
750 Painting
760 Prints and print making
770 Photography
780 Music
790 Recreation

800 Literature

810 American literature in English
820 English and Old English
830 Germanic literatures
840 French, Provençal, Catalan
850 Italian, Rumanian
860 Spanish, Portuguese
870 Latin and other Italic literatures
880 Classical and modern Greek
890 Other literatures

900 History

910 Geography, travels, description
920 Biography
930 Ancient history
940 Europe
950 Asia
960 Africa
970 North America
980 South America
990 Other parts of world

An example of the operation of the plan for subdivision is American literature:

810 General American literature
811 American poetry
812 American drama
813 American fiction
814 American essays
815 American oratory
816 American letters
817 American satire and humor
818 American miscellany
819 Canadian English literature

Use of the decimal point is illustrated by the classification for zoology, 591:

591.1 Animal physiology
591.2 Animal pathology
591.3 Animal maturation
591.4 Animal morphology
591.5 Animal ecology
591.6 Economic zoology
591.8 Microscopic zoology
591.9 Zoogeography

Although this system is used by most public libraries in the United States, most large research libraries use the Library of Congress system because so many of their patrons conduct research in many different subjects that must be divided into minute categories. Introduced in 1897, it was so obviously valuable that many large university libraries adopted it quite early. In recent years, many other university libraries that are likely to develop huge holdings and serve many kinds of specialists have changed from the Dewey Decimal Classification to the Library of Congress system so they can expand their holdings almost infinitely in any discipline. This is a brief outline of the system:

A General Work—Polygraphy
B Philosophy—Religion
C History—Auxiliary Sciences
D History and Topography (except America)
E–F America
G Geography—Anthropology
H Social Sciences
J Political Science
K Law
L Education
M Music
N Fine Arts
P Language and Literature
Q Science
R Medicine
S Agriculture—Plant and Animal Husbandry
T Technology
U Military Science
V Naval Science
Z Bibliography and Library Science

This system is almost infinitely expandable. The principal branches of knowledge represented by the list are subdivided further by adding second letters and by adding numbers up to 9999. For example, P stands for Language and Literature, PQ for Romance literature, and PQ6001-8929 represents divisions of Spanish literature. The classifications also provide for a decimal system—PN6110.H8 designates Humor—which makes expansion so easy that a limit is almost unimaginable.

Using the Card Catalog

With a few exceptions, no matter how vast the holdings of any library, no matter how many branches and subdivisions it may comprise, the card catalog is a key to understanding and using much of it. At Stanford University almost four million books and other materials are housed in the Main Library and in more than forty other special libraries attached to schools, institutes, and departments of the university, yet the card catalog on the second floor of the Main Library records nearly everything in all the libraries except the one maintained by the Stanford Linear Accelerator Center.

More information that is useful in most scholarly research is published in journal articles than in books. Journals are not usually listed in card catalogs, nor are government publications, which are useful to many researchers. Citation indexes, abstracts, and bibliographies (many of which are listed in the next chapter) are the best guides to such information. Librarians include them in the card catalog and usually shelve them in the Reference Section.

Although nearly every library or library system differs from others in some way, the similarities are so obvious and pronounced that one who masters the card catalog system of one large library is likely to be able to use others knowledgeably. These directions for using the card catalog of Stanford libraries illustrate the basic system.

Author, subject, and title cards are interfiled in one alphabetical sequence. The following are some of the important filing rules:

1. *Initial articles.* When the *first* word of a title is an article (*A, An,* or *The,* or their equivalents in foreign languages), it is disregarded in the filing.
   GENIUS (the subject)
   The Genius (a title)
   Genius and stupidity (a title)
   Der Genius im Kinde (a title)
2. *De, Le, Van, Von, etc.* Surnames beginning with a prefix are filed as one word, including names in which the prefix is an article. Disregard the uncapitalized initial articles "*al-*" or "*el-*" prefixed with a hyphen to

Arabic, etc., names and the articles "*ha-*" or "*he-*" prefixed to Hebrew names.

Dean, Joseph
De Andrade, Mario
Deans and advisers (a title)
al-Dig, Muhammed

3. *M' and Mc.* Surnames beginning with *M'* and *Mc* are filed as though they were spelled *Mac,* and are interfiled with other words beginning with *Mac.*

   MacAlister, D.
   McAlister, E.
   MACHINERY
   Macmillan

4. *Vowels: ä, ö, ü à, ø.* In Germanic languages, these are filed as ae, oe, ue, aa, oe.

   Maeder, Clara
   Mäder, Paul

5. *Common abbreviations.* These are arranged as though they were spelled out.

   Dr. filed as Doctor (or Doktor, etc.)
   Mr. filed as Mister.
   St. filed as Saint (or Sankt, etc.)
   U.S. filed as United States

The book or periodical you want may be located outside the Main Library. Locations for books and serials often are shown either on the catalog card below the call number or by a *location card* preceding the author card (see figure 5). In many cases locations are indicated only on a record at the Loan Desk. Locations for periodicals may be obtained at the Serial Records Desk or the Government Documents Library.

Examples of catalog cards are shown in figures 1-5, including approaches:

1. *By author.* Each book in the Library by an individual author is listed under the author's name. Although authors usually are individuals, they may be companies, government departments, or institutions, such as "Pacific Gas & Electric Company," "California Dept. of Water Resources," and "American Chemical Society." The author card always contains the most information about the book.
2. *By subject.* Most are listed in the Catalog under words or phrases describing their subject matter. Be *specific* when looking for a subject. For example, look under "Physics," not "Science," or under "Christianity," not "Religion." A few subjects such as "History," "Description," "Politics and Government," are used as subdivisions of a place. For

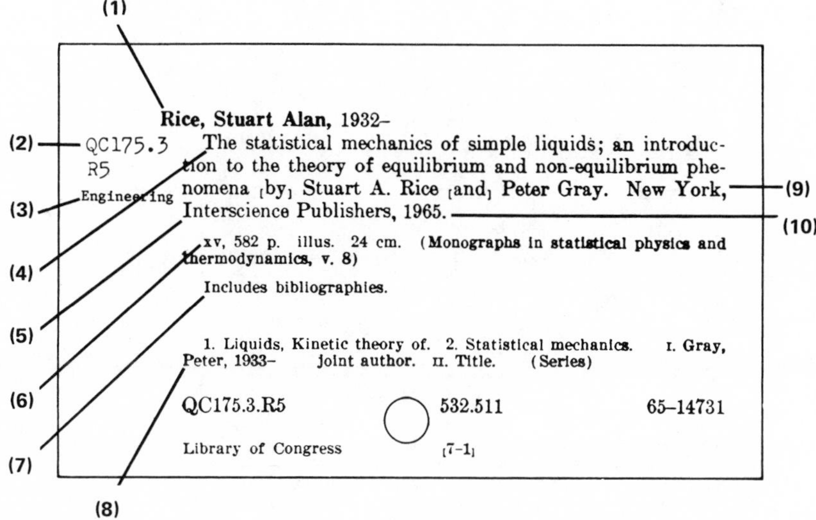

Rice, Stuart Alan, 1932–

QC175.3
R5
Engineering

The statistical mechanics of simple liquids; an introduction to the theory of equilibrium and non-equilibrium phenomena [by] Stuart A. Rice [and] Peter Gray. New York, Interscience Publishers, 1965.

xv, 582 p. illus. 24 cm. (Monographs in statistical physics and thermodynamics, v. 8)

Includes bibliographies.

1. Liquids, Kinetic theory of. 2. Statistical mechanics. I. Gray, Peter, 1933– joint author. II. Title. (Series)

QC175.3.R5 532.511 65–14731

Library of Congress [7-1]

(1) Author's name and date of birth (if this date is easily found)
(2) Call number, a group of numbers and letters used to classify and locate the book
(3) Shelving location
(4) Title of book
(5) Publisher
(6) Paging, illustrations, height (in centimeters), and series
(7) Notes of special interest
(8) Technical processing data used by the library staff
(9) Place of publication
(10) Date published

Fig. 1. Author Card (main entry)

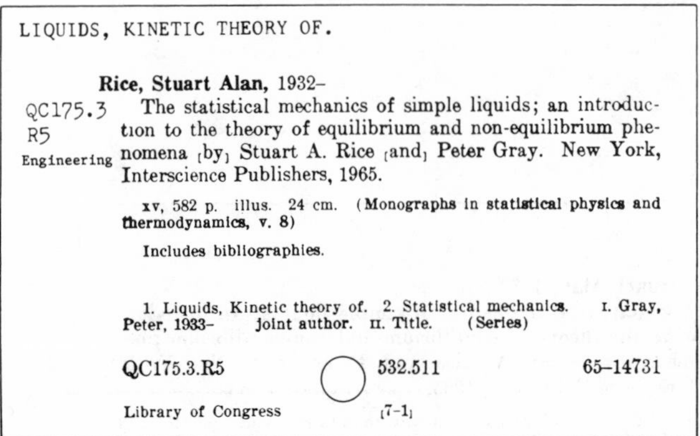
LIQUIDS, KINETIC THEORY OF.

Rice, Stuart Alan, 1932–
QC175.3 The statistical mechanics of simple liquids; an introduc-
R5 tion to the theory of equilibrium and non-equilibrium phe-
Engineering nomena [by] Stuart A. Rice [and] Peter Gray. New York, Interscience Publishers, 1965.

xv, 582 p. illus. 24 cm. (Monographs in statistical physics and thermodynamics, v. 8)

Includes bibliographies.

1. Liquids, Kinetic theory of. 2. Statistical mechanics. I. Gray, Peter, 1933– joint author. II. Title. (Series)

QC175.3.R5 532.511 65–14731

Library of Congress [7-1]

Fig. 2. Subject Card

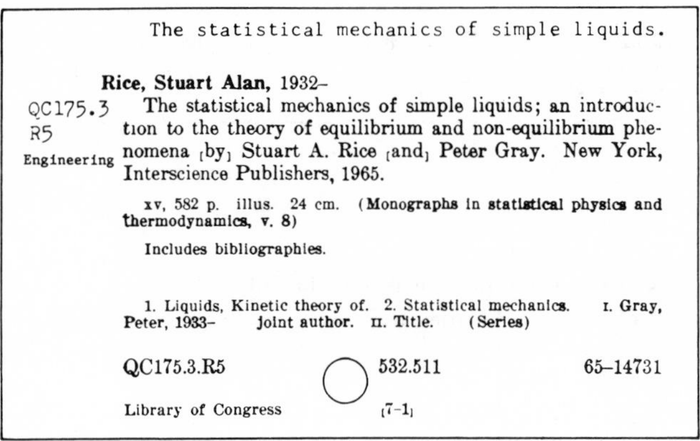
The statistical mechanics of simple liquids.

Rice, Stuart Alan, 1932–
QC175.3 The statistical mechanics of simple liquids; an introduc-
R5 tion to the theory of equilibrium and non-equilibrium phe-
Engineering nomena [by] Stuart A. Rice [and] Peter Gray. New York, Interscience Publishers, 1965.

xv, 582 p. illus. 24 cm. (Monographs in statistical physics and thermodynamics, v. 8)

Includes bibliographies.

1. Liquids, Kinetic theory of. 2. Statistical mechanics. I. Gray, Peter, 1933– joint author. II. Title. (Series)

QC175.3.R5 532.511 65–14731

Library of Congress [7-1]

Fig. 3. Title Card

example, look up "France—History," not "History—France." The subject heading appears above the author's name either in red or in black capitals.

3. *By title.* Many books are also listed in the Card Catalog under their titles. The title appears above the author's name. In turn, some books and many periodicals are listed under title.

The call numbers are the classification numbers by which the books are arranged systematically on the shelves. They are found either in the upper left corner or at the top right of each card. Names following the call number, e.g., Engineering, indicate the specific library in which the volume is located.

There are two systems of classification in the Stanford Libraries: the Dewey Decimal and the Library of Congress. All volumes classified since June 1965 for the Main Library and most departmental libraries are in the Library of Congress scheme; Cubberley Education is the only library still using a Dewey Decimal scheme.

Enjoyment of Fact

Even those who have solved the mystery of the card catalog and thus can trace down most of the books and documents they need are likely to

Monographs in statistical physics and thermodynamics, v.8.

QC175.3
R5
Engineering

Rice, Stuart Alan, 1932–
The statistical mechanics of simple liquids; an introduction to the theory of equilibrium and non-equilibrium phenomena [by] Stuart A. Rice [and] Peter Gray. New York, Interscience Publishers, 1965.

xv, 582 p. illus. 24 cm. (Monographs in statistical physics and thermodynamics, v. 8)

Includes bibliographies.

1. Liquids, Kinetic theory of. 2. Statistical mechanics. I. Gray, Peter, 1933– joint author. II. Title. (Series)

QC175.3.R5 532.511 65–14731

Library of Congress [7-1]

Fig. 4. Series Card

QC175.3 Rice, Stuart Alan, 1932-
R5 The statistical mechanics of simple liquids.

Additional locations for the item described on next card(s) are listed below:

Physics Library	Chemical Engin. Lib.	

Fig. 5. Additional Location Card (first location follows the call number)

consider reference collections a hazard, and perhaps a bore. They may be surprised to learn that some people are fascinated by reference books. The late James Thurber once confessed that he enjoyed reading dictionaries. Seán O'Faoláin, the famous Irish writer, wrote of one reference book:

> The most soothing book I know is *Whitaker's Almanack.* When I have spent weeks struggling with a recalcitrant short story; when the Ecumenical Council seems to have lost itself in a Roman fog; when the bottom seems to have fallen out of sterling; or when the Congo, Cyprus, Vietnam, Tibet, Pakistan and Malaysia make me feel that I never again want to hear the word *insoluble*—what a relief to wander among such undeniable facts as that Stoddart hit 485 for Hampstead in 1886, whereas Bradman only hit 452 for New South Wales in 1929–30; to establish the number of theatres in London or the number of colleges in Oxford; to note that in 1918 the Derby was run at Newmarket and not at Epsom; to know where Ammaputtaland is and who runs the magisterial province of Babanango.
>
> For other men a bit of fox-hunting or hot squash would do just as well, but at my advanced age I agree with that famous old lexicographer, Walter William Skeat, that the most pleasant, bloodless sport in life is to hound an innocent fact to its lair.
>
> . . . Out-of-the-way knowledge you may sniff? Beneath a writer, you may add? Utterly unimportant, you may conclude? But such minutiae are the very stuff of biography, and, indeed, of science, to which no knowledge is unimportant until we examine it. Had Max Planck not been idly inquisitive enough to wonder (on no evidence whatever) whether radiant energy may come out not in a stream but in bits, like shot-gun pellets, we might never have had the Quantum Theory—or TV.[1]

Writers and lexicographers are not alone in enjoying reference works. Indeed, anyone with a special interest may be dedicated to at least one. Many baseball or golf addicts explore sports record books and the sports sections of general references. *The Guinness Book of World Records* is a continuing best-seller in America as well as in England (where it is published as *The Guinness Book of Records*).

But such dedication is selective, and librarians rightly complain that most reference books become dusty with disuse. That would not be true if the millions who regularly seek wide-ranging information would try to become whole researchers, at home with reference sources as well as interviews and questionnaires, capable of finding facts in a variety of fields and disciplines. Many do not because they are at least vaguely aware that the reference apparatus *is* vast and that only expert reference librarians can pick their way through it confidently. But the following section tries to show that the apparatus is not an insoluble mystery.*

How to Use Reference Sources

This chapter, which introduces research in reference sources, emphasizes finding individual facts. That is a small but essential step in developing knowledge.

The nagging problem in most fact research is that the researcher does not know that his task may be simple. All too often, one who looks for a fact that is actually close at hand assumes that his quest is truly novel, that no one ever *had* such a research problem before. He begins a wild search—and sometimes stumbles upon the answer. More often, he becomes frustrated and gives up. Later, in similar situations, he remembers his frustration and refuses to play the game again.

The first principle of library research is that the day is long past when librarians considered it their chief duty to *store* books and documents to protect them from those who wanted to use them. The old attitude may have been epitomized by the strong protests of Columbia University librarians when Columbia trustees voted in 1858 to keep the library open for ten hours a week rather than nine. At about the same time, John Langdon Sibley, head librarian at Harvard, was hurrying across the campus one day when he was stopped by a friend who asked why Sibley looked so happy. He replied, "All the books are in excepting two. Professor Agassiz has those, and I am going after them."

Modern librarians are there to help, but a librarian finds it difficult to help those who are not certain what they want to know. Sally Drew, chief reference librarian of the Redwood City, California, Public Library, said that she is often asked to find material on impossibly broad subjects. On one occasion, she was asked by a patron:

"Where are all your books on houses?"

"What would you like to know about houses? How to build them? How to decorate them? The history of houses?"

"Ah, gee, I don't know. I'll have to think about that." The patron walked away looking distracted.

Even those who seek precise information may be unaware of how many different kinds of specific questions librarians can answer. Thinking

* This section owes much to the work of Will Rogers, a former reference librarian, and especially to the work of William Allan of the General Reference Department of the Stanford University Libraries.

only of vast repositories of books, many are unaware that libraries—especially public libraries—carry copies of local ordinances, laws, community studies, and agendas of local board meetings. A library may have lists of special book collections in its area, descriptions of local public service organizations, clubs, recreational opportunities, and information on local residents who have special talents. The range and volume usually depend on the degree to which reference librarians clip and file newspaper items, but most public libraries try to serve as headquarters for community information. To this end, most of them preserve many old books and other records.

Consider the researcher who hoped to retrace the steps of Mark Twain in Hawaii. Twain had been sent there by the *Sacramento Union* in 1865 to write "lively sketches." In one of his "Letters from the Sandwich Islands" (as Hawaii was then known), Twain mentions a wonderful party at "Sam Brannon's bungalow." The problem: Where was Brannon's bungalow? A hundred years had passed, Honolulu had changed, and everyone living in Brannon's time was dead. The odds were against turning up an aged resident who might remember having heard a grandparent say that Sam Brannon had lived here or there. The researcher gave up.

What he failed to do was put the question in its simplest form, state it in everyday terms. If he had been looking for a living resident of Honolulu, he would have needed only a City Directory and a map. He needed no more to fix the location of Sam Brannon's bungalow. The City Directory of Honolulu for 1865 lists Brannon and his address, and a map shows the precise location—the bungalow once stood on the site of the present Federal Building in downtown Honolulu.*

This example illustrates the principal points stressed by reference librarians. First, the question *must* be well defined. In this case, it was;

* City directories and telephone directories are mines of unused information, much of it valuable.

The typical city directory lists address, telephone number, head of household, occupation, employer, spouse (or whether either spouse is deceased), and indicates ownership or co-ownership of business firms. Preceding the main body of information are "Facts & Figures" on the city: Area, Bank Debits, Bonded Debt, Automobile Registrations, and the like. Following the main body are listings by address, alphabetically by street. Then comes a "Numerical Telephone Directory," which lists all the numbers and exchanges of an area and gives the name of the party to whom each number belongs. Thus, having only an address, or only a telephone number, one can learn much more.

Telephone directories, properly analyzed, yield much more than names and numbers. A Central Intelligence Agency official once admitted that telephone directories are hot items on both sides of the Iron Curtain. Studying directories of military camps and nearby cities reveals much to a perceptive analyst, including dispositions of units and classifications of forces. Sociologists have traced immigration and emigration by analyzing the names that appear over a period of years.

the researcher wanted to know the exact location of the bungalow. Usually, though, librarians are frustrated by vagueness. One points out: "Often, people don't know *exactly* what they want to know because they are vague and hazy about the problem to be solved. Until they can fairly well define what they are after, the professional question-answerer is nearly helpless. Also, people don't want to appear stupid. Most of them don't really mind *being* stupid, they just don't want to appear stupid. So we must somehow elicit exactly what they are after without making them appear stupid."

Reference librarians also stress that researchers should make proper use of what they know. The Mark Twain researcher failed because he made a problem of history difficult by thinking of it only historically. Had he put it in his own time and used his knowledge and experience, the question would have answered itself. One librarian suggests: Take the specific question, turn it into a general problem, then ask yourself how you solved such general problems before. Where possible, try to put a general question in your own time, then ask how you would solve it.

As a rule, general sources should be consulted first. Too many researchers look for the hard-to-find specialized reference when a general source would yield the information more rapidly. For example, a music critic who wants to learn more about the trade name "Chickering," which he has seen on a famous performer's favorite piano, might easily fall into the error of looking through tomes on piano manufacturing. A quick check of the index to the *Encyclopaedia Britannica* would lead him directly to the information. One should always consult the index to an encyclopedia; it is *the* general key to information. But one must use it imaginatively. "Chickering" may not be found under "C," but it will turn up under "Piano Manufacture." (In the older *Encyclopedia Americana,* "Chickering" has no separate entry; it has in the current edition.)

A few research questions suggest that there are clear avenues through the maze of reference sources.

General

The Sacco-Vanzetti Case is an American classic. Where can one find the defendants' words quoted?

This is a specific question that yields an easy answer. The card catalog of any large library and the subject heading "Sacco-Vanzetti" lead to many books, including *The Letters of Sacco and Vanzetti.*

a. *When and where was the ice cream cone invented?*
b. *Who was the first woman executed in the United States for murder?*

c. *Who was the first Negro to obtain a patent?*

a. In 1904 at the Louisiana Purchase Exposition in St. Louis, Missouri.

b. Martha M. Place of Brooklyn, New York, at Sing Sing on March 20, 1899.

c. Henry Blair of Glenrose, Maryland, who obtained a patent on October 14, 1834, on a corn planter.

These are highly specific and odd questions, and they require a special reference. The clue is that all the questions involve conspicuous "firsts." Joseph N. Kane's *Famous First Facts* (subtitled "A Record of First Happenings, Discoveries and Inventions in the United States") is the key. Although this is the sort of book one must simply learn about, imaginative researchers have developed techniques for finding them without knowing they exist. One says, "When I'm looking for special information, I decide what the title of a book would be if someone had written it; then I go to the card catalog and look up the invented title. In a large library, half the time I find it."

In the underworld, what is meant by "the shake"?

Dictionary of American Underworld Lingo defines "the shake" as the extortion racket in general. One who did not know of the existence of this book could find it in the card catalog by looking under "Cant—Dictionaries," or "English Language—Dictionaries—Slang."

What is the origin of the phrase "fifth columnist"?

In *A Hog on Ice and Other Curious Expressions* (New York: Harper & Row, 1948), Charles Funk writes: "The expression arose in 1936, and came to mean, without regard to the numerical sense, a person who acts secretly within a city or country toward furthering the interests of an outside enemy; a secret agent. The expression is attributed to General Emilio Mola, who, leading four columns of armed rebels against Madrid during the revolution in Spain, told the foreign correspondents that he had a 'fifth column' within the city, meaning an army of sympathizers and active partisans waiting to assist in its overthrow."

This is a specific and odd question and requires a specific book—a dictionary or compilation of phrases, idioms, and curious expressions. The researcher who does not know such books can begin in the card catalog with "English Language—Terms & Phrases," or look to a general reference book for guidance.

Biographical

Where can one find a brief biographical sketch of John Steinbeck?

This answer is easy to find (Kunitz and Haycraft's *Twentieth Century Authors* is one of many sources) because Steinbeck is so widely known. In other cases of biographical and biobibliographical research, however, it is especially important to be specific about the identity of the subject. Knowing the nationality, occupation, and approximate period during which the subject lived often lightens the task considerably. The researcher can go to the general encyclopedias and the universal biographical dictionaries for bibliographies that lead to more specific and detailed sources.

When did Walter Reed live?

1851–1902.

If one does not know that Reed is dead and an American, the first source to check is Hyamson's *Dictionary of Universal Biography* (London: Routledge and Kegan Paul, 1951). The information is also in the *New Century Cyclopedia of Names,* which includes both living and dead persons. The researcher who knows that Reed is dead and an American might want to use *Who Was Who In America 1897–1960* (Chicago: Marquis, 1942–1960, 5 volumes).

Geographic

Where is Riobamba?

If you are not sure in what part of the world this is located, try a detailed index to a world map. *The Times Index-Gazetteer of the World* lists it, as does *Webster's Geographical Dictionary,* which devotes a paragraph of description to it. Both are standard research tools that are likely to be carried in even the most limited reference collection.

Literary

What is the origin and the significance of the title of Aldous Huxley's book After Many a Summer Dies the Swan?

Huxley's protagonist is like the mythical personage in Tennyson's poem "Tithonus" (from which the title came) who received immortality from the gods, but not eternal youth, so he became a decrepit old man longing for the sweet release of death.

This involves three research problems, the first of which is identifying the line. Many literary encyclopedias and handbooks to literature list the line and give its source, but it is usually wise when tracing literary allusions to start with standard works like *Bartlett's Familiar Quotations*. *Bartlett's* turns this up under the key words "swan," "summer," and "dies." To understand the significance it is necessary to use *Bartlett's* to find the poem among Tennyson's works (thus solving the second research problem). Then one can consult a classical dictionary of mythology such as *Oxford Companion to Classical Literature* or *New Century Classical Handbook* to learn more about Tithonus—and solve the third problem.

> *What was the leading American fiction best-seller in 1959?*
> *Exodus* by Leon Uris.

Any question involving a particular year can often be answered through the general yearbooks: *World Almanac, Information Please*, and the British *Whitaker's Almanack*. Trade journals in the various fields also publish leading statistics (in this case, *Publishers' Weekly*). Much more detail is available in the general encyclopedia yearbooks—the annual volumes which try to summarize notable events in all areas of human endeavor. The *Britannica Book of the Year* for 1960 (the 1959 statistics on publishing are not compiled until after the turn of the year, of course), carries an index item under "Best Sellers." This leads the researcher to an article on "Book Publishing and Sales," which places the answer in a meaningful context.

> *Where can one find a list of books by David Riesman, author of* The Lonely Crowd?

Building bibliographies is hazardous. Few are complete because periodical literature can turn up almost anywhere, and translations into other languages are sometimes unrecorded. (Several of Riesman's books have already been translated into German, French, and Italian.) Thus, the researcher should define exactly what he wants. Supposing that the aim is a list of books in English alone, the printed card catalog of the Library of Congress is a good beginning. Most books by American publishers turn up there. The next step is a methodical search of *Cumulative Book Index* (or *Bibliographic Index of Contemporary Authors*), which is a world listing of books in English. Other steps—searches in the British Museum Catalogue, for example—may assure reasonable completeness.

> *What is the title and who is the author of the poem in which appears the line, "I am the master of my fate"?*
> "Invictus" by William Ernest Henley.

Although the floods of poetry written during the last two thousand years make it difficult to find isolated lines in undistinguished poetry, finding memorable lines is usually easy. *Bartlett's Familiar Quotations* and

Granger's Index to Poetry are the most often used of the hundreds of research tools. *Bartlett's* has an alphabetical *key word* index which places the quoted passage in the main body of the work. Thus, to identify the line, one looks under "master" or "fate" and is guided to the poem. *Granger's,* on the other hand, is a *title and first line* index. "I am the master of my fate" would be listed under "I" if it were the first line of "Invictus." But it is not.

Since many memorable quotations are from great authors or from the Bible, literary researchers should become acquainted with the concordances, which list very meaningful words and refer to the source. Thus, identifying a line from Shakespeare, the Bible, or James Joyce requires only referring to a Shakespeare Concordance, a Bible Concordance, or a Joyce Concordance. But one should always use the general references first. A quick glance through *Bartlett's* or *Granger's* requires little work; finding specific sources through the card catalog ("Milton, John—concordances") takes more time.

> *Where can one find a review of Margaret Mitchell's* Gone with the Wind?
> *New York Times Book Review,* July 5, 1936, page 1.

As in the preceding case, one asks simple questions: Where are general-interest books reviewed? Answer: In general magazines and newspapers. Where are these indexed? Answer: In *Book Review Digest, Book Review Index,* or *Index to Book Reviews in the Humanities.*

Again, one faces the problem of looking through many volumes of *Book Review Digest* to find the appropriate year. The shortcut is the card catalog in a large library (or the printed catalog in a small one), which will carry the date of publication of the book. With the 1936 publishing date, the researcher can go directly to the 1936 volume of *Book Review Digest,* find Mitchell in the alphabetical list, and read the synopsis of reviews for all the leading media.

> *Ranting about his mother, Hamlet says, among other scathing things, that she was like "Niobe, all tears." Who was Niobe and what is the meaning of the allusion?*
> In Greek Mythology, Niobe boasted of her children and was forced by the gods to watch Leto's children slay them. She wept until, at her request, Zeus turned her into stone.

Although guides like Benet's *Reader's Encyclopedia* and even the general encyclopedias are useful in this kind of search, a dictionary of mythology will usually turn up many more allusions. *Oxford Classical Dictionary* is recommended. Similar volumes can be found in library card catalogs under "Mythology—Dictionaries."

Law and Government

Where can one find legal comment on the last appeal made by Caryl Chessman?

Notre Dame Lawyer, Volume 32, May, 1957, page 522.

American Bar Association Journal, Volume 43, August, 1957, page 735.

For the layman, legal research is a jungle, and it is usually necessary to appeal to a reference librarian. The problem is that to find the text of a court's decision and all subsequent references to it, one must go to a law reporter which reports all appellate cases (those taken to a higher court) to read the case, then "Shepardize" it—search for further developments through a reference series known as *Shepard's.*

Where would you find a biographical sketch of the senior senator from Colorado if you don't know his name?

This could be found with the use of one reference work—*Official Congressional Directory,* issued for each Congress—which includes biographical sketches of the members of Congress. If the researcher seeks information about a former congressman whose name he knows, *Biographical Directory of the American Congress 1774–1961* is useful.

Where can one find congressional committee hearings?

Recognizing the widespread and deep interest in government publications, officials long ago designated many large libraries as depositories for U.S. documents. In a sense, each depository library is a little Library of Congress which receives the majority of congressional or legislative publications (bills and resolutions, hearings, committee reports, Senate and House documents, journals, debates, laws, and codes) and executive publications which deal with the organization, structure, and administration of the executive branch. These arrive in such volume—the Stanford University depository contains nearly two million items—that government documents librarians have become proud specialists. They can guide a researcher quickly to the relevant documents, but only if he knows precisely what he wants. What hearing of which committee in what year?

Music

What was Johannes Brahms's education and musical training?

The first problem in doing research about composers and musicians is to determine in which branch of music the subject is or was active. This can usually be done easily with the help of a dictionary such as Grove's *Dictionary of Music and Musicians.*

For jazz composers and musicians, the best source is Leonard Feather's *Encyclopedia of Jazz,* the greater part of which consists of biographies of jazz celebrities.

Communications

How can I find Nielsen ratings for television programs?

Nielsen is one of the many audience research companies that sell their rating services. Available at first only to clients, Nielsen ratings later are printed, especially in broadcasting trade journals. The broadest research approach is to consult the *Business Periodicals Index* under "Television broadcasting—Program rating." Perhaps the quickest research route is to use the *Wall Street Journal Index* under "Nielsen, A. C. & Co."

Where can one find a review of the movie It Happened One Night, *starring Clark Gable?*

New Republic, Volume 78, May 9, 1934, page 364.
Literary Digest, Volume 117, March 10, 1934, page 38.

To find reviews, one asks first: Where are general movie reviews published? Answer: In general magazines that appeal to the general public. Where are general magazines (*Time, New Republic,* and the like) indexed? Answer: *Readers' Guide to Periodical Literature.*

Now the researcher *could* start back through *Readers' Guide* looking under "Moving Picture Plays—Criticism, plots—Single Works" and eventually arrive at 1934 and be able to trace down the reviews. But he could save hours by posing another question: When was the movie released? He can determine this through *Film Daily Year Book of Motion Pictures,* which carries a section entitled "31,825 Titles released since 1915." There in the alphabetical list he would find "It Happened One Night" and "Col —2-23-34," which means that Columbia Pictures released it on February 23, 1934. Then he can go directly to the 1934 volume of *Readers' Guide.* He could also use *The New York Times Film Reviews,* a seven-volume set of reviews from 1913 to 1970.

Science

Where and how does one find the difference between the atomic bomb and the hydrogen bomb?

Such timely and general questions are easily answered by any of the standard encyclopedias, and *Collier's Encyclopedia* is especially useful to the layman looking into science. The complete answer—sometimes in specialist's language—will be found in a specialist's tool, a general *science* encyclopedia like *McGraw-Hill Encyclopedia of Science and Technology.*

What scientist headed up the development of the atomic bomb at the Los Alamos Scientific Laboratory (also called "The Manhattan Project")?

J. Robert Oppenheimer.

Since this is a fairly well-defined question on a general subject, the first search should be made in the index volume of a large encyclopedia. Under "Los Alamos" and "Manhattan Project," the *Encyclopedia Americana* notes that J. Robert Oppenheimer was director of the research laboratory at Los Alamos. More complete information about Oppenheimer can then be found under his name.

Business

Who was the president of the Bates Shoe Company of Webster, Massachusetts, in 1964, and how many employees worked for the company?

Edgar A. Craven; 475 employees.

Virtually every profession and industry is served by a directory which is easy to locate in a library catalog under the appropriate entry followed by "—Directories" (for example, "Physicians—Directories"). *Poor's Register of Corporations, Directors and Executives* is cataloged under several subject entries, among them "Directors of Corporations—U.S.—Directories" and "Capitalists and financiers—U.S.—Directories."

What was the net income of the New York Times *for 1963?*

$1,069,127.

Every company holding stock must make public its financial situation, and usually does so in an annual report. Any large business library files many annual reports. More important, since the financial condition of all large companies is newsworthy, salient excerpts from annual reports are published in such papers as the *Wall Street Journal* and the *New York Times*, and many business journals analyze annual reports. Thus, the *Wall Street Journal Index* (which began in 1958) and the *New York Times Index* are prime sources, and so is the *Business Periodicals Index*.

Although these examples barely touch the range of possible questions, they suggest the basic method. They also emphasize the importance of being aware of central sources, many of which are described in the next chapter.

6 Central Sources

The researcher who first approaches the reference apparatus in awe may, in time, begin to develop a reasonable attitude toward it. He may have an experience like that of Alfred Balk, a writer who was assigned in 1962 to collaborate with Alex Haley on a magazine article on the Black Muslims. Balk, who is white, was to work outside the Muslim movement. Haley, a black writer, was to work inside it. Balk learned from a widely respected work, *The Black Muslims in America* by Dr. C. Eric Lincoln, that the Muslims were estimated to have 100,000 to 250,000 members. In their subsequent research, which involved traveling extensively, attending meetings and rallies, and talking to Muslims and to local and federal law enforcement officials, Balk and Haley learned that the Muslims may have had 7,000 members, and perhaps 50,000 others might be considered close and consistent sympathizers, but not by any stretch of definition did the Muslim movement approach 100,000 members.[1]

The awestruck researcher should also be aware that in some instances the editors of the otherwise excellent *Encyclopaedia Britannica* assign the writing of *Britannica* biographical articles to friends of the subjects. In the fourteenth edition of the *Britannica*, the article on the late Congressman Sam Rayburn, who was for many years Speaker of the House of Representatives, is signed "L.B.J." Can one expect a balanced picture of Rayburn from his political protégé, Lyndon Baines Johnson? Similarly, the editors of the *Britannica* sometimes assign articles about business firms to those who control them. Frederick R. Kappel was Chairman of the Board of American Telephone & Telegraph Company when he wrote an article on AT&T. And the article on the Federal Bureau of Investigation was written by "J.E.H." The late J. Edgar Hoover certainly knew the organization he directed, but one could wish for an authority with a more detached perspective.

The researcher should also consider the limitations of even the most painstaking compilers of reference sources. In 1972, a team of lexicographers issued the first of three volumes that are designed to supplement the huge and irreplaceable *Oxford English Dictionary*. The team worked on that supplementary volume for fifteen years. In 1,356 pages, it covers English language development from 1884 to the present, letters A to G. But the director of the team, Robert W. Burchfield, said resignedly to a *New York Times* reporter that the volume is not complete: "The right policy is to do things you can do without holding up your dictionary and without killing off your staff." One of the things the compilers could not do was work into the volume some words that have become common in recent years. "Chicano" and "downer" were among those that were being prepared but missed the printing deadline.[2]

In a light article on his research experiences, writer Tracy Early told of finding in one reference book that Martin Luther King, Jr., earned his Ph.D. at Boston University, in another, at Harvard. Also:

> For a recent article, I needed to know how many member churches the World Council of Churches had at its founding in 1948. For such information you are not dependent just on the *New Catholic Encyclopedia,* which says 145. Or on the authoritative *History of the Ecumenical Movement,* edited by Rouse and Neill, which says 147.
> Fortunately, the Council published the official report of the founding Assembly. So you can get the number from the general secretary's report to the Assembly—150. Or, if you don't mind taking the time, you can turn to the back of the book, where the churches represented are listed, and count them—133.[3]

What is the proper attitude toward the reference apparatus? Certainly not to regard it suspiciously, although estimates are sometimes wrong, practices questionable, limitations insurmountable, and sources in disagreement. Just as the awe of the beginner is inappropriate and injurious, so is cynicism. A researcher working with references sources should simply remember that all books, including reference books, are made by people.

The researcher who remembers that all those who write, compile, and edit reference books are subject to certain influences and errors begins to place the research apparatus in a reasonable context. He must also realize, however, that most reference sources are produced by specialists whose ambitions and goals may push them as close to an objective state as humans are likely to reach.

Such beliefs undergird the following descriptions of reference sources. This list is far from exhaustive. Constance Winchell's *Guide to Reference Books* covers 741 pages and lists about 7,500 sources. Nor are the brief listings of scholarly journals complete. Estimates of *their* numbers, worldwide, range from 200,000 to 600,000. More than 700 medical journals are published in Japan alone. This section lists and describes many reference sources useful to those who are not specialists.

Because many of the following sources enable the researcher to find facts in context and to develop relationships among them, studying the sources takes the researcher beyond the pursuit of the single fact that was emphasized in the preceding chapter. The next chapter takes another step in suggesting how the researcher should pursue knowledge and organize it in reporting.

The following terms are used often in reference research and appear throughout this chapter:

Abstract A summary, usually quite brief, that sketches the essential points of a book, pamphlet, article, thesis, or other writing.

Almanac This word has two meanings. (1) An annual publication containing a calendar, frequently accompanied by astronomical data and other information. (2) An annual book of statistics and other information, sometimes limited to a particular field.

Annotation A note that describes, explains, or evaluates, or all three.

Archives This term has two meanings. (1) An organized body of records. (2) An institution that preserves particular records.

Atlas A book of maps, engravings, and tables, with or without descriptive text.

Digest A condensation, sometimes quite brief, of a written work, sometimes in words other than those of the original. In law, a *digest* is a systematic summary of laws, cases, and decisions.

Ephemera This word has two meanings. (1) Current writings, usually pamphlets and clippings of temporary interest and value. (2) Similar materials of the past which have acquired literary or historical significance.

Fugitive publications (or *Fugitive Material*) Pamphlets, programs, and the like printed in limited quantities and usually of interest only at the time or in the place of publication.

Gazetteer A geographical dictionary.

In press Anything that is in the process of being printed.

In print Publications available from the publisher (as distinguished from those out of print, which may be available from another source but are no longer sold by the publisher).

Periodical A publication with a distinctive title intended to appear in successive numbers at scheduled or regular intervals. Most periodicals contain articles by several contributors. Librarians do not consider newspapers as periodicals and do not catalog them as such. Nor are periodic memoirs, proceedings, and journals of societies cataloged among periodicals.

Serials Any publications (including periodicals, newspapers, proceedings, reports, and numbered monographs) published indefinitely.

Standard A work recognized as having permanent value.

In the following lists, the notes reading *1942–*, *1956–*, etc., indicate that the sources so identified are not single or irregular publications but have been issued continually since that date.

General References—Dictionaries

More and more, the function of the dictionary is becoming historical and descriptive rather than critical and prescriptive, much to the dismay of many grammatical purists. Many lexicographers contend that their mission is to record language as it is used, not to cull speech and literature for proper words. Thus, "ain't" is in many dictionaries, and so are hundreds of other improprieties, not to mention the pungent vulgarisms that small boys who learn the facts of life from the neighbors' children would like to be able to look up.

Fad words come flooding into the language, and many of them go out again so rapidly that they are never recorded. But most lexicographers require only that a word make its way into "standard speech and literature" (the standard is usually low) to be included in a dictionary.

Most unabridged dictionaries—"unabridged" might be defined as "paralyzingly extensive"—offer definition, spelling, pronunciation, syllabification, and grammatical usage. They also include illustrative material and some information of an encyclopedic nature, undoubtedly distressing some of those who are trying to make a living in the encyclopedia business.

Dictionaries, then, have come a long way since the fifteenth and sixteenth centuries, when the few English words that were recorded were designed only as an aid to learning Latin. They have also traveled far beyond the highly personal dictionary compiled by Dr. Samuel Johnson, who defined the lexicographer as a "harmless drudge."

Unabridged Dictionaries

A Dictionary of American English on Historical Principles
Chicago: University of Chicago Press, 1936–1944. 4 vols.

William Craigie's great *Dictionary of American English,* which is known as the D.A.E., might be described as the colonial equivalent of the *Oxford English Dictionary.* The O.E.D. must be consulted for the full history of any word that originated in the British Isles, but for the many words of American origin (which are marked with a plus sign), this dictionary is excellent, if a bit dated. It shows when, how, and in what form each word has come into the American version of the English language, and all changes in spelling, meaning, and usage. Compiling it took forty years.

Funk & Wagnalls New Standard Dictionary of the English Language
New York: Funk & Wagnalls, 1964.

The scope of the *New Standard Dictionary* is somewhat comparable to *Webster's.* Both are valuable, and heavy. The editors of the *New Standard* focus on the changes in language: "The vocabulary should . . . embrace *all the live words* of the English language as used in the standard speech and literature of the day." The emphasis on modernity is so strong that it arranges its definitions with the current meaning first.

Oxford English Dictionary on Historical Principles
Sir James A. H. Murray. Oxford: Clarendon Press, 1888–1933. 10 vols. plus supplement. Reissued, 1933, in 12 vols. plus supplement.

The O.E.D., as it is known to professors, graduate students, lexicographers, and those faking erudition, represents the most compelling feat in lexicography. Confusingly, this is also known as N.E.D., for "New English Dictionary." Its purpose: "to furnish an adequate account of the meaning, origin, and history of English words now in general use, or known to have been in use at any time during the last seven hundred years." It shows when, how, and in what form each word has come into the language and the changes in spelling, meaning, and usage. The history of each word is illustrated by a series of quotations ranging from its first known occurrence in the written language to its latest usage. In short, it offers more about the English language than most of us care to know. (As noted earlier in this chapter, Oxford issued in 1972 the first volume of a massive supplement.)

Webster's New International Dictionary of the English Language
Springfield, Mass.: Merriam-Webster, 1961. Third edition.

The oldest and most famous American dictionary, *Webster's* offers excellent definitions (in historic sequence, the oldest meanings first), careful editing, and the largest number of word entries among American dictionaries. Until the publication of the third edition in 1961, "controversial" was a word that one looked for in, rather than associated with, *Webster's*. But "the Third," as it quickly became known, appalled those who believe that dictionaries should prescribe proper usage—or at least indicate preferred usage—not simply describe how words are being used. The editors of the *New York Times* were so dismayed that they directed the *Times* staff to use the new edition only for "new, primarily scientific words." For the rest, the *Times* relies on the old second edition.

Some authorities believe that history will be kinder to "the Third' than contemporary critics have been, but this sounds too much like U.S. Presidents who try to justify their present disasters by imagining that historians will justify them. It can be said of the third edition, though, that it added 100,000 new words or meanings that bloomed after publication of the second edition. Such is the fertility of language.

Shorter Dictionaries

American Heritage Dictionary of the English Language
Edited by William Morris. Boston: American Heritage and Houghton Mifflin, 1969.

A prestigious array of contributors and consultants helped produce this 1,550-page volume. The 155,000 entries are written so that "the first definition is the central meaning about which the other senses may be most logically arranged." Many who use the *American Heritage Dictionary* applaud its readability. It contains many well-chosen quotations from literature to illustrate definitions and carefully explains shades of different meanings among synonyms.

The Random House Dictionary of the English Language
Jesse Stein, editor-in-chief. New York: Random House, 1966.

This volume suggests as well as any what the makers of abridged dictionaries try to do in most instances. Instead of merely reducing the number of words defined, they also reduce the lengths of definitions (usually by giving little attention to word origins), and work hard to include new words and current meanings of old words. In contrast to the 450,000 to 600,000 words in the unabridged dictionaries, this one includes 260,000 words. It emphasizes current meanings and is notable for concise definitions, legibility, and other features that make it easy to use.

Webster's New World Dictionary of the American Language
Prentice-Hall, 1970. Second College Edition.

This dictionary includes over 12,000 Americanisms and emphasizes words, terms, and expressions unique to the American language. It is the first dictionary to list origins and explanations of American place names. All entries, including the names of people and places, foreign expressions, and abbreviations, are listed in a single alphabetical listing, so the reader need not search through numerous appendixes before finding the proper entry. *Webster's New World Dictionary* contains more entries than any other college dictionary, more detailed etymologies than comparable dictionaries, and emphasizes the English language as it is used in America.

Specialized Dictionaries

American Usage: The Consensus
Roy H. Copperud. Van Nostrand Reinhold, 1970.

The American version of the English language has no final authority, no expert or board of experts to decide what usage is correct. That fact makes this book valuable, for Copperud has collected and compared the judgments of the experts who wrote these books:

The ABC of Style by Rudolf Flesch. Harper & Row, 1964.

The Careful Writer by Theodore M. Bernstein. Atheneum, 1965.

Current American Usage by Margaret M. Bryant. Funk & Wagnalls, 1962.

A Dictionary of Contemporary American Usage by Bergen and Cornelia Evans. Random House, 1957.

A Dictionary of Usage and Style by Roy M. Copperud. Hawthorn, 1964.

Modern American Usage by Wilson Follett and others. Hill & Wang, 1966.

Copperud included in his comparison the most respected book on the English version of the English language:

A Dictionary of Modern English Usage by H. W. Fowler; second edition revised by Sir Ernest Gowers. Oxford University Press, 1965.

The result of Copperud's labors is a volume that provides a valuable overview of the various judgments of proper usage. An example:

> *anyplace.* Disapproved by Bernstein and Bryant as colloquial for *anywhere,* accepted by Fowler as a U.S. usage, and considered standard by Evans and Flesch. Among the dictionaries, Webster and American Heritage accept it as standard, but Random House calls it informal. Here, as in other instances when the authorities fall out, the writer may safely make his own decision.

Dictionary of American Slang
Compiled and edited by Harold Wentworth and Stuart Berg Flexner. New York: Thomas Y. Crowell Company, 1967.

The more conventional dictionaries, once chiefly concerned with the language spoken by taste-makers, long left a wide field to the collectors of informal English. That field is narrowing because these days fewer lexicographers sniffily dismiss slang in a few offhand words. There is still room, though, for scholars like Wentworth and Flexner. As they write, "Slang is best defined by a dictionary that points out who uses slang and what 'flavor' it conveys." In other words, look to the lexicographer who really cares.

Wentworth and Flexner cast a wide net, terming all slang used in the United States "American," regardless of its country of origin or use in other countries They define it: "American slang is the body of words and expressions frequently used by or intelligible to a rather large portion of the general American public, but not accepted as good, formal usage by the majority."

The Dictionary of American Underworld Lingo
Edited by Hyman Golden. New York: Twayne, 1950.

This carries gamier fare than Wentworth and Flexner, but it is not, fortunately, everything claimed in the jacket blurb: "an encyclopedia of criminal technique." It is diverting, though, and perhaps not the gift for juveniles who take pride in their delinquency.

Dictionary of Slang and Unconventional English
Eric Partridge. New York: Macmillan, 1970. 2 vols. Seventh edition.

Eric Partridge is the Noah Webster of flavorful English. He published the first volume of this controversial collection in 1937 and has been bringing out additions ever since. These "addenda," as he calls them, have been incorporated into a single volume (as Volume 2) and called the "supplement." In 1949, he also published *A Dictionary of the Underworld, British and American* (New York: Macmillan, 1949). Although Partridge has the scholar's interest in tracing word origins—he includes terms dating back to 1600—the serious purpose of his works does not protect them from the censure of outraged school library committees. Partridge marks with asterisks words that are likely to be considered objectionable, a feature that may be used as guard or guide.

Roget's International Thesaurus
Edited by Robert A. Dutch. New York: St. Martin's, 1965. Revised edition.

Peter Mark Roget was a British doctor whose interests embraced phrenology and chess problems. In 1852, he brought out his first book of synonyms and antonyms. The editors of the latest edition have a much clearer notion than did Roget about how to serve the general reader as well as the word specialist. They have organized and indexed more than 250,000 words and phrases in easy-to-find, readable fashion.

Webster's New Dictionary of Synonyms
Springfield, Mass.: Merriam, 1968. Second edition.

To many a student, a synonym is a word to be used for one he can't spell. This big volume covers many unusual words as well as those most commonly used, giving same and nearly same meanings. It distinguishes carefully among the several meanings of single words.

Encyclopedias

The makers of encyclopedias are futility's traveling companions. Like Bacon, they try to make all knowledge their province. They fail. It is nonetheless true that anyone who can read is in their debt. Even though a researcher must go far beyond an encyclopedia for a detailed examination of almost any subject, he can glean first principles and develop an overview from many of the leading encyclopedias. Most encyclopedias rely on authorities, and most of those authorities are well chosen.

Encyclopedias are, of course, inevitably behind the times. The major companies—Britannica, Americana, Collier's, and others—try to reduce the lag by issuing yearbooks. Most carry obituaries for the year and a chronological index of the year's events. The *New International Yearbook* features an excellent list of leading national and international "Societies and Organizations" giving founding date, president, and current address for each.

(Specialized encyclopedias such as *McGraw-Hill Encyclopedia of Science and Technology* will be listed in this chapter according to various subject fields.)

Chambers's Encyclopaedia
London: International Learning Systems, 1973. 15 vols. Revised edition.

Although the British perspective is obvious in many passages, this 15-volume set ranks in usefulness to Americans with the best of our encyclopedias. Comprehensive, international, accurate, its grace and clarity sometimes make the writing in American volumes seem limp.

Collier's Encyclopedia
New York: Collier-Macmillan, 1972. 24 vols.

Collier's Encyclopedia is resolutely modern. It is so bright with large print and many illustrations and so attentive to today (sometimes scanting yesterday and the day before) that many scholars refuse to rank it with the *Britannica* and the *Americana*. Putting the bibliographies in the index volume instead of attaching them to the appropriate articles is tidy, but inconvenient for the reader. Nevertheless, *Collier's Encyclopedia*, which is supplemented by *Collier's Encyclopedia Year Book*, is useful and authoritative—often used by reference librarians, one said, because it is so "fact-conscious."

Encyclopedia Americana
New York: Americana Corp. (a division of Grolier, Inc.), 1974. 30 vols.

The *Americana* is not the American counterpart of the *Britannica*. Both are published in the United States; both try to cover the world of knowledge. Nevertheless, the *Americana* may be considered appropriately titled because of its attention to American places—some of them quite small—organizations, and institutions. This focus and an unusual collection of articles on the histories of the centuries of mankind make the *Americana* distinctive and valuable. Like the *Britannica*, the *Americana* issues an extraordinarily useful index volume that enables a researcher to winnow subjects and find the right volume rapidly. It also publishes a yearbook, *The Americana Annual*.

Encyclopaedia Britannica
Edited by Warren Preece. Chicago: Encyclopaedia Britannica, Inc., 1974. 30 vols. Fifteenth edition.

Early in 1974, *Britannica* announced the publication of the fifteenth edition, which is called *Britannica* 3 because of its three-part structure. One volume is the *Propaedia: Outline of Knowledge and Guide to the Britannica*, which is both an expanded table of contents and an index. Ten volumes of the thirty-volume set are physically distinct and are subtitled *Ready Reference and Index*, which is more descriptive than the main title, *Micropaedia*. These ten volumes are designed to serve the researcher who is looking for one fact, a few facts, or the essentials in any of the 102,214 short entries, none of which is longer than 750 words. Among the entries are 4,207 digest versions of the 4,207 major articles in the *Macropaedia*, which makes up the other nineteen volumes. The *Macropaedia* provides lengthy articles, an average of five pages per article, all of them written by authorities who were asked to write not for other authorities but for the intelligent layman. The result is a readable and highly innovative encyclopedia that may change encyclopedia-making.

Desk Encyclopedias

Columbia Encyclopedia
New York: Columbia University Press, 1963. Third edition.

The print is small, the articles are short, and some of the information is outdated (a new edition is scheduled for the mid-1970s), but this volume continues to be a valuable tool for many research purposes. Designed for high-school students, adult laymen, and most of those between the two groups, the *Columbia Encyclopedia* is the handiest quick-reference book available. It carries 70,000 entries and 75,000 cross references.

Lincoln Library of Essential Information
Buffalo, N.Y.: Frontier Press, 1969. 2 vols.

Little-known except to librarians and others who specialize in general research, this collection was organized for self-education, but it is also an excellent research tool. A bit superficial for anyone who wants information in depth, it is nonetheless a useful source in literature, fine arts, music, education, and biography. The editors have aimed throughout at providing essential information concisely. The fact that they do so in three and a half million words indicates the broad scope.

Biographical Dictionaries and Indexes

Biography Index
New York: Wilson, 1946–. Quarterly.

The researcher who has always leaned heavily on *Readers' Guide* should introduce himself to *Biography Index*. It has an overwhelming scope, indexing biographical material and articles in current books and in 1,500 periodicals.

Contemporary Authors
Edited by James M. Ethridge, Barbara Kopala, and Carolyn Riley. Detroit: Gale Research, 1962–. Semiannual.

This volume provides information about many authors whose biographies are not published in other sources. Restricted to living authors, it includes many who have written relatively little and many who have written in obscure fields. *Contemporary Authors* is especially valuable because it is continually updated. The two semiannual volumes are bound as one every year.

Current Biography
New York: Wilson, 1940–. Monthly.

Anyone who is prominent in the news of the day may be sketched in the informal word portraits that make up *Current Biography*. (Many of the biographical articles carry pictures of the subjects.) The monthly issues are cumulated in annual volumes.

Dictionary of American Biography
New York: Scribner's, 1928–1973. 20 vols., index, and Supplements I, II, and III.

Widely known as the greatest of all American biographical dictionaries, the D.A.B. has been called "an assessment of what the American people have thus far accomplished in all fields of endeavor." Scholars, divines, politicians, authors—every American is sketched who satisfies two requirements: he must have made a significant contribution, and he must be dead. J. G. E. Hopkins abridged this giant set in 1964, producing the *Concise Dictionary of American Biography*.

Dictionary of National Biography
London: Smith, Elder, 1885–1901. 22 vols. 7 supplements, latest covers 1951–60 (London: Oxford University Press, 1971); corrections and additions 1923–63 (Boston: Hall, 1966).

A monument to biographical scholarship, the D.N.B. came out first in sixty-three volumes. Then it was revised in twenty-two volumes, and many supplements have been published since. Its focus is on more than thirty thousand deceased inhabitants of Great Britain and its former colonies.

A Dictionary of Universal Biography: Of All Ages and of All Peoples
Albert M. Hyamson. New York: E. P. Dutton, 1951. Second edition.

Albert Hyamson measured out his life in the three-by-five index cards that pulled together this excellent source. He wrote upon completing the first edition: "The largest biographical work in existence has not a tithe of the entries which this volume contains." Hyamson had reason for pride, but this is not a biographical dictionary in the conventional sense. Unlike the long articles in *Chambers's Biographical Dictionary* (New York: St. Martin's Press, 1968), which cover the great of all nations and all times, most of Hyamson's "biographies" are entries—single lines made up of name, birth and death dates, nationality, profession, and the reference source which gives full information. Without detracting from the value of Hyamson's work, it is fair to say that he provides a thumbnail of fact and a guide to more comprehensive biographies.

American Men and Women of Science
New York: R. R. Bowker, 1973. Twelfth edition.
Directory of American Scholars
New York: R. R. Bowker, 1969. 4 vols. Fifth edition.
The Physical and Biological Sciences
New York: R. R. Bowker, 1965–67. 6 vols. 2 supplements, 1967–68.
The Social and Behavioral Sciences
New York: R. R. Bowker, 1968. 2 vols.

These companion volumes are indispensable for brief information on the careers of many college and university professors, only a few of whom are in the august general sources like *Who's Who in America*. The entries vary in length, but all give birth date, education, marital status, children, major publications, field of chief interest, and address.

Index to Women of the World from Ancient to Modern Times: Biographies and Portraits
Norma Olin Ireland, Westwood, Mass.: F. W. Faxon, 1970.

This volume indexes almost a thousand biographies that record the chief contributions of women throughout recorded history.

National Cyclopedia of American Biography
New York: White, 1892–1971.

This series, the most comprehensive American reference source, indexes not only biographical articles, but also names, institutions, events, and other items mentioned in the biographies. It is published in two parts, a "permanent" series (numbered volumes) and a "current" series (lettered volumes in loose-leaf form). The permanent series, which carries only biographies of *deceased* persons, is now complete through volume 53, published in 1971. The current series, published in 1967, includes *living* persons. When a biographee dies, his article is brought up to date and permanently entered in the permanent series. Cumulative indexes are published for these series because the articles are not printed in alphabetical sequence.

New Century Cyclopedia of Names
Edited by Clarence L. Barnhart and William D. Halsey. New York: Appleton-Century-Crofts, 1954. 3 vols.

This is a unique work consisting solely of important proper names in the English-speaking world. The editors, who apparently didn't know when to stop, give "the most frequently used English and native spellings and pronunciations, as well as the essential facts, about more than 100,000 proper names of every description—persons, places, historical events, plays and operas, works of fiction, literary characters, works of art, mythological and legendary persons and places, and any other class of proper names of interest and importance today." Naturally, all this spilled over, requiring three volumes.

The New York Times Obituaries Index, 1868–1968
New York Times, 1970.

This is an important tool, a cumulative index to the obituaries that have appeared on the obituaries pages of the *Times.*

Webster's Biographical Dictionary
Springfield, Mass.: Merriam, 1972.

The 45,000 entries in this volume cover a wild range, from brief identifications to profiles of several hundred words. Although *Webster's Biographical* won't work for researchers who need to go into depth, its brief entries are just right for verifying names, dates, and birthplaces.

Who's Who
London: A. & C. Black; New York: St. Martin's, 1849–. Annual.

Who's Who in America was built on this British model, which began publication in 1849. *Who's Who* offers concise biographical information about prominent living Englishmen and a few distinguished foreigners. An "Obituary" section lists those who died during the preceding year. The success of the British *Who's Who* is responsible for the birth of similar books of other countries: *Wer Ist Wer, Who's Who in France,* and *Who's Who in Canada.*

Who's Who in America
Chicago: Marquis, 1899/1900–. Biennial.

Published every other year, this biennial is considered the standard source on notable living Americans. It consists of brief, fact-packed biographies and current addresses supplied by the subjects. A definite status symbol, a listing in *Who's Who in America* sometimes seems to be the American substitute for knighthood. Because women have difficulty receiving recognition for their accomplishments, the same publisher also brings out *Who's Who of American Women* biennially.

Yearbooks and Almanacs

Information Please Almanac
New York: Simon & Schuster, 1947–. Annual.

Some of the information presented in other almanacs is also here, but the editors have been so imaginative in selecting areas to cover that *Informa-*

tion Please Almanac can be used as a supplement to almost any book of facts. It features broad, useful coverage of statistics in geography, U.S. governments, and general biography.

Statistical Abstract of the United States
Washington, D.C.: Government Printing Office, 1878–. Annual.

This is a digest of data collected by all the statistical agencies of the United States government and some private agencies. Another Government Printing Office publication, *Historical Statistics of the United States, Colonial Times to 1957* (Washington, D.C.: Government Printing Office, 1960), is helpful for early records. An updated version, titled *The Statistical History of the United States from Colonial Times to the Present,* was published by Fairfield Publishers, Stamford, Connecticut, in 1965.

In 1967, the U.S. Bureau of the Census began issuing biennially a handier summary titled *Pocket Data Book,* 300 to 400 pages of the central information on this country.

World Almanac and Book of Facts
New York: Newspaper Enterprise Assocation, 1868–. Annual.

Perhaps the most often-used reference in the United States, this is a deservedly famous mine of miscellany. It is not, of course, "complete"—no reference book deserves that adjective—and research specialists can name more comprehensive sources in almost any field. But as a general rapid-reference tool, *World Almanac* is invaluable.

Foreign Yearbooks and Almanacs

Canadian Almanac and Directory
Toronto: Copp Clark, 1847–. Annual.

Unlike the almanacs of infinite scope, this one is resolutely Canadian. Within these limits, it is satisfyingly comprehensive. Little of the wide range of Canadiana has escaped this net—from "abbreviations" to "zoological gardens."

The Europa Year Book
London: Europa Publications, 1959–. Annual.

Once a loose-leaf compilation, this source is now issued annually in two compact volumes. Information on the UN, its agencies and other international organizations is followed by detailed information about each country of the world arranged alphabetically in each volume, giving an introductory survey, a statistical survey, the government, constitution, religion, press, publishers, radio and TV, finance, trade and industry, transportation and tourism, atomic energy, and a brief list of universities.

Whitaker's Almanack
London: Whitaker, 1869–. Annual.

This British counterpart of the American *World Almanac* covers the world, but its British origin shows, especially in its detailed focus on orders of knighthood, Members of Parliament, tables of British rulers, and the like. The statistics on Great Britain and the Commonwealth are excellent.

Books of Quotations

Bartlett's Familiar Quotations
John Bartlett. Boston: Little, Brown, 1968.

Commonly known as *Bartlett's*, this famous source lists sayings and writings of ancient and modern speakers and authors from 2000 B.C. to the present. Its arrangement—chronologically by author—is irritating and mystifying, but the comprehensive index is helpful. Those not familiar with this work may think that using it is like solving a puzzle, but the phrase they want may be *somewhere* among those 113,500 quotations.

Home Book of Quotations
Compiled by Burton E. Stevenson. New York: Dodd, Mead, 1967. Tenth edition.

A comprehensive collection of more than fifty thousand quotations, arranged alphabetically by subject. The author index gives the full name of the person quoted, birth and death dates, and references to all quotations cited. *Stevenson*, as it is known among librarians, is more comprehensive than *Bartlett's*.

Atlases and Gazetteers

Columbia Lippincott Gazetteer of the World
New York: Columbia University Press, 1962.

A remarkable geographical dictionary of the world, this gazetteer lists approximately 130,000 names of places and geographical features, offers pronunciations and variant spellings, and supplies information regarding population, location, altitudes, trade, industry, natural resources, history, and cultural institutions.

Encyclopaedia Britannica World Atlas International
Chicago: Encyclopaedia Britannica, 1967.

Scholarly, current, small enough that the researcher won't dislocate his shoulder in picking it up, this may be the best atlas for everyday use. It sketches many aspects of geography, including world political geography, comparative world distribution maps, and comparative tables and summaries of the political, geographic, and economic makeup of each country.

Rand McNally Commercial Atlas and Marketing Guide
New York: Rand McNally, 1972. Annual.

This atlas, which is revised annually, contains large, clear maps. Its detailed treatment of the states and the outlying possessions of the United States is excellent. More than three-quarters of the maps picture the U.S.

Books of Miscellany

The American Book of Days
Compiled by George William Douglas. New York: Wilson, 1948. Revised edition.

This is a book-calendar of days of celebration and commemoration, including religious and historical holidays, birthdays of famous Americans, local festivals, and unexpected information on such anniversaries as the first balloon ascent. The researcher can get at the entries in two ways: by topic through the index, or by day of celebration through the day-by-day arrangement.

American Nicknames: Their Origin and Significance
Compiled by George E. Shankle. New York: Wilson, 1955. Second edition.

This is a thick volume that testifies to our habit of nicknaming nearly everything. An ingenious cross-referencing system enables a researcher to find the owner of a nickname and the reason for it as well as the names attached to specific persons, places, and events.

Book of Days: A Miscellany of Popular Antiquities
Compiled by Robert Chambers. Edinburgh: Chambers, 1899. 2 vols.

A view of customs and holidays, primarily in Britain, this volume is arranged according to the calendar (with a helpful index). It is excellent for finding out-of-the-way information, and for browsing.

Famous First Facts
Joseph Nathan Kane. New York: Wilson, 1964. Third edition.

A surprisingly popular reference work when it was first published, *Famous First Facts* went into a supplementary edition when the author learned of other firsts, then the original and the supplement were tied together in one volume. The first occurrence of almost anything can be found here: athletic feats, discoveries, inventions, and bizarre incidents.

Festivals of Western Europe
Dorothy Gladys Spicer. New York: Wilson, 1958.

The title is at least a bit misleading. Dorothy Spicer is primarily concerned here with religious feasts and folk festivals which spring from church holidays, not with the entire range including national and political holidays. There are enough church-oriented holidays and feasts described here, though, to cause one to wonder how Europeans get anything done.

The Guinness Book of Records
Compiled by Norris and Ross McWhirter. London: Guinness Superlatives, Ltd., 1973.

What is the longest place name? That of a hill in New Zealand called Taumatawhakatangihangakouauotamatea (turipukakapikimaungahoronuku) pokaiwhenuakitanatahu, of course. What woman holds the record for the most spouses in a monogamous society? Mrs. Beverly Nina Avery, a Los Angeles barmaid, who was married to fourteen different men, five of whom, she alleged, broke her nose. These are the kinds of facts that fill "The Guinness Book." First published in England in 1955 to serve as a Guinness promotion piece in pubs (where drinkers are forever betting on mosts, leasts, longests, shortests, etc.), it has become the best-selling reference book in England and one of the best sellers in the U.S. (where it is titled *The Guinness Book of World Records*).

What Happened When
Stanford M. Mirkin. New York: Washburn, 1966.

Published originally as *When Did It Happen*, this unpredictable compilation features a list of historical and human interest events which happened on each day of the year beginning with January 1. Most of the listings are events of the nineteenth and twentieth centuries. Divertingly written, this volume is much more attractive than the dreary name "fact book" would seem to imply.

Books: Indexes, Lists, Publishers

Book Review Digest
New York: Wilson, 1905–.

This can be considered the book-review counterpart of *Readers' Guide.* It focuses on seventy-five English and American general periodicals, all but ignoring *avant garde* magazines and the literary quarterlies. Within these limitations, *Book Review Digest* does first-rate work: skillfully condensing critical opinion, guiding the researcher to many reviews of many books.

Book Review Index
Detroit: Gale Research, 1965–. Annual.

This is more comprehensive than *Book Review Digest* because it indexes reviews from nearly two hundred journals. It does not digest or quote reviews. *Book Review Index* started as a monthly, then became a bimonthly, and began annual publication in 1969. The citations are indexed by the name of the authors whose works are reviewed.

Books in Print
New York: R. R. Bowker, 1948–. Annual. 2 vols.

A standard source, *Books in Print* lists by author, title, and subject almost all the books in print in the U.S. In one recent year, it listed more than 185,000 titles issued by 1,600 publishers. R. R. Bowker also publishes a companion two-volume index of books in print arranged by subject and appropriately titled *Subject Guide to Books in Print.*

An Index to Book Reviews in the Humanities
Detroit: Phillip Thompson, 1960–. Annual.

Like *Book Review Index,* this volume cites reviews under the name of the author of the book, but it indexes many more reviews, covering nearly seven hundred popular and scholarly journals.

Literary Market Place
New York: R. R. Bowker, 1940–. Annual.

This business directory of American book publishing is so much more than such an identification suggests that it cannot be described concisely. It lists publishers, their addresses, chief publishing house officers and editors, and it identifies publishers by specialty. *Literary Market Place* also lists lecture agencies, literary agents, literary awards and prizes, book clubs, clipping bureaus, and almost any other agency or service useful in placing, promoting, and advertising literary property.

Paperbound Books in Print
New York: R. R. Bowker, 1955–. Three times a year.

PBIP, as it is known to librarians and publishers, is made up of the monthly issues of *The Month Ahead*. It indexes currently available paperbacks—more than 100,000 are now in print—ranging from classics to those hastily written tales designed for travelers who need something to do while airborne so they won't have to think. With author and title entries plus a selective subject index, this source has everything but a sexy cover.

Publishers Weekly
New York: R. R. Bowker, 1955–. Weekly.

This is a basic source for locating books published too recently to be listed in sources published at longer intervals. The weekly issues also announce the forthcoming publication dates of important books. In addition to alphabetical listings of books (with title, publisher, date of publication, edition, and price), *PW* contains general information about book publishing.

United States Catalog and *Cumulative Book Index*
New York: Wilson, 1928 and 1928–.

United States Catalog lists all U.S. books in print as of 1928. *Cumulative Book Index* takes up the same task at that point and lists books in print up to the present. Both are useful in locating titles, publishers, prices, and publication dates.

Newspaper, Magazine, and TV News Indexes and Lists

Ayer Directory of Newspapers and Periodicals
Philadelphia: N. W. Ayer and Son, 1880–.

Known throughout the world of journalism as *Ayer's*, this volume is unique. Some of the material is duplicated elsewhere, but no other reference carries nearly all these data. It covers the United States, Canada, Bermuda, Panama, and the Philippines, trying—and failing by only a little—to list geographically all the daily and weekly newspapers and magazines and to provide the skeletal framework of fact and figure that will enable the researcher to see the publication in its local context.

Editor and Publisher International Yearbook
New York: Editor and Publisher, 1920–.

The international sections are slender, but this annual does offer some data on newspapers over the world. What it does extraordinarily well is to list daily newspapers of the United States and Canada and to provide basic information about them: circulation, advertising rates and regulations, key personnel, and line upon line of other information.

The same company issues the handiest key to information about syndicates, *Editor and Publisher Syndicate Directory*, an annual supplement to *Editor and Publisher* magazine. Syndicates are listed with the features they sell, features are categorized by subject with the name of the author and the syndicate for each, and authors are listed with their features and syndicates.

Facts on File

New York: Facts on File, Inc. Weekly, with annual bound volumes.

This current encyclopedia of events, which is combined in a loose-leaf file, culls the news of the day from many metropolitan daily newspapers. The researchers who compile and compress the record of events work day by day, issue reports weekly, and manage to retain their sanity and perspective throughout. The indexes cumulate, making it unnecessary to consult more than two in any year.

New York Times Index

New York: New York Times, 1851–.

This is a semi-monthly subject index to the issues of the *Times*. Finding an item in the index is occasionally an adventure, but it is a valuable guide to the *Times*. It helps date events and thus often helps researchers locate reports on the same events in other newspapers that are not indexed. The *London Times Index, The Christian Science Monitor Index*, and the *Wall Street Journal Index* are all excellent guides to reports that have appeared in those papers.

Poole's Index to Periodical Literature, 1802–1906

Boston: Houghton Mifflin, 1891. Revised edition. 2 vols. 5 supplements, 1887–1908.

W. F. Poole, a student at Yale, deplored the fact that the information in American magazines was inaccessible because there was so much of it. Judged by current standards, the pioneer index, which is limited to subject entries, is weak. But it indexes periodicals dating from 1802, and is virtually the only research tool of its kind for the nineteenth century.

Public Affairs Information Service Bulletin

New York: PAIS, Inc., 1915–. Annual.

Somewhat similar to the better-known *Readers' Guide, PAIS* has a loftier standard. It indexes selectively by subject (from more than 1,000 periodicals, selected books, pamphlets, federal, state, and city publications, and reports of public and private agencies) materials concerning what is broadly defined as "public affairs."

Readers' Guide to Periodical Literature
New York: Wilson, 1900–.

Readers' Guide, as it is widely known, indexes the contents of more than one hundred general magazines. It is valuable, but it does not include some quality magazines. Published twice a month (once a month in July and August), it is issued also in other paperback cumulations and finally in biennial bound volumes. *Nineteenth Century Readers' Guide to Periodical Literature* (New York: Wilson, 1944) indexes fifty-one periodicals of the last century, primarily in the 1890s.

Social Sciences and Humanities Index
New York: Wilson, 1907–.

Founded in 1907 as *Readers' Guide to Periodical Literature Supplement,* this service became the *International Index* in 1920. The focus shifted in 1956 to exclusive attention to periodicals in the social sciences and humanities, and the name finally settled down to *Social Sciences and Humanities Index* in 1965. It is thus a key to more seriously analytical publications—210 of them—than those covered in most other indexes.

Television News Index and Abstracts
Nashville: Joint University Libraries, Vanderbilt University, 1972–. Monthly.

Since August 1968, Vanderbilt has collected on videotape the evening news broadcasts of the three major television networks. The collection, which is available at $15 per hour, is known as the Vanderbilt Television News Archive. It also includes related programs, primarily documentaries on major news events. In January, 1972, the Archive began issuing *Television News Index and Abstracts* as a guide to the videotape collection. This is an indispensable source for research in news broadcast by network television. Except in unusual instances, neither videotapes nor scripts are available from the networks.

Ulrich's International Periodicals Directory
New York: R. R. Bowker, 1973–74. Fifteenth edition.

Ulrich's lists 55,000 current periodicals and has a "cessation" section that lists more than 1,800 that have died, an index to new periodicals, and the conventional kind of index that lists titles and subjects with cross references. Its worldwide scope makes it especially valuable.

Willing's Press Guide
London: Willing, 1874–.

For a careful overview of the British press, this annual is recommended. It provides much the same kind of detailed information on the British press that *Editor and Publisher International Yearbook* provides on the American press.

A service somewhat similar to that provided by *Willing's* is *Newspaper Press Directory and Advertisers' Guide* (London: Benn Bros., 1946–), which is also an annual.

Guides to Government Publications

The United States government is such a prolific publisher—the largest in the world—that many government workers are frustrated by sheer volume and have trouble locating the more obscure books and pamphlets that carry the proud imprimatur: Washington, D.C., Government Printing Office. The Bureau of National Affairs, a private concern, takes advantage of the confusion by selling to government agencies publications that index and summarize government publications.

It is nonetheless true that there are several handy keys to the masses of government publications. They are needed, because most government-published books and pamphlets cannot be found in lists of books in print, and not all of them are listed in library card catalogs.

(General references on government and political science—some of them issued by government—will be found in the section titled "Law and Political Science.")

Guides to Current Publications

Monthly Catalog of United States Government Publications
Washington, D.C.: Government Printing Office, 1895–.

This catalog, the most comprehensive list of current publications, was started in 1895. An annual index and a Decennial Cumulative Index provide a guide to publications.

Subject Guide to Major United States Government Publications
Ellen P. Jackson. Chicago: American Library Association, 1968.

Major publications cover a wide range. This 175-page volume lists hundreds that researchers have found most useful.

Guides to Early Government Publications

Comprehensive Index to the Publications of the United States Government: 1881–1893
Compiled by John Griffith Ames. Washington, D.C.: Government Printing Office, 1905. 2 vols.

This publication, covering only twelve years, bridges the gap between Poore and the *Catalog of Public Documents*.

Catalog of Public Documents

Washington, D.C.: Government Printing Office, 1896–1945. 25 vols.

These volumes carry government publications up to 1945, at which point the researcher must go to the *Monthly Catalog* (above). The indexes are by author, subject, and sometimes title in one alphabet.

Reference Sources in Specialized Fields— Art, Architecture, Minor Arts

Some Leading Journals

Apollo. H. W. Finnegan Jennings, Editor and Publisher, 225 Molton St., London W.I. Monthly.

Art Bulletin. College Art Association of America. Quarterly.

Art News. Art Foundation Press, Inc. Monthly (September-May); Quarterly (June-August).

Burlington Magazine. Burlington Magazine, Ltd. Monthly.

Gazette des Beaux Arts. Presses Universitaires de France, Paris. Monthly. (Text in English and French.)

Progressive Architecture. Van Nostrand Reinhold Publishing Co. Monthly.

American Architects Directory

Edited by Jacques Cattell Press, New York: R. R. Bowker, 1970. Third edition.

The American Institute of Architects sponsors this listing, which includes the achievements and standards of selection of architects as well as less controversial data such as addresses and positions. The geographical index enables the researcher to locate architects in particular cities.

American Art Directory

Federation of American Artists. New York: R. R. Bowker, 1898–. Triennial.

Once known as *American Art Annual*, this leading directory is a useful catalog of American art, including Canada. It carries information on associations, museums, art schools, magazine and museum publications, scholarships, and fellowships.

The same association and the same publisher issue *Who's Who in American Art*, which, like *American Art Directory*, comes out every three years.

For a longer look into the artistic past, see *The New York Historical Society's Dictionary of Artists in America 1564–1860* (New Haven: Yale,

1957) by George C. Groce and David H. Wallace. This comprehensive volume includes painters, draftsmen, sculptors, engravers, lithographers, and allied artists, native and foreign-born, who worked in the United States—11,000 of them.

Art Index

New York: Wilson, 1929–. Quarterly, with annual cumulations.

This is an index to 130 international publications which deal with archaeology, art history, arts and crafts, fine arts, graphic arts, industrial design, interior decoration, photography and films, planning and landscape design.

Art Prices Current

London: Art Trade 1908–. Annual.

The subtitle describes this service: "a record of sales prices at principal London, Continental and American auction rooms."

Complete Encyclopedia of Antiques

L. G. G. Ramsey. New York: Hawthorn Books, 1969.

The "minor arts"—a term that wounds those who practice and write about them—are beginning to develop a significant literature. This volume is an example: more than 1,500 packed and readable pages.

Dictionary of Architecture and Building

Russell Sturgis. New York: Macmillan, 1901.

This three-volume classic describes famous buildings, sketches the architecture of many countries, and carries biographies of architects. Although its 1901 publication makes it seem far out of date, specialists say the historical value is high, especially because these volumes may be nicely supplemented by Banister Fletcher's *History of Architecture,* which has proved its worth by surviving through seventeen editions (New York: Scribner's, 1961).

Encyclopedia of World Art

New York: McGraw-Hill, 1959–1968. 15 vols.

The publisher devoted ten years to bringing out these volumes, for good reason. This is not so much a set of books as it is a museum containing seven thousand full-page plates and hundreds of essays that embrace all of man's greatest achievements in the visual arts through the centuries. This is the leading historical synthesis in the world of art.

Index to Reproductions of American Paintings
Compiled by Isabel S. Monro and K. M. Monro. New York: Wilson, 1948. First Supplement, 1964.

This unusual reference source helps the researcher locate works of U.S. artists reproduced in more than 520 books and 300 catalogs of annual exhibitions in art museums. It is basically an alphabetical list by author and title (and, in some cases, by subject). The book also locates pictures in permanent collections. The 480-page supplement, which was published in 1964, updates the work to 1961.

The New Encyclopedia of Furniture
Joseph Aronson. New York: Crown. Revised 1967.

Although the first edition was published in 1938, this valuable volume has been updated regularly. It covers American and foreign styles from 1800. The wary buyer will be happy with one special feature: a guide that will help him decide whether a piece is authentic or a copy (Early American or Early Nothing)—and how much he should pay. The book also carries many lengthy articles on periods, a glossary of craftsmen and designers, and 1,400 illustrations.

Oxford Companion to Art
Edited by Harold Osborne. New York: Oxford University Press, 1970.

Like the other Oxford companions, this volume aims to cover a broad field in relatively few pages. Like the others, too, it is authoritative and readable.

History

Some Leading Journals

American Historical Review. American Historical Association. Quarterly.

Journal of American History. Mississippi Valley Historical Association. Quarterly.

Journal of Modern History. University of Chicago Press. Quarterly.

Atlas of World History
Robert R. Palmer. Chicago: Rand McNally, 1957.

The complexities of world history are presented in clear maps, each accompanied by a cogent description. The focus on North America and Europe is strong, but Asia, Africa, and Latin America are also covered. *Historical Atlas* (William R. Shepherd, New York: Barnes and Noble, 1964, ninth edition) is similarly useful. For long the most-used historical atlas, it reaches back to 2,000 B.C. and forward to 1964.

Dictionary of Events
Compiled by George Palmer Putnam. New York: Grosset & Dunlap, 1936.

Historical literature is thickly populated with handy, quick guides to names, dates, events—the bare bones of the past. Only a certified antiquarian would want to *read* this (and similar reference books); many others will find it useful. Putnam's work begins at 5,000 B.C. and works its way forward, year by year and table by table, to 1936.

Documents of American History
Edited by Henry Steele Commager. New York: Appleton-Century-Crofts, 1968. Eighth edition.

"Properly speaking," Henry Commager writes, "almost everything of an original character is a document: Letters, memoirs, ballads, folklore, poetry, fiction, newspaper reports and editorials, sermons, and speeches, to say nothing of inscriptions, stamps, coins, buildings, painting and sculpture, and all the innumerable memorials which man has left in his effort to understand and organize his world." Commager offers this list to indicate the impossibility of including *all* the important documents. But he need not have been apologetic. If this book is incomplete, it is nonetheless the best available guide to the central documents in American history.

The author has wisely avoided the items that make up so many books of "readings"—the uncounted (and uncountable) letters, memoirs, excerpts from diaries, and travelers' descriptions that flavor our past. The focus is on the official and quasi-official familiar documents like the Declaration of Independence, but it includes scores of others which deserve a higher place in the American pantheon than they are customarily granted. Most are introduced concisely, and in a way that emphasizes their significance and value.

Encyclopedia of American History
Edited by Richard B. Morris. New York: Harper & Row, 1970. Revised edition.

Even those historians who quarrel with Richard Morris on points of fact and interpretation recognize the unique value of this book. He has organized it both chronologically and topically so that influential persons and notable dates, achievements, and events stand out, but the whole can be read as a narrative. It is comprehensive in that it provides the essential historical facts about American life and institutions. Although there have been many challengers over the years, this remains the handiest single work endeavoring to summarize and revitalize the facts of the American experience.

Encyclopedia of World History

Edited by William Leonard Langer. Boston: Houghton Mifflin, 1972. Fifth edition.

Basically a series of outlines running from prehistoric eras to the middle of the twentieth century, it is so neatly compiled that a researcher can find any important historical event that occurred at any time in any part of the world.

Guide to Historical Literature

Edited by G. F. Howe and others. New York: Macmillan, 1961.

For three decades it was necessary to get along with the 1931 edition of this guide. The 962-page revision that came out in 1961 brings the work closer to the present. It is a careful survey of the entire range of historical writing: bibliographies, encyclopedias and dictionaries, general and specialized histories, biographies, government documents, and printed collections of sources. Compiled by many experts, the *Guide* points up the best books for scholar, student, and layman.

Literature

Some Leading Journals

College English. National Council of Teachers of English. Monthly (October-May).

ELH. English Literary History. The Tudor and Stuart Club; Johns Hopkins University. Quarterly.

Modern Fiction Studies. Purdue University, Department of English. Four times a year.

Philological Quarterly. State University of Iowa. Quarterly.

PMLA. Modern Language Association of America. Five times a year.

Twentieth Century Literature. The Swallow Press. Quarterly.

American Authors and Books, 1640 to the Present Day

Edited by W. J. Burke and Will D. Howe. New York: Crown, 1972. Third revised edition by Irving Weiss and Anne Weiss.

Any compendium of more than three hundred years of writing is necessarily less than exhaustive, but this text may provide the most useful overview. Although the focus is on authors, the editors have carefully searched the crannies of the American literary experience, looking for the unheralded illustrators, editors, publishers, booksellers, reviewers, and collectors —the specialists who shape and color manuscripts and those who react to them in ways that may have as much to do with an author's fate as his own talents. The result is an unusual and valuable perspective.

The Cambridge History of English Literature
Cambridge: University Press, 1907–33. 15 vols.

These fourteen volumes (the fifteenth is the index) sketch English authors and their work and define literary allusions and fictional names from the time of *Beowulf*. A new edition of a companion, *Concise Cambridge History of English Literature,* extends the reach by assessing recent literature, including that written in the United States and the Commonwealth countries. Written by George Sampson, the thousand pages of this volume make it seem concise only by comparison with the basic set. Its sparkle is indicated by Sampson's assessment of Henry James: "painfully explaining the farthest reaches of the obvious."

Granger's Index to Poetry
Edited by William J. Smith. New York: Columbia University Press, 1973.

Granger's latest edition indexes 514 volumes of poetry anthologies with (1) a title and first-line index, (2) an author index, and (3) a subject index.

The Library of Literary Criticism of English and American Authors
Charles Wells Moulton. Buffalo, N.Y.: Moulton, 1901–1905. 8 vols.

Moulton, as this series is known to many critics, was *the* compilation of critical reviews for more than five decades. The tracing of criticism begins with *Beowulf* and ends in 1904, but it has more than antiquarian value. The editor was a shrewd judge of standards, and some authorities hold that his selections set the tone for English and American criticism until the coming of the New Critics. *A Library of Literary Criticism: Modern American Literature* (New York: Ungar, 1969, fourth edition) can be considered an extension of *Moulton* for Americans. It includes excerpts from the major criticisms of 300 authors. The New Criticism is represented, in remarkable balance with the more traditional approaches to literary judgment.

Literary History of the United States
Edited by Robert E. Spiller and others. New York: Macmillian, 1963. Third edition.

Each chapter of this work is the product of a qualified writer. All the writers interpret "literary history" in broad terms, sketching in the influences that have shaped our literary life. It is the most recent comprehensive literary history.

The Oxford Companion to American Literature
James D. Hart. New York: Oxford University Press, 1965. Fourth edition.

The faint flavor of condescension apparent in many British surveys of American literature is absent here. The definitions and descriptions of American literary schools and movements are especially acute. The aim throughout has been to treat the tides of literature concisely, but it is difficult to find anything properly describable as scant. In short, although the researcher who is deeply involved in a study of any particular author or period must look beyond this source, others will find its scope impressive. The updating of the fourth edition is quite evident in the many notes on the period from 1957 to 1965.

The Oxford Companion to English Literature
Compiled and edited by Paul Harvey. Oxford: The Clarendon Press, 1967. Fourth edition.

Primarily a dictionary of concise articles about English authors and their writings, this book also identifies and explains allusions and fictitious names. It is useful for specialists and laymen, and even the appendices are richly informative.

The Reader's Adviser: A Guide to the Best in Literature
Winifred F. Courtney. New York: R. R. Bowker, 1968. Eleventh revised and enlarged edition. 2 vols.

Once limited to investigation by specialists, each succeeding edition has tended to make these volumes a wide-ranging guide for anyone who cares about books. It is not quite true that it covers "absolutely everything," as one admiring librarian holds, but it ranges across fiction, poetry, essays, foreign literature, travel and adventure, Bibles, and reference books. The concise annotations make it much more than a listing. *The Reader's Adviser*, as it is usually known, suggests which translations of foreign works are preferred. It notes, for example, that there are hundreds of bad translations of Cervantes, but Putnam's and Motteux's are the best.

The Reader's Encyclopedia
William Rose Benet. New York: Thomas Y. Crowell, 1965. Second edition.

Issued again in 1965 after long languishing as a well-remembered but outdated reference, this 1,118-page edition is a triumph of literary memorabilia: characters, themes, authors, artistic and literary movements, names of famous swords, and the reason for Mona Lisa's enigmatic smile (it was a convention of the time). This is a small part of an imposing array.

Short Story Index

Compiled by Dorothy Cook and Isabel S. Monro. New York: Wilson, 1953. Supplements extend coverage from 1950–.

This is an index to 60,000 short stories in 4,320 collections. The stories are indexed by author and title (and, in some cases, by subject).

Twentieth Century Authors

Edited by S. J. Kunitz and H. Haycraft. First supplement edited by S. J. Kunitz and V. Colby. New York: Wilson, 1942, 1955.

This widely known work consists of 1,850 biographies and 1,700 portraits of contemporary authors over the world. Useful bibliographies for each writer contain separately published works.

Music and Theater Arts

Some Leading Journals

Dance Magazine. Rudolf Orthwine Corp. Monthly.

Drama: The Quarterly Theatre Review. British Drama League. Quarterly.

High Fidelity. Billboard Publishing Co. Monthly.

Musical Quarterly. G. Schirmer & Co. Four times a year.

Music and Letters. Prof. Sir Jack Westrup, Editor and Publisher. 44 Conduit St., London. Quarterly.

World Theatre. Les Editions et Ateliers d'Art Graphique, Brussels. Quarterly. (Text in English and French.)

Annals of the New York Stage

George C. D. Odell. New York: Columbia University Press, 1927–49. 15 vols.

Despite the growth everywhere of Little Theatres, drama guilds, and theatre workshops, New York has always been the American drama capital. This makes Odell's painstaking labors valuable, at least for antiquarians. From playbills, pamphlets, autobiographies, from yellowing letters, diaries, and account books, he has re-created the rich history of American drama from the beginning to 1894.

Baker's Biographical Dictionary of Musicians

Revised by Nicolas Slonimsky. New York: G. Schirmer, 1958. Fifth edition, with 1971 Supplement inserted.

Although the definitive work does not exist, *Baker's* tries comprehensively to sketch musicians of all periods and countries in one huge volume. It is excellent. "Musicians" is interpreted broadly; composers, musicologists, performers, and outstanding music teachers are sketched here.

The Best Plays Of . . .
New York: Dodd, 1899–. Annual.

This annual reference appears shortly after the close of each theatre season and, in addition to abridging the texts of "the ten best," lists statistics, awards, long runs, and other facts that excite the passions of drama buffs.

The Dance Encyclopedia
Compiled by Anatole Chujoy and P. W. Manchester. New York: Simon & Schuster, 1967.

Dance, dancers, dancing—this volume covers everything from folk to ballet. It contains long, signed articles as well as brief identifications and similar short references.

The Encyclopedia of Jazz
Leonard Feather. New York: Horizon Press, 1960.

Leonard Feather is known as the Boswell of Basin Street. There is almost nothing about jazz—from instruments to foot-tapping with an appropriate beat—that he does not consider worthy of lengthy treatment. Fortunately for those who are not as dedicated but who are interested in jazz, Feather writes informatively and readably about his love. He has also published a continuation, *The Encyclopedia of Jazz in the Sixties* (Horizon, 1961).

The Film Daily Year Book of Motion Pictures
New York: Film Daily. 1915–.

This continuing service lists more than thirty thousand titles released since 1915, but its focus is current. For each new film, the book carries information on everything but the leading lady's latest loves.

Grove's Dictionary of Music and Musicians
Edited by Eric Blom. New York: St. Martin's, 1954. Fifth edition. Nine basic volumes, A-Z, and one supplement, 1961.

These volumes are written in English rather than in musicologese; clarity certainly is a hallmark. So is comprehensiveness. *Grove's* takes all music since 1450 as its province: terms, history, theory and practice, instruments, musicians, songs, and operas.

International Encyclopedia of Film
New York: Crown, 1972.

More than a thousand entries in this unusual volume cover technical terms, biographies, national film histories, a chronological outline of film history, and a selected bibliography of historical and critical writing on film art. Many photographs are included.

International Motion Picture Almanac
Edited by Charles S. Anderson. New York: Quigley Publications, 1929–.

The saving quality of this diverse service is that it carries information on movies and the movie industry which is not available elsewhere. One can mine from these pages data on an aspect of motion pictures that is usually hidden: the corporate structure, including organization and personnel, distributing services, circuits, and organizations.

Motion Pictures, 1894–1912, 1912–1939, 1940–1949, 1950–1959
Washington, D.C.: Government Printing Office, 1951–60. 4 vols.

These lists enable the researcher to determine when particular movies were released and to find the source of a movie based on a book. Other information on thousands of motion pictures is available here. A successor, *Library of Congress Catalog: Motion Pictures and Filmscripts*, (1953–), brings this information up to date.

The Music Index
Edited by Florence Kretzschmar. Detroit: Information Service, 1949–.

This is a monthly subject index to more than 225 periodicals, some of them foreign. It cumulates annually and carries some author entries.

The Oxford Companion to Music
Percy A. Scholes. New York: Oxford University Press, 1970. Tenth edition.

This is a collection of over 10,000 articles covering history, composition, and performance. The book contains more than 1,000 illustrations and many biographies. An appendix lists a pronouncing glossary of more than 7,000 music terms.

The Oxford Companion to the Theatre
Edited by Phyllis Hartnoll with 57 contributors. London: Oxford University Press, 1967. Third edition.

The editors say in the preface: "A representative selection of what was most likely to interest the English-speaking reader was aimed at, and the emphasis throughout has been on the popular rather than on the literary theatre. More space has been devoted to melodrama and the music-hall than to comedy and tragedy, literary quarrels have been ignored, actors have been rated above dramatists. In short, this is a companion to the playhouse, and is meant for those who would rather see a play than read it, for those whose interest is as much in the production and setting of a drama as in its literary content."

Philosophy and Religion

Some Leading Journals

Journal of Jewish Studies. Jewish Chronicle Publications. Quarterly.

Journal of Philosophy. Philosophy Hall, Columbia University. Fortnightly.

Journal of Religion. University of Chicago Press. Quarterly.

Journal of Symbolic Logic. Association for Symbolic Logic. Quarterly.

Philosophical Review. Goldwin Smith Hall, Cornell University. Quarterly.

Religion in Life. Abingdon Press. Quarterly.

Catholic Periodical and Literature Index
Haverford, Pa: Catholic Library Assocation, 1930–. Bimonthly.

More than two hundred Catholic periodicals, newspapers, and bulletins are indexed here. The range is broad, serving as a guide to Catholic interests and concerns besides religion. A detailed book review index is included.

Encyclopaedia Judaica
Edited by Cecil Roth. Jerusalem: Macmillan, 1972. 16 vols.

This excellent encyclopedia provides a detailed and comprehensive picture of all aspects of Jewish life and knowledge from ancient times to the present. It updates the *Jewish Encyclopedia* and is the best English-language guide to the world community of Judaism.

Encyclopedia of Religion and Ethics
Edited by James Hastings. New York: Scribner's, 1908–27. 12 vols. and Index.

The words *religion* and *ethics* are both used in the most comprehensive sense. These volumes contain articles on all the religions of the world and all the leading systems of ethics. In her *Guide to Reference Books*, Constance Winchell calls this, "The most comprehensive work in this class, in English."

Encyclopedia of Philosophy
New York: Macmillan, 1967. 8 vols.

Written for the nonspecialist, these volumes nonetheless take a comprehensive, critical stance. Over 1,450 signed articles, which range from half a column to more than fifty pages, analyze the philosophies of every era.

Handbook of Denominations in the United States
Edited by Frank S. Mead. Nashville, Tenn.: Abingdon, 1970. Fifth edition.

This is the quickest guide to various church histories and doctrines. It sketches in brief, impartial accounts the histories and current beliefs of more than two hundred denominations.

The Interpreter's Dictionary of the Bible
Edited by George A. Buttrick and others. Nashville, Tenn.: Abingdon, 1962. 4 vols.

This is so ambitious that most -ologies—phil-, the-, arche-, and the like—are woven into the text. Considered by specialists to be one of the great Biblical reference works of all time, these four volumes present all the major findings of recent scholarship.

New Catholic Encyclopedia
New York: McGraw-Hill, 1967. 15 vols.

This series is difficult to classify. The title is a bit misleading because these volumes are so broad in scope and concern that one hesitates to include them among religious references. The fifteen volumes that make up the set answer questions on medieval history, literature, philosophy, and art, although there is an emphasis on Catholic doctrine and history.

Rand McNally Bible Atlas
Edited by Emil G. Kraeling. Chicago: Rand McNally, 1966.

The editor introduces his atlas too modestly: "The book exists for the maps." The maps are detailed and alluring, but the text is a compelling narrative. Designed for the general reader, the extensive text is a historical discussion of geographical references in the Bible.

Yearbook of American Churches
New York: National Council of the Churches of Christ in the United States, 1916–.

So many religious bodies issue their own yearbooks that this volume may seem superfluous. It is, however, the handiest summary of church organizations and agencies, theological seminaries, colleges and universities, religious periodicals, and church membership statistics.

Biological Science: General

Biological Abstracts
Philadelphia: University of Pennsylvania, 1926–.

The researcher who hopes to pick his way through the masses of biology literature must begin with a large view. The semi-monthly *Biological Abstracts* provides that scope, guiding the researcher to works in general biology, basic medical sciences, microbiology, immunology, public health and parasitology, plant sciences, animal sciences, and a host of other subjects.

Biological and Agricultural Index
New York: Wilson, 1916–.

More than one hundred periodicals in agriculture and associated fields are covered here in a subject index.

The Encyclopedia of the Biological Sciences
Edited by Peter Gray. New York: Van Nostrand Reinhold, 1961.

This encyclopedia, which is designed for laymen, is authoritative in its coverage of a wide range: developmental, ecological, functional, genetic, structural, and taxonomic. In 1967, the same author and publisher brought out *The Dictionary of the Biological Sciences*.

Gray's Manual of Botany
M. L. Fernald. New York: American Book, 1950. Eighth edition.

The subtitle of this basic work describes it well: "A handbook of the flowering plants and ferns of the central and northeastern U.S. and adjacent Canada."

Larousse Encyclopedia of Animal Life
New York: McGraw-Hill, 1967.

This 649-page volume covers the world of animals from protozoans to mammals. Richly illustrated, with some of the pictures in color, the *Larousse Encyclopedia* includes a classification table, a glossary, and an extensive bibliography.

Putnam's Nature Field Books
New York: Putnam's, various dates.

More than twenty of these small volumes on trees and shrubs, wild flowers, birds, fishes, rocks and minerals, insects, mushrooms, and other subjects have been issued since 1928. They are as understandable to the casual reader as they are authoritative for the researcher. They carry many excellent illustrations.

The World Book of House Plants
Evan McDonald. New York: Popular Library, 1963.

This is a wide-ranging and thorough guide to house plants. It includes careful instructions on propagating and feeding.

Medicine

Some Leading Journals

American Journal of Medicine. American Journal of Medicine. Monthly.

American Journal of Physiology. American Physiological Society. Monthly.

Journal of the American Medical Association. American Medical Association. Monthly.

Journal of Clinical Investigation. American Society for Clinical Investigation. Monthly.

New England Journal of Medicine. Massachusetts Medical Society. Weekly.

Psychiatry. William Alanson White Psychiatric Foundation, Inc. Quarterly.

American Medical Directory
Chicago: American Medical Association, 1906–.

This is a Register of Physicians of the U.S., the Canal Zone, Puerto Rico, the Virgin Islands, and U.S. physicians located temporarily in foreign countries. For each physician it lists primary specialty, secondary specialty, type of practice, and related information.

Index Medicus
Washington, D.C.: National Library of Medicine. 1960–. Monthly.

The monthly issues of *Index Medicus*, which index several hundred thousand articles in medical and related periodicals, are cumulated annually in the *Cumulated Index Medicus*, which is the most comprehensive guide to advances in the health sciences.

Psychiatric Dictionary
Leland E. Hinsie and Robert Jean Campbell. New York: Oxford University Press, 1970. Fourth edition.

A few of the articles in this dictionary are encyclopedic, but brevity is the rule. The framework of the book is built on psychiatric terms, with allied fields well represented: clinical neurology, constitutional medicine, genetics and eugenics, mental deficiency, forensic psychiatry, social service, nursing, and occupational therapy.

Stedman's Medical Dictionary

Edited by Isaac Asimov and others. Baltimore: Williams & Wilkins, 1972. Twenty-second edition.

Long a standard, *Stedman's Medical Dictionary* is described well by its subtitle: "A vocabulary of medicine and its allied sciences, with pronunciations and derivations."

Psychology

Some Leading Journals

American Journal of Psychology. University of Texas Department of Psychology. Quarterly.

Journal of Abnormal and Social Psychology. American Psychological Association. Bi-monthly.

Journal of Applied Psychology. American Psychological Association. Bimonthly.

Journal of Social Psychology. Provincetown, Mass.: Journal Press. Quarterly.

Encyclopedia of Psychology

Edited by Hans Jurgen Eysenck. London: Herder and Herder, 1972.

This is an encyclopedic survey containing more than 5,000 entries written by authorities. The entries range from succinct definitions to extensive articles. The major articles carry bibliographies.

Psychological Abstracts

Washington, D.C.: American Psychological Association, 1927–.

Psych Abstracts, as it is generally known, abstracts U.S. and foreign books, journals, dissertations, monographs, and reports. It is classified by subject, with separate author and subject indexes in each issue.

Physical Science: General

Applied Science and Technology Index

New York: Wilson, 1958–. Monthly.

The successor to the *Industrial Arts Index* (1913–1957), this monthly service indexes more than 200 of the leading American and British scientific and technical periodicals.

Engineering Index
New York: American Society of Mechanical Engineers, 1920–. Monthly.

Although some of the publications covered by this service are also covered by *Applied Science and Technology Index, Engineering Index* is much more extensive and more strongly keyed to engineering. It covers over 1,000 publications, many of them foreign.

McGraw-Hill Encyclopedia of Science and Technology
New York: McGraw-Hill, 1971. Third edition. 15 vols.

Booklist calls this "the first modern, multivolume encyclopedia aimed at authoritative, comprehensive coverage of the physical, natural, and applied sciences." The fifteen fat volumes that make up this set carry more than seven thousand articles. They are updated annually by the *McGraw-Hill Yearbook of Science and Technology.*

Scientific and Technical Societies of the United States
Washington, D.C.: National Academy of Sciences, 1971. Ninth edition.

Keeping up with the world of science is like trying to catch a waterfall in a tin cup, but one can measure growth roughly by marking the increases in scientific societies. This volume provides more than conventional directories, offering details of history, aims, memberships, libraries, research funds, medals and awards, and a list of serial publications for more than 1,000 societies.

The same publisher issues other specialized guides, among them *Industrial Research Laboratories of the United States* (thirteenth edition, 1970), which contains information on more than 5,000 laboratories and 20,000 workers.

Van Nostrand's Scientific Encyclopedia
36 contributing editors. Princeton, N.J.: Van Nostrand Reinhold, 1968. Fourth edition.

Long one of the leading publishers of handy science references, Van Nostrand issues publications that are useful to the scientist and understandable to most interested laymen. This volume is a standard source that explains more than 16,000 science, engineering, mathematics, and medical terms.

Chemistry

Some Leading Journals

Accounts of Chemical Research. American Chemical Society. Monthly.

American Chemical Society Journal. American Chemical Society. Fortnightly.

Inorganic Chemistry. American Chemical Society. Monthly.

Journal of Organic Chemistry. American Chemical Society. Monthly.

Chemical Abstracts

Easton, Pa.: American Chemical Society, 1907–. Weekly, cumulated every five years.

The citation to each article in this useful index to periodicals is accompanied by an abstract. Each issue is arranged by topic with an author index. Beginning in 1958 a patent number index was added, and in 1963 a key-word index was added. At the end of each year, the American Chemical Society issues indexes to authors, subjects, formulas, patent numbers, and ring systems.

Chemical Formulary

Compiled by Harry Bennett. Brooklyn: Chemical Publishing, 1933–.

This is a handy guide to the formulas used in making thousands of things, from complex industrial chemicals to perfumes and cosmetics.

Condensed Chemical Dictionary

New York: Van Nostrand Reinhold, 1966. Seventh edition.

Each entry in this dictionary includes the name of the chemical, the chemical formula, physical properties, derivation, grades, containers, uses, and shipping regulations. In some instances the trade name is included.

Handbook of Chemistry

Norbert A. Lange and Gordon M. Forker. New York: McGraw-Hill, 1967. Tenth edition, revised.

The subtitle describes this book neatly: "A reference volume for all requiring a ready access to chemical and physical data used in laboratory work and manufacturing."

Earth and Space Sciences

Some Leading Journals

Aerospace Historian. Kansas State University. Quarterly.

AIAA *Journal.* American Institute of Aeronautics and Astronautics. Monthly.

Astronautics and Aeronautics. American Institute of Aeronautics and Astronautics. Monthly.

Earth Science. Earth Science Publishing Company. Bimonthly.

Environmental Space Sciences. Plenum Publishing Company. Bimonthly.

International Geological Review. American Geological Institute. Monthly.

Journal of Astronautical Sciences. American Astronautical Society. Bimonthly.

Atlas of the Universe
Patrick Moore. New York: Rand McNally, 1970.

This large and beautifully colored volume, which carries more pages of pictures than text, covers Observation and Exploration of Space, Atlas of the Earth from Space, Atlas of the Moon, Atlas of the Solar System, and Atlas of the Stars.

Bibliography and Index of Geology
Boulder, Colo.: Geological Society of America, 1969–. Monthly.

The monthly issues are cumulated in a four-part annual index, the first two parts made up of an author index of more than 80,000 entries. Parts 3 and 4 are made up of a cumulative index of subjects with more than 100,000 entries. It is worldwide in scope and, according to one authority, "includes more geologic references than any other existing work."

The Climates of the Continents
Wilfred G. Kendrew. Oxford: Clarendon Press, 1961. Fifth edition.

This 608-page volume provides a worldwide view of climates, including information on altitude, temperature, and monthly precipitation for all of the great cities of the world and for many other cities.

A Dictionary of Geology
John Challinor. New York: Oxford University Press, 1967. Third edition.

The editor is careful to flesh out many of the 1,500 terms he defines here with apt quotations from the literature of geology.

Encyclopedia of Oceanography
New York: Van Nostrand Reinhold, 1966.

In more than a thousand fact-packed pages, this volume provides information on the oceans of the earth in language that can be understood by laymen. Among many central items are diagrams and charts that show ocean currents and subsurface topographical maps.

McGraw-Hill Encyclopedia of Space
New York: McGraw-Hill, 1968.

Written in popular style for the nonspecialist and the student, this profusely illustrated encyclopedia contains many articles on space, space exploration, and space travel. Organized in nine sections, the 831-page volume contains information on rockets, artificial satellites, astronomy, astrophysics, conquest of the moon, and life in the universe.

Minerals Year Book
U.S. Bureau of Mines. Washington, D.C.: Government Printing Office, 1932–.

So much information is gathered on metals, minerals, and fuels that the U.S. Bureau of Mines must issue its annual in several volumes. Reports on individual commodities give information about production, consumption, stocks, prices, and other data.

Engineering and Mathematics

Some Leading Journals

American Journal of Mathematics. American Mathematical Society. Quarterly.

American Mathematical Monthly. Mathematical Association of America. Monthly.

Engineering and Science. California Institute of Technology. Monthly.

Power Engineering. Technical Publishing Company. Monthly.

Engineering Index
New York: American Society of Mechanical Engineers, 1920–.

International in scope, this service indexes many foreign journals among the more than 1,000 technical journals and other publications it covers. It abstracts the articles it lists and provides an author index.

Handbook of the Engineering Sciences
Princeton, N.J.: Van Nostrand Reinhold, 1967. 2 vols.

This comprehensive handbook contains definitions of terms and long articles in every engineering specialty. Volume 1 covers the basic sciences, Volume 2 the applied sciences.

International Dictionary of Applied Mathematics
Princeton, N.J.: Van Nostrand Reinhold, 1960.

The central value of this dictionary is that it defines the terms and describes the methods in the application of mathematics to thirty-one fields of physical science and engineering. Mathematical terms in French, German, Russian, and Spanish are listed in a special index.

The Universal Encyclopedia of Mathematics
New York: Simon & Schuster, 1964.

Written for the high school and college student, this 715-page volume covers topics, concepts, and methods in part 1, mathematical formulae in part 2, and mathematical tables for roots, powers, logarithms, and trigonometric functions, among other tables, in part 3.

Physics and Electronics

Some Leading Journals

American Journal of Physics. American Institute of Physics. Monthly.

Annals of Physics. Academic Press Monthly.

Journal of Applied Physics. Argonne National Laboratory. Monthly.

Physical Review. American Institute of Physics. Monthly.

Reviews of Modern Physics. American Institute of Physics. Quarterly.

Solid-State Electronics. Pergamon Press. Monthly.

American Institute of Physics Handbook
New York: McGraw-Hill, 1963. Second edition.

Among the many subjects treated here are mathematical aids to computation mechanics, optics, atomic and molecular physics, nuclear physics, and solid state physics.

A Dictionary of Electronics
Baltimore: Penguin, 1971. Third edition.

This 413-page volume, which was first published in 1962 in a smaller edition, includes more than 5,000 definitions. It is suitable for the nonspecialist; the definitions are concise and readable. The text contains illustrations and an excellent system of cross-references to guide researchers to related topics.

Dictionary of Physics
H. J. Gray. London, New York: Longmans, 1958.

The moderate size of this dictionary expresses its aim: to give a brief overview. Few of the articles are lengthy, but the book deals with applied as well as general physics.

International Dictionary of Physics and Electronics
Edited by Walter C. Michels and others. Princeton, N.J.: Van Nostrand Reinhold, 1961.

The editors have tried to show the connection between classical and modern physics. The book is designed for students, professional physicists, and others who usually work in a different area of science.

Social Science: General

Census of Population, 1970
U.S. Bureau of the Census. Washington, D.C.: Government Printing Office, 1961–.

Of the many census publications, this is the most widely known and used. The Bureau of the Census also publishes many special reports and special censuses of agriculture, housing, business, and other fields.

A Dictionary of the Social Sciences
Edited by Julius Gould and W. L. Kolb. New York: Free Press, 1964.

This UNESCO-sponsored dictionary emphasizes terms used in political science and sociology, but its scope is general for the most part and it is more than a dictionary of terms. It provides definitions, history of usage, and usage in various fields of social science.

Encyclopedia of Associations
Detroit: Gale Research, 1973. Eighth edition. 2 vols.

Subtitled "National Organizations of the United States," this useful reference lists more than 12,000 organizations in business, religious, horticultural, athletic, cultural, educational, and scores of other fields. Each organization is identified by address, date of founding, name of a leading official, number of members and staff members, function, and publications issued.

The Foundation Directory
Foundation Library Center. New York: Russell Sage Foundation.

More than 7,000 nonprofit foundations are listed in this 1,200-page volume. Each entry contains address, date of establishment, donor, purpose and activities, and financial data.

International Encyclopedia of the Social Sciences
New York: Macmillan, 1968. 17 vols.

Written for the educated layman as well as the specialist, this encyclopedia emphasizes the analytical and comparative aspects of the social sciences and their theory and methodology. Each article is followed by a bibliography. Unlike its predecessor, *Encyclopedia of the Social Sciences* (New York: Macmillan, 1930–1935. 15 vols. Reissued in 1937 in 8 vols.), it gives relatively little attention to the historical, descriptive, and practical. Volume 17 of the *International Encyclopedia* is an exhaustive index. The new set also contains about 600 biographies of key figures in the social sciences.

Sources of Information in the Social Sciences
Carl M. White and Associates. Chicago: American Library Association, 1973. Second edition.

This guide to the literature of the social sciences covers eight divisions: social science in general, history, economics and business, sociology, anthropology, psychology, education, and political science. Specialists in each present bibliographic reviews of basic works, which are followed by annotated lists of reference sources.

Business and Economics

Some Leading Journals

American Economic Review. American Economic Association. Quarterly.

Econometrica. Econometric Society. Quarterly.

Harvard Business Review. Harvard University. Bi-monthly.

Journal of Accountancy. American Institute of Certified Public Accountants. Monthly.

Management Review. American Management Association. Monthly.

Accountants' Index
New York: American Institute of Accountants, 1921–.

One basic volume covers the literature of accounting up to 1921; supplements have been issued in periods of one to four years since that date. Periodicals, pamphlets, and books are indexed by author and subject.

Best's Insurance Reports (Fire and Casualty)
and *Best's Life Insurance Reports*
New York: Best Company, 1899–, 1906–.

These useful services, which cover the fields designated by their titles, are published annually and supplemented by weekly and monthly publications.

Business Periodicals Index
New York: Wilson, 1958–.

Known from 1913 to 1957 as the *Industrial Arts Index*, this useful service indexes 120 periodicals in accounting, advertising, banking, finance, business, insurance, labor, marketing, taxation, and similar fields.

Commodity Year Book
New York: Commodity Research Bureau 1939–. Annual.

This is a compilation of data on approximately 100 commodities—hogs, cotton, coal, corn oil, glass, lard, honey, and soybean oil are examples—that covers production, prices, imports, exports, and the like.

Custom House Guide
New York: Custom House Guide 1862–.

Heavy with data on the leading customs ports in the United States—such as steamship lines, banks, warehouses, foreign consuls, lists of commodities with import duties—this annual publication is supplemented monthly by *American Import and Export Bulletin.* Similar information about foreign ports is carried in *Exporters' Encyclopaedia* (New York: Thomas Ashwell, 1904–).

Encyclopedia of Banking and Finance
Glenn C. Munn. Edited by F. L. Garcia. Cambridge, Mass.: Bankers Publishing, 1974. Seventh edition.

When F. L. Garcia took over in the 1950s as editor of this old standard, he set out to provide a comprehensive exposition of the financial system. This is the result, an authoritative volume covering money and credit, banking history and practice, trusts, securities, and almost any other term or concept relating to banking and finance.

The McGraw-Hill Dictionary of Modern Economics: A Handbook of Terms and Organizations
New York: McGraw-Hill, 1965.

The subtitle is descriptive: This volume combines a dictionary of terms and a directory of organizations concerned with economics. Part 1 defines approximately 1,300 terms (Quasi-Rent and Regression Line, for example) and includes graphs and charts. Part 2 is a directory of approximately 200 public and private agencies.

Moody's Manual of Investments, American and Foreign
New York: Analyses Publishing, 1904–1914, Moody's Investment Service, 1915–. Annual.

One of the most important business research tools, *Moody's*, as it is widely known, is a leader in compiling current data. Five annual volumes —on Transportation, Public Utility, Municipal and Government, Bank and Finance, and Industrial Securities—are updated by semi-weekly supplement sheets.

Poor's Register of Corporations, Directors and Executives, United States and Canada
New York: Standard and Poor's, 1928–. Annual.

This widely used annual (which is supplemented three times a year) is in three parts: (1) a list of about 35,000 corporations and their officers and directors, (2) an alphabetical list of more than 70,000 directors and executives, with brief biographical data, and (3) a list of industrial products and the companies selling them.

A similar service is provided by *Who's Who in Commerce and Industry* (Chicago: Marquis, 1936–).

Thomas' Register of American Manufacturers
New York: Thomas Publishing, 1905–.

Issued annually since 1905, this is one of the most useful buyers' guides in the world of business. It is arranged according to products, with the manufacturers of each listed geographically, and it provides an alphabetical index to manufacturers, another to trade names, and still another to specific products. Thus, though the first look at product listings may suggest that this is a generalized maze, there are tools between the covers for the researcher on the track of specific game.

Kelly's Directory of Merchants, Manufacturers, and Shippers (London: Kelly's Directories, 1887–) has a slightly different cast, but it supplements *Thomas' Register* by putting a focus on Great Britain.

Communication: Broadcasting, Magazines, Newspapers

Some Leading Journals

Columbia Journalism Review. Columbia Graduate School of Journalism. Bi-monthly.

Journal of Communication. International Communication Association. Quarterly.

Journalism Quarterly. Association for Education in Journalism. Quarterly.

Journal of Advertising Research. Advertising Research Foundation. Quarterly.

Journal of Broadcasting. Association for Professional Broadcasting Education. Quarterly.

Public Opinion Quarterly. Princeton University Press. Quarterly.

Television Quarterly. National Academy of Television Arts and Sciences. Quarterly.

(*Note:* Several of the most widely used reference works in mass communication are listed earlier in this chapter under "Newspaper, Magazine, and TV News Indexes and Lists.")

Aspen Handbook on the Media: Research, Publications, Organizations
Edited by William L. Rivers and William T. Slater. Aspen Program on Communications and Society, 1975. Second edition.

This slender volume focuses on research, including descriptive lists of leading research institutions and foundations and other agencies that support research in communication, but it also lists U.S. and international organizations and associations and many publications.

Broadcasting Yearbook
Washington, D.C.: Broadcast Publications, 1935–. Annual.

This annual supplement to the weekly *Broadcasting* magazine is heavy with useful information. Although it contains a wide range of other data, the main section is devoted to separate directories of radio and television stations.

Handbook of Communication
Edited by Ithiel de Sola Pool, Wilbur Schramm, and others. Chicago: Rand McNally, 1973.

If "handbook" suggests a slender volume, the word is misleading as a description of this text. Pool and Schramm engaged more than thirty researchers to contribute to "a collection of review articles outlining the present state of research" on the mass media of communication and the process and effects of communication in general. The result is a book of more than a thousand pages written by political scientists, psychologists, sociologists, and others. The volume is divided into three parts: The Communication Process, Communication Settings, and Communication Research.

International Television Almanac

Edited by Charles S. Aaronson. New York: Quigley, 1956–.

Both the formal name and the nickname—"Who's Who in Television"—are somewhat misleading. Although there are sections on Great Britain and the world market, this is not nearly so "international" as the title implies. The focus on the United States is quite strong. It is much more than a personality book, carrying lists of television stations; producers; distributors; services; regular programs with star, producer, network and the like; and many other features.

Standard Rate and Data Service Publications

Skokie, Ill.: Standard Rate and Data Service.

SRDS, as this company is known in the trade, issues huge collections of facts and figures on the mass media. Used primarily as a guide for placing advertising, *SRDS* publications are also helpful to anyone looking for a statistical picture of the mass media. In the monthly *Consumer Magazine and Farm Publication Rates and Data* (one of 15 SRDS publications), for example, one can find these facts about *Mademoiselle* magazine: address, advertising personnel, branch offices, advertising representatives, commission and cash discount, advertising rates (in a full column of detail), mechanical requirements, issuance and closing dates, and circulation.

Reference Books in the Mass Media

Eleanor Blum. Urbana: University of Illinois Press, 1972.

This is an annotated, selected booklist covering book publishing, broadcasting, films, newspapers, magazines, and advertising. The preface states the purpose: "This booklist is compiled for beginning students and other laymen in mass communications. It is intended to provide sources for facts and figures, names, addresses, and other biographical information, and to suggest starting points for research."

World Radio Handbook for Listeners: Broadcasting, Television

Copenhagen: O. Lund Johansen, 1967. Twenty-first edition.

So few directories really cover the world of broadcasting that *World Radio Handbook* is unusual. Truly international, it carries long accounts of the organization and structure of broadcasting in each country. The data on leading networks and stations are set forth clearly, including local times of broadcasts, language or languages used, etc.

Writer's Handbook
Boston: The Writer, 1936–. Annual.
and *Writer's Market*
Cincinnati: Writer's Digest, 1930–. Annual.

These are competing publications, both of which attempt to serve free-lance writers by offering thumbnail sketches of the needs of thousands of magazines. Both also carry advice from professional writers.

Education

Some Leading Journals

Educational Record. American Council on Education. Quarterly.

Harvard Educational Review. Harvard University. Quarterly.

Journal of Higher Education. Ohio State University. Monthly.

Teachers College Record. Columbia University. Eight issues annually.

American Universities and Colleges
Edited by W. Todd Furniss. Washington, D.C.: American Council on Education, 1973. Eleventh edition.

This frequently revised reference is a useful survey of higher education in the United States. It begins with wide-ranging articles: "The Evolution of Higher Education," "The Federal Government and Higher Education," and "The Foreign Student in the United States." The second section is a subject listing for professional education—everything from architecture to veterinary medicine. Next is a directory of universities and colleges covering type, history, requirements, fees, departments and staff, degrees, enrollment, library, publications, finance, buildings and grounds, and names of administrative officials.

The College Blue Book
Edited by Max Russell. New York: Crowell, Collier and Macmillan, 1969–70. Thirteenth edition. 10 vols.

Highly recommended by reference librarians, these volumes are a comprehensive guide to higher education. They sketch 3,400 colleges in easy-to-read tables, describe them fully, and cover most of the central features of college life, including scholarships, fellowships, and grants. The last volume provides information about 30,000 junior and senior high schools in the United States.

Comparative Guide to American Colleges

James Cass and Max Birnbaum. New York: Harper & Row, 1969.

This is one of the best guides to higher education for prospective students, parents, and counselors. Cass and Birnbaum provide information on more than 1,100 American colleges and universities: enrollment, affiliation, location, admission selectivity and requirements, academic atmosphere—almost everything but the latest student fad.

Current Index to Journals in Education

New York: Crowell, Collier and Macmillan. Annual.

This provides detailed indexing for more than three hundred education and education-oriented journals. It is a monthly companion to *Research in Education* (Washington, D.C.: U.S. Office of Education), which lists approximately one thousand new reports every month, many of them unpublished.

Digest of Educational Statistics

Washington, D.C.: U.S. Office of Education, 1962–. Annual.

This useful digest offers current information on schools, enrollment, teachers, graduates, educational attainment, finances, federal education programs, and research and development.

Education Index

New York: Wilson, 1929–. Monthly except in July and August.

The focus of this index is on educational trends, teaching, and educational administration. It is primarily useful to teachers and educational administrators because it ranges widely over the literature to include books and pamphlets as well as journal articles and some of the many publications of the U.S. Office of Education.

The Encyclopedia of Education

New York: Macmillan, 1971. 10 vols.

The scope of this comprehensive encyclopedia is international, but its primary concern is education at all levels in the United States. It contains more than 1,000 signed articles, a bibliography with each.

Encyclopedia of Educational Research

Robert L. Ebel. New York: Macmillan, 1969. Fourth edition.

Synthesizing and interpreting recent studies, this volume covers such topics as grades and grading systems, child guidance clinics, teacher effectiveness, and diagnosis in teaching. It can be supplemented for analysis of more recent articles with *Review of Educational Research* (American Educational Research Association, 1931–), which is issued five times a year.

International Yearbook of Education

Geneva: International Bureau of Education: Paris: Unesco 1948–.

This annual sketches current educational conditions in eighty-seven countries, giving information on developments during the preceding year in administration, curricula, teaching staff, and auxiliary services.

The World of Learning

London: Europa, 1947–.

Broader in scope than most such directories, this annual carries information on colleges and universities, learned societies and research institutions, libraries and archives, and museums. Arranged alphabetically by country, *The World of Learning* also features an international section that covers UNESCO and international councils and organizations.

Law and Political Science

Some Leading Journals

American Journal of International Law. American Society of International Law. Quarterly.

American Political Science Review. American Political Science Association. Quarterly.

Foreign Affairs. Council on Foreign Relations. Quarterly.

Harvard Law Review. Harvard University. Quarterly.

Journal of Politics. Southern Political Science Association. Quarterly.

Political Science Quarterly. Academy of Political Science. Quarterly.

Public Administration Review. American Society for Public Administration. Quarterly.

Review of Politics. University of Notre Dame. Quarterly.

Stanford Law Review. Stanford University. Quarterly.

Yale Law Review. Yale University. Quarterly.

The American Political Dictionary

Jack C. Plano and Milton Greenberg. New York: Holt, Rinehart & Winston, 1967. Second edition.

The authors group terms under eighteen topics (such as U.S. Constitution, civil liberties, the legislative process, and foreign policy) and provide information on important agencies, cases, and statutes as well as definitions.

Black's Law Dictionary: Definitions of the Terms and Phrases of American and English Jurisprudence, Ancient and Modern
Henry C. Black. Revised by the Publisher's Editorial Staff. St. Paul, Minn.: West Publishing, 1968. Revised fourth edition.

Designed primarily for law students and lawyers, and thus a bit legalistic for the researcher who doesn't know a tort from a tart, this volume is nonetheless useful. It contains terms used in Old English, European, and feudal law as well as those of recent origin and reports on legislation and many court opinions. *Black's* has long been standard.

Book of the States
Chicago: Council of State Governments, 1935–. Biennial.

This volume, which is kept up to date with supplements that provide listings of newly elected officials, provides a quick overview of each state: nickname, motto, flower, bird, song, legislative reference service, leading officials, and other details.

Congressional Directory
U.S. Congress. Washington, D.C.: Government Printing Office, 1809–. Annual.

Congressional Staff Directory
Compiled by Charles B. Brownson. Washington, D.C.: Congressional Staff Directory, 1959–. Annual.

The *Congressional Directory* is one of the most widely used government publications. It is the best source for biographical information on members of Congress and their committee assignments. It also provides maps of congressional districts, information on leading congressional staff members, and directory information on the executive and the judiciary.

Charles Brownson, who was a congressman from 1951 to 1958, knew the pivotal roles of congressional staffers and began publishing his *Congessional Staff Directory*. It includes reports on State Delegations; Staffs of the Officers and Members of the Senate; Staffs of Joint Committees; Staffs of Miscellaneous Offices of the Capital; Staff of the General Accounting Office and the Library of Congress; Staffs of the Officers and Members of the House; Staffs of the Committees and Subcommittees of the House; 5,800 Major Cities—Their Congressional Districts and Representatives; and Key Personnel of Executive Departments.

Congressional Quarterly Weekly Report
Washington, D.C.: Congressional Quarterly, 1945–. Weekly.

CQ, as it is widely known, is the best continuing record of action on bills, roll-call votes of members of Congress, and many other congressional activities. The weekly reports can be analyzed easily through a quarterly index that is cumulated annually. As the publisher points out, the annual *Congressional Quarterly Almanac* "distills, reorganizes and cross-indexes" the year of congressional action. The same publisher produced *Congress and the Nation 1945–1964,* which is a summary of the first twenty annuals and includes other reports on Congress. In 1971, Congressional Quarterly, Inc., published a huge and valuable volume titled *Congressional Quarterly's Guide to the Congress of the United States: Origins, History and Procedures.*

Congressional Record
U.S. Congress. Washington, D.C.: Government Printing Office, 1873–. Daily.

It is not quite true that this is the record of every word spoken on the floor of the House and the Senate. In cooler moments, members of Congress sometimes have second thoughts about what they have said and edit the *Record.* But their second thoughts must come fast. The *Record* is set into type a few hours after the House and Senate complete the legislative day (and is available early the next morning). Almost every word of Senate and House debate and many other congressional actions are recorded, which makes the *Record* indispensable for tracing the full development of legislation—and for providing *The New Yorker* with the gaseous sentences it memorializes under the general heading "Wind on Capitol Hill."

Documents on American Foreign Relations
Council on Foreign Relations. New York: Simon & Schuster, 1938–. Annual.

The prestigious Council on Foreign Relations sponsors this useful annual, which provides in convenient reference form the most important documents that define the degree of our entanglements. It includes presidential messages, speeches, reports, letters, communiques, news conferences, comments, official statements, and resolutions.

A companion annual, *The United States in World Affairs* (New York: Harper & Row, 1931–, suspended 1941–44), gives a comprehensive narrative account.

Facts about the Presidents
Joseph Nathan Kane. New York: Wilson, 1968. Second edition.

This widely used source covers the presidents from Washington to Johnson. Part 1 is made up of a chapter on each president and includes family history, election date, and highlights of the life and administration of each. Part 2 deals with collective data and statistics on individual presidents and the office.

Federal Register
Washington, D.C.: Government Printing Office, 1936–.

This is the chief reference source for federal regulations which have the force of law. It includes applicable presidential proclamations and executive orders. Published daily, except Sundays, Mondays, and days following holidays, it is indexed quarterly and annually to simplify research.

Index to Legal Periodicals
New York: Wilson, 1908–.

Sponsored by the American Association of Law Libraries, this excellent service indexes about 300 legal periodicals.

International Yearbook and Statesman's Who's Who
London: Burke's Peerage, 1953–.

A good first source for short profiles of countries and the names of officers in power, this annual is in three parts: International Organizations, States of the World, and Biographical Section—the last, a world who's who.

Martindale-Hubbel Law Directory
New York: Martindale-Hubbel, 1931–. 4 vols. Annual.

Primarily a directory of United States and Canadian attorneys, this noted source also provides a digest of state, Canadian and foreign laws. Volumes 1–3 are arranged geographically by state, then by city and town. Here, the directory lists firms and lawyers, provides a selected list of foreign lawyers arranged by country, gives a roster of patent attorneys, and sketches biographies of many attorneys. Volume 4 includes digests of the laws of the states, territories and possessions of the U.S. and Canada, and other valuable data.

Municipal Year Book
Chicago: International City Managers Association, 1934–. Annual.

Although the emphasis in this yearbook is on cities rather than on towns, the definition of "municipality" the editors favor is so broad that only hamlets seem to be omitted. The book contains a directory of chief officials for cities of 10,000 or more (mayors and clerks are listed for municipalities of 5,000 to 10,000). Useful sections provide information on governmental units, personnel, finance, housing, public welfare, and similar subjects, most of them revised for each new edition to keep pace with rapid changes.

Statesman's Yearbook
London and New York: Macmillan, 1864–.

One of the famous reference sources, this annual carries concise, readable information on the governments of the world: constitution and government, economic conditions, education, religion, defenses, agriculture, commerce, diplomatic representatives, etc.

A Statistical History of the American Presidential Elections
Svend Petersen. New York: Ungar, 1968.

This volume includes 133 tables that spell out the votes and percentages for each election in each state and for eleven political parties. This compilation is as good as any other for research about the major political parties' fortunes in presidential elections, and it may be better than any other in providing statistics that trace the rise and fall of minor parties.

U.S. Code
Washington, D.C.: Government Printing Office, 1965.

The Code, as it is known to legal researchers, is the basic set of documents in a pyramid of publications that seek to bring order to research in law. Revised fairly frequently, it includes all laws passed by Congress and still in force. Supplements are cumulated annually to enable researchers to find up-to-date information between editions. An annotated version of the Code is titled *United States Code Annotated.* It offers additional information, such as judicial interpretations, opinions of attorneys general, and historical and critical essays.

U.S. Government Organization Manual
Office of the Federal Register, National Archives and Records Service, General Services Administration. Washington, D.C.: Government Printing Office, 1935–.

This is to the executive what the *Congressional Directory* is to the legislative, an anatomy in print. Congress gets a few pages of attention here, but most of the volume is devoted to the vast reaches of the executive. The section on the Department of Commerce is fairly typical. It begins by listing the secretary of commerce and his deputies, assistants, and bureau heads (of the National Bureau of Standards, Coast and Geodetic Survey, and the like), spells out the department's purpose, and describes the offices and bureaus. Nearly half the manual is given over to the boards, commissions, and committees that are not part of departmental structures, among them the Interstate Commerce Commission, the National Aeronautics and Space Administration, and the Veterans Administration.

Who's Who in American Politics
New York: R. R. Bowker. Biennial.

Compiled by questionnaire, this volume provides information on 12,500 "current political figures who direct and influence American government at all levels." Although many of the biographies are available in other publications, such as *Who's Who in America*, this work is especially useful because it provides information on local and minor office holders and party officials.

Worldmark Encyclopedia of the Nations
New York: Harper & Row, 1971. Revised edition. 5 vols.

The mammoth subtitle describes these volumes: "A Practical Guide to the Geographic, Historical, Political, Social & Economic Status of All Nations, Their International Relationships, and the United Nations System." For each country, information is provided on trade, industry, income, labor, migration, armed forces, flora and fauna, and population.

Yearbook of International Organizations
International Publications Service. Biennial.

This much-used source is an encyclopedic dictionary of currently active international organizations and associations. It covers their aims, functions, finances, activities, publications, and leading officials.

Yearbook of the United Nations
New York: United Nations, Department of Public Instruction, 1947–. Annual.

Many publications provide more information on particular activities of the United Nations, but this volume offers data on nearly all of them. It is organized in two parts, the first covering the year's activities, the second specialized agencies of the UN. Like most of the documents of international organizations, the *Yearbook* must be written with thought of the sensibilities of its diverse membership. But it is as honest and useful a summary as a huge committee can be expected to produce.

Sociology and Anthropology

Some Leading Journals

American Anthropologist. American Anthropological Association. Bi-monthly.

American Journal of Sociology. University of Chicago Press. Bi-monthly.

American Sociological Review. American Sociological Association. Bimonthly.

Human Organization. Society for Applied Anthropology. Quarterly.

Journal of American Folklore. American Folklore Society. Quarterly.

Population Bulletin. Population Reference Bureau. Eight issues yearly.

Rural Sociology. Cornell University Department of Rural Sociology. Quarterly.

Encyclopedia of Social Work

New York: National Association of Social Workers, 1929–. 2 vols.

Once known as *Social Work Year Book*, this is one of the few sources in this field. A collection of articles on social work and related topics, it also contains biographies of those prominent in social work and enough additional information to be considered both an encyclopedia and a directory.

The Forgotten American—American Indians Remembered: A Selected Bibliography for Use in Social Work Education

New York: Council on Social Work Education, 1972.

This 83-page booklet is intended only to provide background for social work education. A partially annotated bibliography, it includes sections on tribal history, government-Indian relations, missionaries and the Indian, the military and the Indian, biographies, American Indians in fiction, and books by Indians about Indians.

Index to Literature on the American Indian

American Indian Historical Society. San Francisco: Indian Historian Press, 1972.

ILAI, as this is known to researchers, is a relatively new venture. Although it is a strong effort to provide an overview of the quantities of literature on the American Indian, an authority who analyzed it in *Library Journal* lamented that the volume is too selective in its coverage and failed to match an earlier venture, *American Indian Index* (Chicago: Huebner, 1953–1968). It is nonetheless useful to researchers who do not require a complete listing of sources.

The Mexican-American People: The Nation's Second Largest Minority

Leo Grebler, Joan Moore, and Ralph Guzman. New York: Free Press, 1970.

This socioeconomic study of the Mexican American in the Southwest is not a conventional reference book but a close analysis, and a readable one, that contains much information useful to researchers. The statistical appendix and the lengthy bibliography are especially valuable. A detailed index is a good guide to information in the three parts of the volume: Historical Perspective, The Individual and the Social System, and Political Interaction.

A Modern Dictionary of Sociology
George Theodorson and Achilles Theodorson. New York: Thomas Y. Crowell, 1969.

Although the emphasis in this volume is on sociology, many terms are defined that are more often used in cultural anthropology, psychology, statistics, philosophy, and political science. Designed primarily for students, the dictionary is also useful to others. Current usage is emphasized; the most relevant definition is the first provided.

Mythology of All Races
Boston: Marshall-Jones, 1916–32. 13 vols.

Despite the age of this work, it continues to be the best of the comprehensive treatments of mythology. The myths are arranged by race, richly illustrated, and easily located through a general index.

Negro Almanac
Edited by Harry A. Ploski and Ernest Kaiser. New York: Bellwether, 1971.

This comprehensive collection is divided into thirty-two sections, most of which contain useful statistics. Among the topics are historical landmarks, legal status, soul food, black artists, and black jazz.

Negro Handbook
Chicago: Johnson, 1966.

Compiled by the editors of *Ebony*, the leading black magazine, this is a collection of essays on the contribution of blacks to life in the United States. The volume is in eighteen sections on subjects such as civil rights, crime, education, sports, and farming.

Reference Encyclopedia of the American Indian
Edited by Bernard Klein and Daniel Icolari. New York: Klein, 1967.

This wide-ranging handbook is not encyclopedic, but it is useful in itself and for an excellent bibliography that guides researchers to mines of additional information. The volume is divided into seventeen sections on subjects such as government agencies, reservations, schools, visual aids, government publications, magazines, and newspapers. One section is a Who's Who among American Indians.

Sociological Abstracts
New York: Sociological Abstracts, 1952–.

Like *Psychological Abstracts,* this source indexes and abstracts periodical literature. It contains author, periodical and subject indexes and is international in scope. All abstracts are in English, but *Sociological Abstracts* contains articles in more than twenty foreign languages as well as in English.

Sports, Games, Hobbies

Baseball Record Book
St. Louis: Sporting News. Annual.

Published every year in March, this source is much used by sports writers and broadcasters. It includes records of year-by-year leaders and almost every imaginable outstanding feat in a sport that dotes on statistics. The same publisher issues the annual *Baseball Register,* which focuses much more on current players, some of whom are not stars whose exploits have reached the record books.

Encyclopedia of Sports
Frank Menke. New York: Barnes, 1969. Fourth edition.

Every other razor blade company promotes its product by issuing little booklets of sports records, and other publishers come out with more up-to-date information, especially records. But this 1,100-page volume is the most complete treatment of all sports, major and minor. Menke provides information on sports history, rules, and organizations as well as records, and his scope is so broad that chess, curling, and the seating capacities of stadiums find a place.

Football Register
St. Louis: Sporting News. Annual.

Published every September, this volume covers professional football in detail, listing statistics for all active players and coaches.

Guide to Legal Gambling
Harland B. Adams. New York: Funk & Wagnalls, 1969.

This 192-page book focuses on gambling in the United States and tries (probably vainly) to persuade compulsive gamblers that there are games to avoid. Adams also offers tips on the games that bring the best return and the betting systems that should bring riches at the races.

Index to Handicrafts

Eleanor Cook Lovell and R. M. Hall. Boston: Faxon, 1936–65. 4 vols.

This is a guide to how to make practically anything from snowshoes to sod houses. The volumes index references to thousands of books and articles.

Tom McNally's Fisherman's Bible

Tom McNally. Chicago: Follett, 1970.

In these 321 pages are thirty-seven short articles with sharp photos and diagrams that cover where to fish, how to fish, and much more. McNally gives world and state fishing records, information on state conservation departments and professional and sportsmen's organizations, and a directory of fishing tackle manufacturers and importers.

7 Reporting on Research

Every week or so, a young woman who works evenings in a New York City public library is confronted by a man sent by a group of blue-collar workers who have been arguing in a bar a few blocks away. She knows before he speaks that he will ask a question that will send her to the reference shelf for *Famous First Facts,* the *World Almanac, The Guinness Book of World Records,* or a similar book.

One evening he asked, "Didn't Walt Frazier lead the New York Knicks basketball team in scoring and assists in 1971?" When she found the answer, the man took the book to a xerox machine located in a library alcove, copied the relevant page, then returned to the bar, where his friends were waiting to learn who had won the bet that had grown out of the argument.

This incident reflects the three basic methods of research sketched in this book. The man who visited the library had once heard an assistant coach of the New York Knickerbockers say that Walt Frazier was the most valuable Knick player because Frazier always led the team in scoring and assists. But another barroom patron argued that he had *seen* all the Knick's home games in 1971 and was certain that Willis Reed was the leader. Other patrons of the bar were drawn into the argument. A bet was made, and the men decided to conduct their usual research in the nearby library.

The lessons of this incident could be spelled out almost endlessly, but consider a few that are central. The casual conversation with the assistant coach was not a useful interview. Unless one sets out to find particular facts, what is asked, answered, heard, and remembered during a general conversation is so likely to be distorted by interviewer and interviewee that the results are probably useless. The observations of the man who watched the Knicks play were equally useless. An observer who is emotionally involved in what he sees—especially if he is not then trying to focus on particular facts—is a poor witness. But the concluding act in the bar can be trusted: In the best tradition of research, the man who visited the library consulted an authority and reported his findings with documentary evidence.

This suggests what is worth reporting. Vague memories are suspect; verifiable facts are not. Unfortunately, few research projects are so simple. Instead of finding one fact that speaks for itself, a researcher must usually gather scores—if not hundreds or thousands—choose among them, and stitch them together in an informative report.

For example, digging up and choosing among many facts is the foundation of television news, even though most news reports are short. Sally Galvin, a researcher in the Washington Bureau of NBC News, described her work in 1973: "The job is challenging—researching the cases of Sherman Adams, Calhoun, Andrew Jackson, Spiro Agnew, succession to the Presidency and Vice Presidency, gas rationing—and it's rewarding: finding the information! In reality I'm a trivia-tracker-downer, constantly searching for 'Who said. . . ?' or 'What led to. . . ?' or responding to 'Get me a rundown on Joe Schmoe' while I'm wondering *which* cabinet post he's taking." Research in history was vital when Vice President Agnew resigned. And with the Nixon administration in turmoil, a researcher had to check the background of each newly appointed official.

Although Sally Galvin referred lightly to her work as tracking down trivia, she and other researchers know the value of small but revealing facts. Plutarch, one of the greatest as well as one of the earliest biographers, wrote: "Sometimes a matter of less moment, an expression or a jest, informs us better of characters and inclinations than the most famous sieges, the greatest armaments, or the bloodiest battles."

A striking example is Jim Bishop's *The Day Lincoln Was Shot,* which was published in 1955 and achieved the unusual dual distinction of becoming a best seller and winning the applause of historians. John P. Marquand, a leading novelist of that time, explained why:

> Though some of the episodes Mr. Bishop retails are so familiar as to be part of America's folklore, their combination with myriad lesser-known facts lends the whole an amazing freshness. Did you know that the President ceased rocking in the chair provided for him by the management but did not immediately slump forward? Did you know that when Booth said "Sic semper tyrannis" he spoke in such a low voice that very few in the audience heard him? [1]

Kinds of Research Reports

Research is reported in hundreds of forms, from memos to multi-volume books. Even if it were possible to describe all of them, the result would be longer than it would be useful. One who knows where and how to find facts can learn to report them in any of the appropriate forms by analyzing a few of the most important.

Journalistic Forms

When a prominent industrialist refused a reporter's request for an interview, the reporter asked why.

"Because of that editorial," the industrialist replied, referring to one opposing the industrialist's favorite project. The reporter protested that he had had nothing to do with the editorial—that, indeed, he had never written *any* editorial—but the industrialist went on, "I don't mind if you fellows slant news stories, but you shouldn't do that to editorials."

Like the industrialist, most people are confused about journalistic jobs and forms of reporting. Only in extraordinary cases does any reporter ever write an editorial. More important, most reporters try to present news objectively, leaving it to editorial writers to state opinions, to editorialize—to "slant." True, reporters may be as fallible as other humans, but their training and their objectives are different. Perhaps the chief problem in understanding what reporters do and how they do it grows out of the fact that they report in several forms.

The most common is the *straight news report*—also known as the *objective report*—which is a timely account of an event. A newspaper report of a speech is usually straight news. Because it covers only what happened during a brief period, straight news provides a valuable focus. It is also valuable because it makes such limited demands on the reporter that he can come close to presenting an objective report of verifiable fact. Straight news is written by a formula which requires that the first few sentences (in some cases the first sentence alone) report at least the who-what-when-where of an event, with the details strung out in descending order of importance. Because this formula gives the reporter little leeway to express himself—and especially because the reporter is instructed neither to editorialize nor to use words that even hint at his opinion—the report usually lives up to its name: straight.

But if writing according to the formula prevents the reporter from editorializing, it also prevents him from helping readers understand events. Because straight news isolates a small slice of life at a particular time and reports none of the surrounding facts that might provide meaning, it is usually superficial. That is why many reporters argue that nothing like the full truth can emerge from such reports, that straight news is a straitjacket. They are aware, of course, that some events are not *worth* more time and attention than a straight news report provides, but their arguments for more complete reports on important events are the principal reason other forms have emerged.

The *depth report* takes a step beyond straight news. Instead of trying merely to mirror the highlights of an event, the reporter gathers additional information that is independent of the event but related to it—as when Sally Galvin turned up information on other vice-presidents to flesh out reports on the resignation of Vice-President Agnew. A reporter who covers a speech on medical practices in China may consult experts and reference sources, then present the speaker's words in a larger framework. In some cases, additional information is placed in the speech report; in others, it is reported separately. In either case, depth reporting calls for transmitting information, not the reporter's opinion. Verifiable fact is as pivotal in depth reporting as it is in straight news reporting.

Although the writer's opinion has no place in a depth report, the facts he gathers may rebut or refute the speaker—in which case the speaker or his supporters may charge that the report is slanted. Perhaps it is. The crucial point is *which* of the many available facts a reporter uses to build the larger framework.

Interpretive reports—also known as *news analyses*—are another step beyond straight news. They usually focus on an issue, problem, or controversy. Here, too, the substance is verifiable fact—not opinion. But instead of presenting facts in straight news or depth report fashion and hoping that they will speak for themselves, the interpretive reporter clarifies, explains, analyzes. The interpretive report usually focuses on *why:* Why did the president take that trip, appoint that man, make that statement? What is the real meaning of the event?

Whatever his intention, a reporter who is given the leeway to interpret events may inadvertently offer his opinion; he is always in danger of using words that steer his readers toward his desires and beliefs. Because clarification, explanation, and analysis require that the reporter weigh and filter facts, the interpreter enters the reporting process much more personally than other reporters. And because an interpretation is not written by formula, the reporter has latitude that makes it easier for him to disguise his opinions.

Investigative reporting, which some call "muckraking," is the practice of opening closed doors and closed mouths. As in interpretive reporting, the focus is on problems, issues, and controversies. In fact, interpretive and investigative reports are the same in cases in which the reporter must dig up hidden information in order to clarify, explain, and analyze. In most cases, though, an interpretive reporter has relatively little trouble because he is explaining public events and can find many sources who are happy to help him. (In fact, one of the chief dangers in all reporting is that some sources want to provide information that will serve their own interests.) In contrast, the investigative reporter must try to dig up facts that have been hidden for a purpose—often an illegal or unethical purpose.

Features differ from news reports primarily in their intent. Whereas a news report ordinarily presents information that is likely to concern readers, a feature is usually designed to catch their interest. The feature reporter casts a wide net in his search for facts, sometimes pulling in and using things a news reporter would consider frivolous. The feature writer's report provides a reading experience that depends more on style, grace, and humor than on the importance of the information. (This difference is reflected in the fact that those who produce features exclusively are called "feature writers," not "reporters.")

To understand all these journalistic forms, consider a hypothetical case. Imagine that university administrators, discovering that too little dormitory space is available for all the students who want to live on the campus, have leased one hundred trailer homes and have parked them on the edge of the dormitory area to house four hundred students.

Assigned by the editor of the campus paper to write a straight news report, a reporter would quote the speech or the press release in which the administration announced the establishment of "Trailer Dorm." If student leaders spoke for or against the conditions of trailer living, the writer would quote them as well. If students held a protest rally, the writer would report its highlights dispassionately.

Assigned to write a depth report, one might gather opinions by questioning students, compare home campus housing to that at a nearby university, or report the results of any or all of a dozen quests related to student housing. The limit is marked only by the imagination the reporter brings to the research.

Assigned to write an interpretive report, one might interview administrators to determine why they decided to lease trailers rather than make other arrangements and interview student leaders to determine why they support or oppose the trailer park. Again, the reporter can use many approaches to gathering information that will enable him to clarify, explain, and analyze.

Assigned to write an investigative report by an editor who suspects that the administration was lax in not planning for more dormitory space, or that an administrator's brother owns the trailers, a reporter must interview widely and adroitly and check financial records. The most difficult kind of journalism, investigative reporting requires a researcher who is imaginative, industrious, and aggressive. He must write a hard-fact report, not speculation.

Assigned to write a feature, the writer looks for the color and flavor of trailer life. Do trailer residents live differently from other students? How? Have they painted their homes in wild colors? Are they planting gardens? Who does the cooking—and with what results?

These are not rigid categories. Like all other writing, journalistic forms sometimes overlap. Traces of depth or interpretive reporting may appear in a straight news report. An interpretive report may have investigative elements. A feature may seem to be weighted as heavily with matters of concern as with matters of light interest. But occasional mixtures are not as important as the fact that definable forms exist. Nearly every large newspaper carries reports in these forms. Reading them will show how journalists use different kinds of information to shape the structure of each kind of report.

Academic Forms

William James once said that there is only one kind of scholarly report: the research paper. If the paper is short, it is an article; if long, it is a book. Established scholars can talk off-handedly with one another about the length of their writing; most of it is article or book length. But unless they are having trouble trimming an article to size for publication or deciding whether to devote another year to expanding a long article into a book manuscript, they regard discussions of the length of their work as little more than cocktail party talk.

Unfortunately, the proper length sometimes seems to be the principal concern of students. Most seem to resemble the amateur writer who called a publisher and asked, "How long is the average novel nowadays?"

"Oh, between 75 and 90 thousand words."

"Well, then, I've finished!" [2]

Perhaps he had actually finished, perhaps he should have written more—or perhaps he should never have written a word. In any case, length was not the proper criterion. There is no appropriate length for novels in general. Ernest Hemingway's *The Old Man And The Sea* is fewer than thirty thousand words. Tolstoy's *War and Peace* is more than three hundred thousand. Similarly, student research reports should cover the subject, whatever the length.

The trouble is, of course, that students are accustomed to having the lengths of their reports prescribed—or at least the minimum length. That is probably inevitable. Ideally the instructor in any course would have to do no more than say that he expected a research paper. Each student would soon become so caught up in the substance of the course that he would read widely, noting how, and at what length, different researchers treat different topics. Then the student would say, "The topic that intrigues me is this, and I can treat it that way if I do this and that." By the middle of the term, each student would be able to outline his topic; the instructor would do little more than nod approvingly to encourage each student to develop his excellent idea. One student's report would cover twenty pages, another ten, another fourteen—each an appropriate length because it suited the topic and the purpose of the assignment.

But an instructor is fortunate to find one or two such students in the average course. As a result, he must assign topics and lengths to everyone and encourage those who are caught up in their own ideas to develop them. An instructor may sigh and assign his students to prepare for more demanding work by writing finger exercises: papers that do not demand the time, the attention, or the sophisticated understanding of research and writing that go into a research paper.

The simplest kind of academic paper is the *precis*. Pronounced *pray-see*, it is a specialized summary of a passage from a book or article. Written in the basic order of the passage, it also maintains the same proportions of part to part.

Next is the *summary*, which is usually a compact version of an article or book. It covers all the main points and reports them in the same relation to one another found in the work.

The *book report* is both summary and something more. Most instructors require some information on the author and much more on the book itself—identification of it as novel, biography, etc., its subject, the author's theme and interpretation, the organization, and the tone or style. Because few books carry enough on their author's background, other writings, and reputation (some that *do* carry enough background material tend to make the author more important than he is), the student must find the relevant reference sources described in the preceding chapter of this book.

Book reports should not be confused with the *book reviews* published in newspapers, magazines, and professional journals. Reviewers and critics seldom provide all the detailed information about author and book that can be found in a formal book report. Although they are likely to provide much of it, they usually have a larger purpose: comparing the book to similar works and assessing its value.

Nor should book reports and book reviews be confused with *Reports*, which were once formal documents like research papers (the capital "R" is to distinguish this use of the word from the other references to "report"). Some instructors still require formal Reports properly footnoted and spell out everything that must be included.

Most assign informal Reports, some of them like the journalistic accounts described earlier in this chapter. Other instructors require students to report on a group of readings assigned during the term. The informality is reflected in this Report by a student, June Bube, on eight publications. She is able to cover all of them fairly satisfactorily in relatively few pages because she developed a theme. Although here and there she touches on other qualities of these publications, the focus is on these qustions: How can one be truly informed? What informational purpose is served by each publication?

> To be truly informed on international, national, state and local events and issues, you have to read more than one publication, more than one magazine or newspaper, unless you live in New York City. The inadequacy of a local paper like the *Palo Alto Times* is readily apparent: it *is* local. The inadequacies of the *San Francisco Chronicle* can also be easily seen, but for different reasons. Magazines like *National Review, The New Republic,* and *Harper's* seem to be to some extent like clubs appealing to members who have a common body of knowledge and acquaintances, a slightly distinct vocabulary, and similar viewpoints. *Newsweek* and *The New York Times* come closest to being sufficient in themselves. But how do you find out about local entertainment, the California Teachers Association, or Bay Area transportation facilities, regardless of the radio or television, by reading these two publications? Because each publication has a different focus and purpose, the best way to evaluate each is to determine its intention and try to evaluate briefly how well it is fulfilled.
>
> *Newsweek* provides an in-depth summary of primarily national and international events and issues. It does especially well in re-creating events, putting them in context (often in chronological order), and analyzing the consequences. It gives the atmosphere of the color story while presenting the relevant details. In an article telling about Nixon's announcement of his choice for the new vice-president, the reader is told what the party looked like, what the attitudes of the guests were, and how Nixon responded to their reactions. Within the same article, the reader learns something about the background of Gerald Ford, the new developments in Nixon's hassle over the tapes, and Nixon's rating in the polls. The writing is compact and vivid without sacrificing the facts. In articles on Agnew, *Newsweek* follows him through the stages leading up to his resignation. The reader knows what he looked like during the courtroom sessions. When *Newsweek* discusses the energy crisis, it probes the facts and relationship to the Middle East War, not just what happened, but how it came about and what it means.
>
> The editorials also contribute to the sense of objectivity and thoughtful interpretation. Theodore H. White and Stewart Alsop express their former admiration for Agnew, why they think he was valuable to the

country, and what the implications and consequences of his exposure and betrayal are for the country.

Newsweek has inherent limitations. It cannot cover all the news of one week and it has to be enlightening to a reader who probably already knows what has happened. Therefore, it works to achieve complete coverage of the news it does select.

The New Republic does not strive to give even an interpretative account of significant events of the week. Its choice of articles usually assumes that the reader has some knowledge of the news. Through editorials, it makes no attempts to hide making judgments, but it bases its interpretations on facts. The subjects of the articles are designed to give insight into things that people are concerned about now. An article on the absence of peace in Vietnam recounts what has been going on and suggests how this might effect Nixon's future actions. An article on oil in Maine discusses peripheral aspects of the energy crisis. Another article discusses the results of elections at the gubernatorial and city levels in the light of Watergate's effect on the nation.

The style of *The New Republic* is somewhat rhetorical, posing questions and then answering them persuasively. With gentle convincing it leads the reader along toward accepting its point of view. The political issues discussed are highly selective and so are the books reviewed. Particularly in the reviews the language is intellectual and assumes a fairly high level of education on the part of the reader.

The *National Review* resembles *The New Republic* in that it examines news events in the abstract, in principle. *The New Republic* discusses alternatives to impeachment to rid the government of Nixon; the *National Review* compares our constitutional republic to other parliamentary governments and speculates how they would handle a crisis like Watergate.

Within a conservative framework, the *National Review* tries to be factual and objective. It also tries to put news in context. One article looks at the Middle East War by examining Russia's past and present and probable future motives.

It makes a conscious effort to see events from a different perspective, occasionally trying to be clever. One article gives a view of the Middle East War from the battlefield. Another story turns the firing of Cox into a soap opera.

The *National Review* is an insiders' magazine. A large part of this issue is devoted to tributes to people I have never heard of. Not so much the movie reviews, but the book reviews seem to be about books that would appeal to a select group.

Harper's definitely has its special group of readers too. To those not in the group, it seems aloof and seems to be trying very hard to find subjects which some other magazine is not covering. It seems to edge around the big political issues, presenting not vital information, but sideline information that would appear to be good conversational topics. It does not discuss hamburger shortage; it dwells on soybean experiments. It does not discuss Watergate; it talks about bringing the CIA home. It does not mention Kohoutek; it discusses eclipses.

It seems to be quasi-political, quasi-literary, and quasi-scientific. Some of the articles are very interesting, but what are they? Some of the language is a blend of esoteric literary references and political jargon. *Harper's* is a magazine for people who are taking several other magazines and at least one newspaper.

Of the newspapers, *The New York Times* has the biggest scope and the greatest depth. It focuses on international and national affairs (and state) and the business world. It provides a clarity of vision and meaty news. In a recent issue, there were six articles about Rockefeller's resignation and one editorial. The articles covered the event from every possible angle: what his resignation means for Malcolm Wilson, what it means for the GOP at the state and national levels, his personal and political reasons for resigning, a review of his past political career, a transcript of his news conference, a discussion of other governors who have resigned, and a discussion of what Rockefeller plans to do now. On the international level, several articles dealt with the problems that NATO is facing, what happened at a recent meeting, how the problems developed and what can be done about them. *The New York Times* is interested in the why and the how behind the what. It has so many important things to say that (at least in this particular issue) there was only one article on corpses and murder—and that was on page 30. The impression is that *The New York Times* has neither time, need, nor space for fillers.

The *San Francisco Chronicle's* primary purpose is to be a paper that is enjoyable, entertaining, and easy to read. Even its organization, continuing news articles from the front page on the last page, makes it easy to read. It mentions national and international events and then goes on to lighter things. In this issue, Cambodia, the development in the tapes crisis, and Nixon's income were large-scale news. Besides articles presenting different aspects of the energy shortage, the reader is struck by the amount of trivia. The paper is filled with colorful local news: the delivery boy who becomes rich, the possibility of bilingual education in San Francisco schools for the Chinese population, the tearing down of the Dumbarton Bridge, shootings, suicides, and problems with the nudies in San Francisco. Also, stories about pets and wild or zoo animals are popular. For some people, these things must be what they really want to read about, but more important aspects of the news are omitted.

The *Palo Alto Times* has much of the same subject matter as the *Chronicle,* but somehow its limited focus seems more justified because it is a paper for a smaller town. Besides the most important international and national news, it focuses on local business, local scientists, its high schools, Stanford, transportation all over the Bay Area, weather, the California legislature, and the energy crisis and the way it will affect Palo Alto residents. Its front page is about a third local, a third national, and a third international news. An account of a police breakthrough in Menlo Park and a Palo Alto burglary were the biggest news items on the front page of this particular issue. The *Palo Alto Times* also uses tidbits like short murder stories from Memphis, Tennessee; however, it emphasizes issues that concern everybody, like the energy crisis.

What papers and magazines people enjoy must depend on what they consider to be news, how informed they want to be, what interests them, and how much time they have to spend reading newspapers and magazines. Ideally, it would be nice to have time to read *The New York Times,* the *Palo Alto Times,* and *Newsweek* on a regular basis.

Formal Research Papers

A fun-loving professor once gave a class a list of topics for a research paper, all but one of which were reasonable. That one was:

> Describe the history of dramatic poetry from its origins to the present, concentrating especially but not exclusively on its social, political, religious, and philosophical impact on Europe, Asia, America, and Africa.

To the professor's dismay, most of the students considered that to be seriously intended as a topic. Three chose to write on it. Perhaps nothing else could have demonstrated more clearly that the students did not understand the goals and limitations of research. Unless a teacher explains them in some detail, few students ever seem to understand, if one judges accurately by the many who sigh, "I have to write a paper tonight," as though a research paper represented only meaningless hard labor that actually could be completed properly in one night.

Considered as a negative example, the grotesque topic quoted above shows the goals and limitations of research papers. The most important point is that the topic is impossibly broad. If it can be undertaken successfully, only a specialist should try it, one who is prepared to spend years —probably decades—writing several volumes. A student could do little more with it than pull scraps of information from several books, quote several passages and paraphrase several more, then use a few of his own sentences to string the hodge-podge together.

That approach points up flaws common to many research papers that cover reasonable topics. Written by a student who does not understand what he is about, even a paper on a topic narrow enough to provide a suitable foundation for research and writing is likely to be made up of pieces of the findings and ideas of others. This process can be described as transferring bones from one graveyard to another. Instead, the student should *use* the writings of others, but produce a research paper that bears the clear mark of his own thoughts. That is the scholar's way.

Why should a student who cares not at all about becoming a scholar imitate one? The answer lies at the center of learning. To mingle the works of others in a form whose only claim to originality is that no one has ever placed them in quite the same order is to learn nothing of much value. But a student who analyzes the research and insights of others and responds to them creatively is engaged in the best kind of education. He may undertake research paper after research paper in course after course without reading anything or developing any ideas that will seem to him in later life to have practical value. That is much less important than the real value: learning to think. Gail Thain Parker, who became president of Bennington College when she was 30, said that "The best ideas I have about college administration came from courses in nineteenth century novels. They taught me to think."

Choosing a Topic

The student must first choose a topic that he believes will interest him, for without interest, research and writing are not just hard labor but drudgery. Choosing should be a long process, in part because one must be sure that the topic actually is narrow enough to be explored—not just touched on—in the length assigned. To make certain, a beginner must read widely, weighing his own topic in a balance with published work to determine whether it actually is suitable.

Reading will do more for the researcher—and more *to* him. It should show whether the topic is so simplistic that it is not worth the work or whether he is planning to explore a much-traveled path. Although finding that a topic that seemed attractive either is too simple or has been exhausted may be disheartening, it should not be. Anyone who hopes to produce something ambitious and fresh should realize that his first topic is not likely to be adequate because it *is* the first. Rarely does one who has just been introduced to a field of learning hit upon a unique idea. Working on and discarding the first topic—and probably others—is not wasted effort. To shape and refine topics through thoughtful reading is to learn and to think. One who looks back on the first topic he considered interesting and shakes his head, wondering how he could have been so naive, has learned and has thought.

Selecting Sources

Whatever the topic, the two preceding chapters are guides to many sources of basic information. A researcher should always seek *primary sources* (first-hand information) rather than *secondary sources,* which are one step removed from the original. For example, William Faulkner's writings are primary; analyses of them by a literary critic are secondary. A president's book on his administration is primary, a critical review of it secondary. A painting or any other artistic production is primary, a description or analysis of it by an art critic or historian secondary.

Most authorities define primary sources differently. A researcher examining a book by William Faulkner is not consulting a primary source. The original manuscript is the primary source. The book is at least one step removed and thus is a secondary source because editors and others probably produced a book that is at least slightly different from the manuscript. Similarly, a researcher must examine the original of a painting—not a reproduction—to use a primary source.

Although these are important distinctions for many scholars, for the present purpose the examples in the first paragraph of this section may provide the most useful distinction. To analyze the printed works of Faulkner or the president or to examine a good reproduction of a painting is to avoid relying on what *someone else* has written about the works. The important matter is that the researcher must make his own analysis and think for himself rather than relying on someone else to do his thinking for him. In practice, a researcher considers the analyses of authorities *and* examines for himself. The ultimate value of a research paper pivots on the writer's own thoughts.

Taking Notes

The order of the sections of this chapter—first choosing a topic, then selecting sources and taking notes—may suggest that all research projects proceed step by step: choosing the topic, reading, note-taking, outlining, and writing following upon one another in marching order. Few projects are so neat. In fact, a researcher who can make his work march along crisply is either extraordinarily well-organized or produces sterile papers—or both. In many cases, one chooses a topic, begins reading, develops a vague notion for a outline while taking notes, rejects the first topic and chooses a related one, reads more and takes more notes, starts outlining, reads again and revises the outline, reads, changes the focus of the topic in a way that requires additional reading, note-taking, and outlining, and so on.

Chaotic as this may seem, it is a kind of a map of the mind

at work. The researcher cannot take each step mechanically; he is thinking as he steps. Because thinking—having new and different thoughts—is central to reading, taking notes, outlining, and writing, the researcher sometimes takes one step forward and two steps back. Even when he steps backward, he should consider taking with him what he picked up along the way. He should not, for example, automatically discard his notes when he decides to undertake a new topic. The new is likely to be related to the old and may even be a different version of it.

Although seasoned researchers may differ markedly from one another in many opinions, they seem to agree that a researcher must make as many complete notes on three-by-five cards as his time and temper allow. Perhaps nothing is more irritating in research than discovering that more of a quotation is needed than one has copied, or that one has not noted some of the facts needed for footnotes and bibliography.

Researchers also seem to be nearly unanimous in believing that a photocopy machine is no substitute for handwriting. The researcher who writes out an important quotation or set of facts rather than merely making a photocopy of the relevant page fixes it in his mind, giving it a central place that will help him later in writing. Many modern researchers both write notes and photocopy pages. Although they are likely to find later that they use only the notes, having the photocopy at hand enables them to refer to the context in which it appears.

If this seems to be curious duplication of work, consider a similar journalistic practice. Some journalists both take notes *and* tape record interviews and news conferences, then refer only to their notes in most cases, with the tape recording used only occasionally for checking and for providing the context of a quotation. To fail to take notes and rely on the recording alone would require struggling through so much extraneous material that the reporter might not be able to fix again on the highlights that had seemed to shine during the event.

By the same token, the library researcher who does not take notes but relies on photocopies of many pages that include both primary and secondary points may discover as he shuffles through them that he has lost the focus that occurred to him when he decided to photocopy the pages. This page was photocopied because it carries this quotation that must be used because I was thinking then that. . . . What *was* that point?

Photocopying is more useful, of course, than this analysis indicates. In an earlier time, many researchers used three-by-five cards for short quotations and other material that would fit in little space, larger cards to note summaries of long passages or to paraphrase them. Many of them now use the three-by-five cards as they did before, but photocopy passages that are to be summarized or paraphrased, thus doing away with the larger cards.

Photocopying may also enable the researcher to consider a much wider range of material for writing. If the focus of the topic should shift, material that was once considered secondary is now at hand, not back in the library. Even if the topic remains the same, the many photocopied pages may be useful because they enable the researcher to select from much material rather than little, which is always valuable in writing. But to avoid being overwhelmed by a jungle of photocopied pages, a researcher should organize them by scribbling notes about them on cards. If this use of cards in addition to the use suggested above seems to build the stack alarmingly, the researcher should be aware of the basic value of cards: No other form of writing is easier to organize.

Outlining

In a companion volume that covers many forms of writing, this author presents arguments for and against making outlines. The book suggests that setting down a full outline before beginning a short piece of writing is ordinarily useless but that some form of outline is valuable in writing longer pieces. Even in writing at some length, it is argued, the full, formal outline that uses I–II–III–1–2–3–A–B–C–a–b–c cuts a precise pattern before one begins to write that can bear little resemblance to what one will produce in shaping sentences that grow out of one another as the writer thinks through what he is saying.

That is a strong argument when it is applied to *any* form of writing. A full outline of some kind is often useful in planning a research paper, however, because the writer usually depends heavily on many sources. It is foolish to begin to write an ambitious paper after making a plan no more precise than arranging note cards in a semblance of order.

Cards can be used to help shape an outline; then the outline helps the researcher reorganize the cards. Consider the most common kinds of outlines.

The *scratch outline*, which is usually made up of notes scribbled on one or two pages, is a preliminary survey of the research the writer has assembled and his thoughts about it. Before writing, one should consider imposing more order on the material than the scratch outline is likely to have. One can, of course, develop and write from a more organized and detailed scratch outline. Many researchers do. Others use the scratch outline to develop one of the more formal outlines described below.

The *topic outline* is ordinarily made up of both the topics and the subtopics that will form the bulk of the paper. Although designed to show general relationships—topics are more important than the subtopics under them—the topic outline does not usually represent the full shape of the paper. Again, however, some researchers are content to write from a topic outline. Others use it to build a more formal outline.

The *sentence outline* is full-fleshed, with each item written in the form of a complete sentence, and with the relationship of each item to the others made clear by symbols: Roman numerals identify sentences on topics, capital letters those on the most important subtopics, Arabic numerals those on the next most important subtopics, lower-case letters those on the least important.

Whatever the form of outline one uses, it should be considered a guideline, not an unchangeable set of rules. The important point is that research material must be organized in some systematic way before writing and reorganized as the work progresses. Because individuals are different, the form most useful to one may not be to another. Moreover, a form that is most useful to a researcher who is trying to organize material in one case may not be the best for him in another. This is a good general rule: the longer and more complex the research paper, the fuller the outline.

Footnotes

Because most college students have been required to use footnotes since junior high school, they know that footnotes are an explicit means of expressing debts to other writers—and they should know that a writer must avoid any form of plagiarism, including paraphrasing the ideas of another and passing them off as his own. Many students, however, are depressed by the very word "footnotes," in part because using them requires assembling dull details in a form that has no color or flavor. Perhaps more important, many dislike footnotes because they worry almost endlessly about *what* to footnote.

To a casual reader, footnotes *are* dull details. They are not likely to disappear or change form very much, though, because many serious readers value them and can use them most easily in the economical form in which most footnotes appear. The best one can do to reduce footnote worry is to try to understand why footnotes are valuable and how one should decide which items deserve them.

The student can begin to understand if he realizes that established scholars, too, are sometimes uncertain how many footnotes they should use. Giving credit to other writers who unearthed facts and clothed them in ideas is an almost automatic practice for most scholars. Their principal problem is deciding what they need to cite (footnotes are often called "citations," or "cites") to enable their readers to find a particular item so that it can be read in context.

The scholar has three general guidelines: *credit*, *confidence*, and *retrievability*. He wants to give credit to pay his debts to other researchers. Because he wants his readers to have confidence in his published work, a scholar ordinarily cites those important aspects of it that are not common knowledge. He also cites important aspects to enable his readers to retrieve them.

Who deserves credit is not usually difficult to determine, but how does the scholar know what to cite to give his readers confidence? How does he know what they will want to retrieve? He can usually judge fairly accurately because he knows his readers—not each reader but the *kind* of readership. A professor of English, for example, shares a common fund of information with most other professors of English who specialize in his field. Writing for a journal that is read primarily by those who teach much the same courses, he has some sense of the knowledge they share and thus can judge what aspects of his research he must cite.

No scholar, however, can really judge *precisely* what his colleagues know and would like to know. Although the editors of the journal in which the scholar's work is to appear can help, *they* cannot be certain of all the knowledge, interests, and needs of all their readers. So it is that a reader occasionally writes to an author or to a journal editor, irritated because an article was not properly footnoted. In some cases, *many* readers are irritated by inadequate citations and related matters.

All this helps to shape the strategy a student should use in citing sources. Like the scholar, he should use footnotes to express debts, to establish confidence, and to help readers retrieve information. Like the scholar, too, the student must develop a sense of who his readers are and what they know. In writing an article that he hopes to publish in a journal, the student must think of the knowledge and needs of those who read the journal. In the absence of any such well-defined readership, he should probably try to write for his fellow students. Whatever the readership, the writer uses citations to serve it.

Like the scholar, the student will make mistakes—and probably more of them—even if he follows the guidelines of scholarship. But he will not make the absurd mistake of the student who, acting on the naive principle that the more footnotes one provides the better the research paper, cited a biography in order to make the point that George Washington was the first president of the United States.

What is the proper footnote style? Several are widely used. And why not? The purpose in citing sources is not to observe rules but to enable readers to find basic information readily. To avoid confusing readers, a writer must use one style throughout his research paper, but if the instructor does not prescribe a style, any that provides information briefly can be used. (Most teachers of English seem to prefer the style recommended by the Modern Language Association, the MLA Style Sheet;

some prefer that developed by the University of Chicago Press. Many psychologists and other social scientists have adopted the quite different style —remarkable for brevity—developed by the American Psychological Association.)

Most styles are alike in basic prescriptions. They require, for example, that an article or book cited in a footnote be identified fully the first time it is cited, briefly in succeeding footnotes. The various styles also prescribe that one should underline titles of periodicals and books but use quotation marks for titles of items published in periodicals.

These examples indicate the central characteristics of most footnote styles:

Book Footnotes

[1] Edward Jay Epstein, *News From Nowhere* (New York: Random House, 1973), p. 81.

[2] Harold L. Nelson and Dwight L. Teeter, Jr., *The Law of Mass Communications:* Second Edition (Mineola, N.Y.: The Foundation Press, 1973), p. 70.

[3] James McCartney, "Vested Interests of the Reporter," in *Reporting the News,* ed. Louis Lyons (Cambridge: Belknap Press of Harvard University Press, 1965), p. 98. [Note that this entry cites a contribution to a volume made up of writing by several authors. The first name identifies the writer, the second the editor.]

Periodical Footnotes

[4] Alfred Werner, "The Angry Art of Chaim Soutine," *The Progressive,* 37 (Feb. 1973), 43. [The first number identifies the volume of the periodical, the last identifies the page. Had the volume number been omitted, the page would have been indicated by "p. 43."]

[5] "Limping From Crisis to Crisis," *The Progressive,* 35 (Sept. 1971), 3 [A researcher cites unsigned editorials and articles with the details in the usual order, omitting unavailable information.]

In each case, the footnotes above are the first referring to these publications. To refer to them again, the researcher may use one of several forms. If the second footnote had cited the book by Epstein and the page that is identified in the first footnote, it could have been written

[2] *Ibid.*

If the second had been from the same book but not the same page, it could have been written

[2] *Ibid.,* 93.

Or it could have been written

[2] Epstein, 93.

When a footnote refers to a work already cited but does not appear immediately after the citation that carries full information, it can be written

[3] Epstein, *op. cit.*, 114.

or

[3] Epstein, 114.

When two footnotes have appeared citing different books by Epstein, another footnote referring to a page in one of them must be written

[11] Epstein, *Counterplot*, 88.

Although Latin abbreviations are used less often today, researchers run across them in many older works and should know what they mean. Some of the more commonly used are:

anon. Anonymous.

c. or *ca.* (*circa*) This refers to an approximate date when the actual date cannot be determined.

cf. (confer) Compare.

et al. (*et alii*) And others, an abbreviation often used for works by several authors. The first author is named, the others referred to by *et al.*

f. or *ff.* One or more pages following the page indicated.

ibid. (*ibidem*) In the same work cited in the immediately preceding footnote.

infra Below.

op. cit. (*opere citato*) In the work cited.

passim In various places, or here and there. Used to indicate that information appears on several pages.

supra Above.

Like footnote style, the location of footnotes varies. In an earlier time, many writers often used footnotes to provide information that was related to the subject but was not essential and might interrupt the flow of the narrative. They also used them to provide additional evidence or to illustrate important points. Writers who still use footnotes for these purposes usually place them at the bottom of the page so that readers can consult them while reading the narrative. Increasingly, however, many writers use footnotes primarily to give the sources of facts or quotations and sometimes to add related information that is not worth a place in the narrative. Such footnotes can be placed at the end of the narrative.

Bibliography

The value of bibliographies should be obvious to anyone who begins research by reading general articles on his subject in encyclopedias (which is sometimes a good way to begin). Most of the articles carry bibliographies that will enable the researcher to find more narrowly focused articles—which may in turn carry bibliographies leading to still other articles. In this progression, the researcher begins with the broad overview an encyclopedia provides and expands his search even as he narrows his focus from broad subject to specific topic.

Because it is designed for use, not show, a bibliography must be constructed carefully. A book or article one has merely scanned or thumbed through has no place in the bibliography. Even works a researcher has examined should not be listed unless they are reflected in his paper. The purpose is not to persuade readers that one has been industrious but to list useful works. The temptation to list too much is likely to be so strong that the researcher who is uncertain about one item or another should probably err on the side of omission.

Like the footnotes, the bibliography provides all the information needed to retrieve each item, but bibliographic style differs from footnote style. One important difference is that the author's last name is written first. That is essential because a bibliography must be alphabetized to be most useful. When a work is not signed by the author—a fairly common omission in some magazines and newspapers—it is placed in the alphabetical list by the first important word (not "A," "An," "The," etc.) of the title. (An extensive bibliography may be arranged in several alphabetical lists—one for books, another for periodicals, another for documents, etc.) The works that were cited above to show a style of footnoting might be placed in a bibliography in this style:

Epstein, Edward Jay. *News From Nowhere*. New York: Random House, 1973.

"Limping From Crisis to Crisis," *The Progressive*, 35 (September 1971), 3–4.

McCartney, James. "Vested Interests of the Reporter." *Reporting the News*. Edited by Louis Lyons. Cambridge: Belknap Press of Harvard University Press, 1965. 97–106. [Note that the page numbers at the end indicate the citation of an essay in a collection.]

Nelson, Harold L., and Dwight L. Teeter, Jr. *The Law of Mass Communications*, Second Edition. Mineola, N.Y.: The Foundation Press, 1973.

Werner, Alfred. "The Angry Art of Chaim Soutine," *The Progressive*, 37 (February 1973), 49–50.

Writing Papers from Library Research

In an earlier time, most research papers were written in a formal tone and in a rigidly formal structure. Some are still written that way, with the writer stating his subject and goals at the beginning, laying out his findings at length, then summarizing the whole—all in heavy detail. Many modern teachers and students sneer at the tone of such papers and ridicule the structure with, "Yeah, first you tell 'em what you're gonna tell 'em, then you tell 'em, then you tell 'em what you told 'em."

When a writer is so grimly serious that he writes a kind of parody of a research paper—his voice frigid, the structure a formula, footnotes sprouting everywhere—he deserves ridicule. But those who overreact to the formality may forget that it is essential to steer the reader, to tell him near the beginning of the paper where the researcher is going and how he expects to get there. This is especially essential when one reports complex research at length. Without direction, readers will become lost in thickets of facts and ideas.

That is the principal reason the first chapter of a doctoral dissertation should be an extensive guidebook, although not all dissertations are constructed from the same blueprint. Here is one blueprint for the first chapter of a dissertation.

> *Introduction*
>
> The writer begins with at least a few introductory paragraphs to provide an overview. These are ordinarily broad-brush strokes that put the reader in the large picture. The other sections of the first chapter will narrow the focus. In some cases, the introductory paragraphs are largely a review of all important research conducted by others that is related to or touches on the dissertation. The rest of the first chapter runs:
>
> *I. The Problem*
>
> First the problem is stated: a few sentences (or one sentence) that describe precisely the goals of the writer's research. The most common fault in writing dissertations is failing to describe precisely and concisely the problem investigated. This usually springs from the fact that the researcher has never actually fixed his goals but knows only that "It's in the general area of . . . ," which is almost fatal.
>
> A statement of the importance of the study is part of setting forth the problem. Unfortunately, many researchers treat it vaguely, some offhandedly. The importance of the study should be a careful statement, for a dissertation must make an original contribution to knowledge, and the writer should be able to state the value of his contribution.

II. Definition of Terms

Although the writer must define a few terms, he should not provide a detailed glossary. Those who will read the dissertation know nearly everything the writer knows about the general subject of which his topic is a part. They may not know unusual terms that the writer has come across in his research and has decided are essential to his dissertation. Such terms must be defined. The writer must also define any terms he employs in an unusual way.

III. Review of the Literature

The review of related research should be covered at this point if it was not used at the beginning of the chapter. The aim of the writer is to place his research in the realm of related studies: Researchers A, B, and C showed this, this, and this; the present study is like theirs (or builds on theirs) in that it ____________. It is unlike theirs in that it ____________. In cases in which the writer's work challenges the findings of the interpretations of another researcher—which is not unusual—he should state it at this point. In cases in which a dissertation is complex and the related research extensive, the writer may describe the various research studies in the chapters that cover related matters.

IV. Development of the Study

Here the writer should include information on his own background if it was important in his undertaking the dissertation successfully and describe the help and guidance he received. But this section centers on research methods. As methods have become more complex, descriptions of them have become more important—and usually longer. Whatever the length, readers must be told exactly how the researcher went about his work. In some cases, the "Methodology Section," as it is called, is too extensive to be merely a part of the first chapter and is itself a chapter, usually the second.

The writer must also define the limits of his study by devoting at least a few sentences to aspects that he has not examined that others might expect to find in his dissertation. The limits can usually be expressed fairly briefly, like this: "This study of Supreme Court decisions on obscene literature covers only those decisions handed down since . . . because. . . ."

V. Organization of the Remainder of the Dissertation

This section briefly describes all the other chapters, usually with a short paragraph for each.

Almost anyone who reads primarily for pleasure surely considers this structure deadening. But some such guidelines are essential if those who try to read a complex dissertation are really to comprehend it. Moreover, the writer who ignores structural guidelines is almost certain to wander for weeks in a swamp of his own words, usually because he tries to apply the principles of the essay to writing that is quite different.

But the writer of a short research paper or a journal article cannot borrow dissertation guidelines, if only because the structure they build is much too imposing. The writer can, however, borrow the idea of beginning in a way that indicates where he is going. This is indicated by the following, the first four pages of "The Abortion Dilemma," a short research paper written by a student, Diane Norburg.

COMMENTS

This paper is designed to argue a case as well as to describe and analyze. The writer wisely begins with a definition so that readers will know the basis of the argument as well as that of the description and analysis. Similarly, the focus of the argument is defined: morality.

Note that the writer manages at the outset to define the subject (abortion) and her topic (the morality of abortion) even as she provides a brief overview of the attention both receive.

Just as the writer has put first things first above, she does so here by recognizing that not every question can be answered readily, if at all.

PAPER

Abortion is the deliberately induced miscarriage of a potential human being in the embryonic or fetal stages of its growth. The purpose of this paper is not to outline the various procedures employed to effect an abortion, but rather to concentrate on the morality of the issue. Abortion is one of the most widely discussed contemporary controversies. Many organizations and religious and ethnic groups have felt a pressing need to formulate positions which indicate who they believe should be allowed to receive abortions and what stipulations must be met for the act to be justifiable. These statements rely in part on the laws drafted by the American Law Institute and encompass forced impregnation, age and marital status of the woman, medical evidence that an abortion is advisable, and criteria for the proper and legal performance of the abortion.

However, the vast majority of position papers fail to state an answer to the question which lies at the heart of the abortion controversy—Where does one draw the fine line between "murder" of a living human and abortion of a potential human? In short, the question is, "When does life begin?"

The reason for this omission is obvious. The answer cannot be deduced, even with the aid of elaborate modern science. First, one must realize that science is merely a human construct to aid in interpreting our environment; therefore, any "scientific definitions" are necessarily arbitrary. The men of science draw their own lines; they do not suddenly discover Almighty Truths which describe the natural world.

It is doubtful that science will ever be able to pinpoint the exact moment when life begins by choosing one hypothesis from among the several in existence today. When, and if they do, the abortion decision will be removed from the individual and be regulated by the penal codes of the world. Until that unlikely time, however, the question of abortion will remain a personal and moral one, and will continue to comprise one of the greatest issues in science and religion which mankind labors to solve.

It is the contention of this paper that until the debate regarding the beginning of life is brought to a final close, one must regard the issue of abortion in the light of *potential* human life. The welfare and rational desires of the future mother must be weighed against the right of the original fertilized zygote to grow and experience life after birth. Therefore, the abortion decision rests solely upon individual conscience.

It would appear reasonable, however, to assume that no person has the right to deny existence to one who was created just as he was, unless the reasons for so doing are such that *all* those involved in the considered abortion could not function healthfully and normally if the pregnancy were carried to term.

In order to include the beliefs and present viewpoints which aided in the formulation of this opinion it is necessary to begin with the existing laws.

Throughout this passage, the writer is calling upon an amalgam of information and ideas. To try to cite sources in these paragraphs would be futile. The mixture of what she knew before she began research for the paper is so mixed with her reading since she began it that singling out this source or that one is not possible.

In a more extensive paper, a writer would be wise to cite sources for several points that crop up from point to point in this passage. For example, a source that discusses the limitations of science would be in order, even a general source that does not discuss science in connection with the problem of abortion.

Having stated her beliefs, the writer is now concerned to make it clear that they are not based on pure emotion but grow out of reasoning based on research. This is central in research papers that state a position and argue a case. Although a writer need not ordinarily show that the position taken and the argument reflect the opinions of most authorities, the position and the argument are not likely to be persuasive if they are not solidly grounded.

The most recent draft of the Model Penal Code (1962), set forth by the American Law Institute, treats justifiable abortion in Section 230.3. It reads,

> *A licensed physician is justified in terminating a pregnancy if he believes there is substantial risk that continuance of the pregnancy would gravely impair the physical or mental health of the mother or that the child would be born with grave physical or mental defect, or that the pregnancy resulted from rape, incest, or other felonious intercourse.*[1]

This passage and most of the others are artfully constructed. The writer is simultaneously arguing and informing. Readers who might reject her argument can nonetheless learn from her research—enjoyable learning because the information is not presented woodenly but is entwined in the context of her argument.

The Institute also requires that two physicians certify in writing "the circumstances which they believe to justify the abortion."[2]

Different states have adopted liberal or conservative variations on the rules in the Model Penal Code. Only one state, California, does not list the *possibility* of an imperfect child as a justifiable cause for abortion. This paper holds the omission to be laudable. In the light of recognizing the sanctity of human life, potential or actualized, one must look to the existence of those handicapped individuals already born, many of whom have made valuable contributions to society. To have denied them life would have been barbaric and not in keeping with the idea of *everyone's* right to life. Few people, born deaf because their mother contracted rubella in the early weeks of her pregnancy, would opt for death simply because of their handicap. Yet, some people would have had them aborted.

The kind of information presented *here* does not call for a citation because it is general. Should the writer have cited the source of the information on spontaneous abortions of nature? That depends on a writer's judgment of the needs of readers—which is sometimes faulty. Surely most readers would accept that as a verifiable fact without documentation. It probably need not be foot-

Nature spontaneously aborts one in six babies conceived. Thus, selection is canalized to the development of only those fetuses which have the best chance for survival. When modern

noted. (But researchers must always keep in mind that a few readers are not likely to accept important information on faith, and perhaps at least one reader would wish that a source had been cited so that he could read more about it.)

obstetrics and gynecology find a fetus to be grossly malformed, the question of euthanasia might vie with that of abortion to determine whether the deformity is so severe that life would not be a gift. Once again, it is doubtful that even the most sophisticated experimentation could set up a value scale to make such a determination. One can call to mind the renowned thalidomide babies of a few years ago. Now, many of them are excelling in school and enjoying the company of their playmates. Especially noticeable is the fact that they all, without regard to the extent of their deformity, have been an addition of love to their families, just as any normal child would have been.

Like the other facts drawn from sources cited by the writer, the information on the AMA platform is valuable. It supports the writer's argument, and it provides facts that will interest anyone who cares enough about the topic to read this paper. Moreover, the writer would have been at fault had she not done research on the AMA platform. The leading association of physicians is one of the most obvious and important sources on a subject involving human life.

The platform of the American Medical Association parallels the law quite closely. In their policy adopted in June, 1967, they opposed induced abortion except in the following instances:

1. when there is a threat to the health or life of the mother,
2. when medical evidence indicates deformity in the fetus,
3. when two competent physicians concur in writing,
4. when rape or incest cause a mental or physical threat to the mother,
5. when the abortion is performed in an accredited hospital.[3]

The writer did not cite a source for this information on the number of illicit abortions because it had become common knowledge by the time she wrote.

A look at these criteria, coupled with a look at the actual statistics on abortions, shows that the majority of abortions do not legally fit into one of these categories. In spite of leniency in respect to the clause concerning the mental health of the mother, most abortions remain illicit. Many women seek abortions because the child was conceived out of wedlock or because they already have enough children and another would be too great a financial burden. If they are denied aid through legal channels, they can receive the help they want elsewhere. This situation once again points to the undeniably personal and moral aspects of abortion. In the final analysis, the lawyers and doctors have little part in the decision.

Because of the moral nature of abortion, many religious groups have formulated guidelines for their members to follow. The most outspoken criticism of abortion comes from the Roman Catholic Church. Papal encyclicals have repeatedly stressed that the only legal abortion is an *unintentional* one, in which the fetus is incidentally killed during attempts to save a mother's life. The 1968 encyclical, *Humanae Vitae*, issued by Pope Paul, states,

We must once again declare that the direct interruption of the generative process already begun, and above all, directly willed and procured abortion, even for therapeutic reasons, are to be absolutely excluded as licit means of regulating birth.[4]

Although it was not essential that the writer follow the progression from law to medicine to religion—the order depends on the structure of the paper, which might have placed them in another order—all three are certainly essential to any cogent discussion of abortion, which has obvious legal, medical, and religious qualities.

Diane Norburg ended her paper with this paragraph:

So also must abortion be available in instances in which it offers the best choice. Lest this paper seem to imply an unequivocal support of abortion when social, psychological, and economic pressures call for one, it might be wise to conclude with a saying promoted by the "Chance of a Lifetime" group in Washington: "Abortion is not healthy for children and other living things." [8] Abortion should be a ready exception, but never the rule.

Note that more sources are listed in the following bibliography of "The Abortion Dilemma" than in the list of footnotes. That is because some of the items in the bibliography contributed to Diane Norburg's knowledge of her topic but were not used in such a way that she could cite them as footnotes. That is standard practice in most research paper writing.

Footnotes

1. Society of American Friends, *Who Shall Live? Man's Control over Birth and Death* (New York: Hill and Wang, 1970), pp. 105–106.

2. *Ibid.*, p. 106.

3. *Ibid.*, p. 99.

4. *Ibid.*, p. 96.

5. John T. Noonan, *The Morality of Abortion* (Cambridge: Harvard University Press, 1970), p. 9.

6. Daniel Callahan, *Abortion: Law, Choice and Morality* (London: The Macmillan Company, 1970), p. 414.

7. Virgil C. Blum, "Public Policy Making: Why the Churches Strike Out," *America,* 124 (March 6, 1971), p. 224.

8. "Anti-Abortion Campaign," *Time,* 97 (March 29, 1971), p. 73.

Bibliography

1. "Anti-Abortion Campaign," *Time,* 97 (March 29, 1971), pp. 70–73.
2. Blum, Virgil C. "Public Policy Making: Why the Churches Strike Out," *America,* 124 (March 6, 1971), pp. 224–225.
3. Callahan, Daniel. *Abortion: Law, Choice and Morality*. London: The Macmillan Company, 1970.
4. Edmiston, Susan. "New York City—Abortion Capital," *San Francisco Chronicle* (April 21, 1971), p. 21.
5. Friends, Society of American. *Who Shall Live? Man's Control over Birth and Death*. New York: Hill and Wang, 1970.
6. Granfield, David. *The Abortion Decision*. New York: Doubleday and Company, Inc., 1969.
7. Noonan, John T. (editor). *The Morality of Abortion*. Cambridge: Harvard University Press, 1970.
   (essays used for reference include those by Paul Ramsey, James M. Gustafson, Bernard Haring, and Noonan)
8. Olds, Sally. "What We Do and Don't Know About Miscarriages," *Today's Health,* 49 (February, 1971), pp. 42–45.

"The Abortion Dilemma" is a research paper that explores a problem, a fairly common assignment in many kinds of courses. In the excerpt below from "The Novel as History: Aptheker Versus Styron," a research paper written by Don Dodson when he was a student, the writer analyzes a literary controversy, which is also a common assignment. Note that Dodson does not state explicitly the subject of his paper or his own position. But he does both implicitly, an acceptable practice that is preferable to explicit statement when it is written as artfully as this example.

COMMENTS

The artfulness of this research paper is apparent from the beginning. The writer states that the novel has been received enthusiastically and uses as counterpoint two compelling quotations by authors who consider the novel damaging to Negroes. That enables the writer to state two assumptions that are pivotal in this research paper, thus carrying readers into intellectual argument at a fast pace.

Note that Aptheker, one of the two principals in the controversy implied in the title of the paper, has not yet been mentioned, but the writer has focused immediately on the intellectual root of the controversy.

The writer properly lays a strong foundation for this ambitious paper by quoting several authorities on the relationship between history and historical fiction. It is important that he does *not* quote only those whose opinions support the argument he will make later.

PAPER

William Styron's *The Confessions of Nat Turner* is "the worst thing that's happened to Nat Turner since he was hanged," says Harlem writer William Strickland.[1] Dampening the enthusiastic response the novel has received from both readers and critics, many Negroes have asserted that it is a racist fantasy. Remarks John Henrik Clarke, an editor of *Freedomways:* "Coming at this time, it's not accidental that a white Southerner should write about Nat Turner, altering his character to express and justify a lot of current white Southern anger."[2] Such charges rest upon two assumptions: (1) there is an objective historical truth to which an historical novelist should adhere and (2) the novel reveals as much about the period in which it is written as the period it is written about.

These two assumptions are intertwined although together they are somewhat contradictory. Lion Feuchtwanger, an historical novelist of some renown, states the rule that "creative writers desire only to treat contemporary matters even in those of their creations which have history as their subject."[3] But if they want only to "discuss their relation to their own time, their own personal experience, and how much of the past has continued into the present," as Feuchtwanger says, then historical novelists must relinquish any claim to objective historical truth. "Incapsulated" history, as R. G. Collingwood calls the body of contemporary ideas about past events, is not the same as "objective" history. The two assumptions underlying attacks on *The Confessions of Nat Turner* are compatible only if they are interpreted in this way: When historical novels depart from objective truth, they demonstrate the incapsulated history in which the novelist has become ensnared.

James F. Davidson seems to share that line of reasoning when he calls for social scientists to use political fiction as signals of opinion (incapsulated history), aids to teaching, or misrepresentations to be corrected (objective history).[4] One social scientist who has appropriated Davidson's first and third uses of political fiction is Herbert Aptheker, director of the American Institute for Marxist Studies, member of the national committee of the U.S. Communist Party, and author of *American Nego Slave Revolts* and *Nat Turner's Slave Rebellion*. Aptheker attempts in a review in *The Nation* to demolish Styron's history.[5] His major points are:

When Aptheker enters, the writer not only colors in his background but is careful to be fair to Aptheker (and strengthen the research paper) by quoting and paraphrasing at length to give full expression to views he will counter later in the paper.

(1) Styron underplays the impact on Turner of the anti-slavery feelings of his peers. Nat ran away from his owner during the mid-1820s, returning after about a month because of religious qualms. He states in his confessions recorded by Gray that "the negroes found fault, and murmured against me, saying that if they had my sense they would not serve any master in the world." [6]

(2) Styron shows Turner as a broken man at the conclusion of the book. But when Gray asked whether or not he saw that he had been mistaken, Turner retorted: "Was not Christ crucified?"

(3) Styron seems to accept the "Moynihan thesis" about the disintegration of American Negro family structure at the expense of historical fact. The actual confessions indicate that Turner knew his grandmother before she died and his father before he ran away, contrary to what Styron pictures in his novel. Although Styron repeatedly

The writer provides several footnotes in the passage in which he states Aptheker's position because the points cited come from different works. (When a long passage of a research paper is given over to citations from one work, whether the writer should provide only one footnote or several usually depends upon the length of the work he cites. Several footnotes are ordinarily used in the case of a long article or a book to guide readers to the appropriate page. It is not usually necessary to use more than one citation of an article or review that covers only a page or so.)

stresses the benevolence of the master who undertook Turner's education, "Turner tells us that his parents taught him how to read—though he adds that he has no memory of just how early this occurred," according to Aptheker.[7]

(4) Styron has Turner reject the Great Dismal Swamp as a possible refuge since he thought the slaves could not survive in it. But the fact is that the swamp *was* a refuge for runaway slaves for generations.

(5) Styron describes the Turner rebellion as an almost unique expression of slave discontent. It was just one out of 250 slave uprisings, plots and conspiracies, however—and not even the longest or most deadly one at that.

(6) Styron ignores the repressive laws that were passed throughout the South just before the rebellion. Virginia in 1831 passed legislation allowing free Negroes to be sold into slavery, making it unlawful assembly for free Negroes or mulattoes to meet to learn how to read or write, and forbidding any white person to instruct Negroes for pay.[8]

(7) Styron portrays Will as a mad monster whose sadistic lust distressed Turner. But in the actual confessions he tells Nat that "his life was worth no more than others, and his liberty as dear to him." Said Turner: "This was enough to put him in full confidence." [9]

(8) Styron stresses that Turner was able to recruit only 70 or 75 men in a county with more than 7,000 slaves. But considering the obstacles—"the system of control, the stakes involved, the apparent lack of prior preparation"—the number was impressive.[10]

(9) Styron has a master arm his loyal slaves to resist the rebels. This figment of his imagination has no evidence to substantiate it.

Like the first few paragraphs, this passage makes it evident that the writer has ranged widely in research. It would have been simpler for him to continue to focus on Aptheker versus Styron and thus devote the rest of his paper to the center of that controversy. But he has wisely added a dimension by exploring other elements. The research that went into this passage taught the writer, who then uses it to teach readers.

About the only historical criticism that Aptheker misses in *The Nation* review is that Turner was married. That he should be portrayed as a lifelong celibate who lusted after a white teenager is offensive to some Negroes. Howard Meyer, a white New York lawyer who has written a biography of Thomas Wentworth Higginson, colonel of a Northern black regiment in the Civil War, says: "In an 1861 essay in *Atlantic Monthly* Higginson clearly states that Turner had a young wife and that she was a slave belonging to a different owner." [11] To accept these criticisms founded in the notion of an objective history is to come to one conclusion about the incapsulated history embodied in *The Confessions of Nat Turner:* Styron has systematically etched a "pattern amounting to consequential distortion—a distortion widespread in the United States at the present time." [12]

What is that distortion? As Aptheker and others interpret the novel, Styron has systematically reworked historical fact to turn the Negro into a Sambo. Why else have a Negro turn in the runaway Hark just as he is about to achieve his freedom? Why else have a jealous black toady haul young Nat before his master for taking a book? Why else have loyal slaves fire upon their fellows and kick the wounded Hark? Styron himself admits it in a review of Aptheker's *American Negro Slave Revolts:* "The character (not characterization) of 'Sambo,' shiftless, wallowing happily in the dust, was no cruel figment of the imagination, Southern or Northern, but did in truth exist." [13]

In this important passage, the writer seems to argue with Aptheker against Styron. That is not actually a contradiction of the position the writer takes later, however, because

So, under Aptheker's scalpel, what at first appeared to be unpleasant truths about the Negro now seem to be unpleasant untruths. What do the Negroes in *The Confessions of Nat* he uses qualifying words ("seem," for example) and poses questions (consider the last sentence in this paragraph) instead of making statements. The effect is to pull readers on to discover the writer's real belief, much as a novelist pulls his readers on by using suspense.

Turner desire? Hootch and poontang. How do they act? They thieve and dissemble, they wheedle and flatter, they scrape and shuffle, they smirk and giggle, they sing and dance. No noble savages, they are merely children—ignorant, superstitious, gullible and trusting. Such qualities are not those of the intractable rebels Aptheker paints in *American Negro Slave Revolts*. It seems, then, that however great *The Confessions of Nat Turner* may be as literature, it is somehow morally defective. It is marred by the insidious racism of American culture. Such a conclusion demands a reassessment of the novel. It may be technically brilliant, but as literature it must also stand on its moral presuasiveness. For must not great literature express a moral vision? And must not that vision be humane? Styron seems to suffer not from a failure of his imagination, but from a failure of his humanity.

Here, the writer signals his belief and begins to spell out the reasons for it. As always in this paper, the writer does not ask readers to trust his bald judgment of the facts; he guides them to his sources with appropriate footnotes.

But wait. Before *The Confessions of Nat Turner* is condemned, one question must be answered: Are Aptheker's criticisms valid? Consider some of them. He says Styron makes Nat reject the Great Dismal Swamp as a refuge. In the novel, however, Turner jots down the following notes: "*'Dismal swamp' grand retreat for my force. . . . Many fresh water springs & unbelievable profusion of game . . . Fish by millions. . . . Some land c'ld be cultivated for vegtbls. Of course endless supply of timber for shelter, revetments, etc.*" [14]

Although Aptheker says Styron portrays Nat as a broken man as death approaches, the novel belies his charge:

And already the quill pen was out, the paper laid flat on the lid of the writing box, and the sound of scratching as Gray hastened to get down to busi-

ness. "What'd the Lord say to you again, Nat? 'Confess your sins, that' —what?"

"Not confess you sins, sir," I replied. "He said confess. Just that. Confess. That is important to relate. There was no your sins *at all.* Confess, that all nations may know . . ." [15]

And as the jailer comes to take Nat to hang: "*Yes,* I think just before I turn to greet him, *I would have done it all again. I would have destroyed them all.*" [16] All except Margaret Whitehead. Is this a broken man? The actual confessions—in which Turner uses words like "stone," "helpless," and "forsaken"—denigrate his morale more than Styron does.

Here, the writer uses close analysis to challenge Aptheker's point of view, quoting Aptheker's source against him. (Matching the two quotations in this paragraph teaches an important lesson. One must be certain—as Aptheker obviously was not—that his paraphrase is an accurate interpretation of his source.)

To repeat a statement from Aptheker's review: "Turner tells us that his parents taught him how to read—though he adds that he has no memory of just how early this occurred." Compare this to his more accurate statement in *Nat Turner's Slave Rebellion:* "Nat himself was unable to account for his ability to read and write, though this is often ascribed to his parents' instructions." [17] In Nat's confessions to Gray, the only record of his words, Nat makes absolutely no reference to learning to read from his parents. But Gray, a secondary source for the historian, states parenthetically "(it was taught him by his parents)." [18]

The writer is making a serious charge and knows that it must be supported. That he does support it seems clear from the evidence he offers. (But one who makes such a charge without evidence is as unethical as he is unpersuasive.)

If Aptheker is a skillful pedant, he is a vulgar scholar: vulgar, not because his central thesis of slave rebelliousness is untenable, but because he maintains it with such shoddy evidence and such unrelenting dogmatism. Aptheker, as the historian, should be wary of literalism in using historical sources. He should realize that the discipline of history is the most personal, intuitive, and aesthetic of social sciences. It

Note especially that the writer demonstrates here as he has earlier that the structure of the research paper, like the structure of history, is not a prison. To present research persuasively, a writer need not send fact and idea plodding after fact and idea like convicts lining up for a meal. The graceful essay style that lights this passage makes it a pleasure for a reader to absorb information.

cannot be conducted without the active engagement of the historian's creative imagination. The structure of history is not a cell in which the historian must imprison himself, but an open field in which he is free to move as long as he does not trample the grass underfoot. Objective historical truth is unknowable. To make that statement is not to succumb to obscuratism. It is rather to underscore the essential difference between truth and fact—a qualitative, not quantitative, difference. Aptheker, the historian, does not understand this. Styron, the novelist, does.

That is not to say fiction and history are interchangeable. They are not. While the historian is free to organize known facts into a creative whole (which then allows him to speculate where facts are lacking), he is still subservient to the most trifling fact—to the tiniest blade of grass in the field. The novelist is thrall to a different master: psychological consistency rather than historical fact.

Dodson ends his paper with these sentences:

> It is Aptheker who muddles the distinction between fiction and history by denying any autonomy to the former, with a dogmatism lacking in Davidson's suggestion. The problem of historical fiction is indeed a knotty one. But the knot hangs Aptheker, not Styron.

Dodson's paper, which covers more than twice the length quoted above, carries thirty-five footnotes and a bibliography listing fourteen sources. Because his footnotes and his bibliography are written in the form of earlier lists, it is not necessary to reprint them here.

Writing Papers: Three Kinds of Research

A researcher who limits his exploration of a topic to reading books and periodicals is always in danger of writing a one-dimensional paper. Instead of using the living world as a source, he uses only what is in print. It is true that the authors of books and articles have captured much of the world and have expressed its essences. It is also true that a thoughtful student who bases his writing on what has appeared in print is not actually limiting himself to it. Because he brings to his reading a self that has seen and heard and acted, his writing is invariably informed by his experiences. One can grant all this, however, and still argue that the researcher who chooses a topic, then explores it in the living world as well as in the library is much more likely to describe and analyze reality. (He is more likely, too, to prepare himself for a challenging career. Most interesting work involves asking intelligent questions, observing accurately, and reading analytically.)

That is why this book describes all three research methods. And that is why it ends with a research paper based on all three. The writer, a student named Peter Aleshire, interviewed, observed, and read to produce his paper on "The Journalistic Excellence of *The Christian Science Monitor*."

COMMENTS

Like the research paper by Don Dodson, this begins with no explicit statement of purpose. Instead, readers are told implicitly in the first three paragraphs that the promise of the title will be carried out through close examination of the newspaper. Like this writer, one who *unfolds* his report, somewhat in the form of story, must be careful that the opening paragraphs give the readers a sense of the purpose and direction of the paper.

No footnotes are needed until the end of the second paragraph because the preceding references to publications indicated on which page each story could be found. Because the reference to the *Monitor* story in the issue of June 6 does not indicate on which page it appears, a footnote is needed to enable readers to find the story easily.

PAPER

On the afternoon of June 3, 1973, the Soviet equivalent of the Concorde crashed during an air show in France. On the morning of June 4, many American newspapers carried banner headlines like the one that appeared in the San Jose, California, *Mercury:* "FIERY SST CRASH KILLS 14."

In contrast, the lead story in *The Christian Science Monitor* on June 4 was headlined "Dean Vs. Nixon: The crucial credibility gap." On June 5, the *Monitor* carried a front-page picture of a Soviet Tupelov SST waiting on a runway, while a Concorde took to the air in the background. The caption on the photo mentioned the tragic crash of June 3. On June 6, the *Monitor* carried a story headlined "Impact of Soviet SST Tragedy," in which the ramifications of the air crash were explored.[1]

This suggests the philosophy that distinguishes the *Christian Science Monitor* from most other newspapers. Its philosophy, to "harm no man but bless all mankind," has both religious and journalistic roots. The method used is interpretative reporting, for those who write and edit the *Monitor* are more interested in the implications of events than in details. Underlying all *Monitor* articles is the assumption that news must be placed in a framework to have meaning.

The high quality of the *Monitor*'s effort can be verified through both its professional standing and close analysis of its coverage. In polls of publishers, editors, journalism professors, and Washington correspondents, the *Monitor* was rated among the top newspapers in the nation.[2] It is even more impressive on close inspection.

The first three paragraphs focused on newspapers as sources. In the third and fourth paragraphs, the writer provides information from two books and cites them.

The *Monitor* is certainly a national newspaper, and probably an international one. Its slogan is unambiguous, "an International Daily Newspaper," which is not simple boasting. The *Monitor* maintains offices in Bonn, Beirut, Hong Kong, Latin America, London, Moscow, Nairobi, Paris, Saigon, Tokyo, the United Nations, and seven major American cities. The international attitude is revealed by the change, in 1920, from designating reporters abroad as foreign correspondents, to calling them "Overseas Correspondents." [3]

To cite these issues of the *Monitor* in a footnote would be useless. This paragraph provides all the detail readers need to find each story.

The international orientation is obvious on every front page. From June 4 to June 8, 1973, the paper carried 38 front-page stories, 14 of them on international affairs or the internal affairs of a nation other than the U.S.

This international outlook has several roots. The paper has a faintly missionary flavor and diffuse geographic support. Though there are no exact records, it is likely that the core of the *Monitor*'s subscribers are Christian Scientists, who are scattered widely.

Relying on geographically diffuse

subscribers has a number of effects. Because there is a time-lag between printing the paper and distributing it so widely, the *Monitor* is at a serious disadvantage in printing hot scoops. In a sense, radio and television have disqualified all the print media from competition for fast-breaking news, but the *Monitor* cannot even be in the running with other newspapers. So instead of working to place news on the front page first, the *Monitor* works to place it in context. The value of the *Monitor* is not the facts it prints, which are available faster elsewhere, but in the understanding it offers.

Most of the information in this short passage is common knowledge among those who are interested in the reporting of public affairs and no sources need be cited. Part of the passage, including the sentence beginning "The value," is not cited because it offers an insight by the writer.

The *Monitor*'s time-lag forces it to give less dramatic play to the news. The San Jose *Mercury* announced in a banner headline on June 8 "BOLD ASTRONAUTS SALVAGE SKYLAB," but the *Monitor* had to drop the same story in its June 8, 1973, issue to the middle of the page, with a modest headline noting, "Space walk scores." [4] Because most *Monitor* readers receive the paper the day after it is printed, it would look faintly silly trumpeting news the readers had heard and read the day before.

Footnotes 4 and 5 represent the kind of citation the careful writer provides to make certain that readers can find sources easily. The dates of the issues the writer refers to are included in the text, but the page numbers are not.

The paragraphs beginning "This emphasis" and "The *Monitor* has" show how a writer develops insights—from reading, thinking, and interviewing—and offers them as his own (properly), then illustrates them with examples. The examples help support his judgment and provide specific information that will interest and inform readers.

This emphasis on the long-range meaning of news gives rise to *Monitor* specialties. One is the "relationship" story. On June 6, for example, the paper published a story on the fact that a group of Greek colonels had deposed of King Constantine.[5] Not content merely to report this bit of news, the *Monitor* compared it to the situation of the Spanish Monarchy. The result for the reader was an increased understanding of each.

The *Monitor* has also made an art of the follow-up story. During a confrontation at Wounded Knee, South Dakota, between Indians and federal officials, the *Monitor* ran a six-article series followed by an editorial statement.[6] Between June 4 and June 8, the editors published a front-page article on the Watergate scandal every day. In that same period, the *Monitor* published a three-article series on integration and an editorial statement. Such continuing coverage emphasizes that the *Monitor* is not restricted to trailing passively after the breaking news of the day.

It should be obvious that a writer cannot always find in print everything he should know to explore a topic. This short quotation suggests the value of interviews. It is footnoted primarily to cite the *time* of the interview, which is important because conditions may have been different before and may be different later.

David Holmstrom, San Francisco Bureau Chief for the *Monitor*, explained the *Monitor*'s goals with, "You can't come up with a good handle, but here's what you ought to be thinking about. It's more important to know *why* than anything else. The compelling thing for the correspondent is that he take a harder look at things and put a little less emphasis on the short-term news." [7]

These goals have a decisive impact on the way news stories are written and enable writers to use a variety of lead styles. One of the most distinctive—one in keeping with the interpretative tradition—is the lead which provides perspective by relating current news to associated events and historical causes.

Again, examples are valuable to support the writer's judgment and to interest and inform readers. The three paragraphs in this passage that begin with dates show *exactly* how *Monitor* reporters provide "perspective by relating current news to associated events and historical causes."

On May 10, 1973, a single headline, "Double trouble in Cambodia" linked two stories: one on Congress and funding for the war, the other reporting from Cambodia. The lead on the Cambodia story ran: "American Diplomats are struggling once again with the problems involving a pair of brothers running a Southeast Asian Government. Ten years ago, it was the Diem brothers in South Vietnam. Today it's the Lon Brothers in Cambodia." [8]

On May 21, an article covered Russian leader Brezhnev's trip to West Germany with a lead beginning,

Footnotes 8 through 15 might have been eliminated had the writer chosen to include the page numbers of each issue carrying the sentences he quotes. Except for the paragraph that includes the information cited in Footnote 12, the text carries all the information needed except page numbers.

Why did the writer not include the page numbers (and eliminate the footnotes)? So few readers are likely to want *all* the information provided in footnotes that including page numbers would weight the text too heavily with detailed information. In fact, the passage might have been more readable had the writer eliminated from the text some of the dates of *Monitor* issues and provided them in footnotes.

"Leonid I. Brezhnev's visit to West Germany is just as dramatic, just as radical, just as freighted with long meanings, just as important to other peoples around the world as was President Nixon's trip to Peking." [9]

On April 24 appeared an article headlined, "Will non-whites some day rule South Africa?" It began: " 'Black consciousness' is sweeping South Africa as nothing has since Afrikaner nationalism caught fire here some 30 years ago."

Another often-used *Monitor* lead is more conventional, serving to introduce the article directly. On April 24, an article headlined "Watergate alters U.S. political arena," began: "The Watergate scandal already has given the U.S. political outlook a mighty shake." There followed an itemized survey of the major presidential hopefuls. The writer used one of the *Monitor*'s standard techiques, introducing major points in the article with a dot at the beginning of each paragraph.[11]

Monitor styles enable reporters to give a light touch to news stories. One headlined "On a hairy forest-eater," begins, "What is two inches long, has tufts of hair, five pairs of blue spots, six pairs of red spots, sometimes travels by trailer, and has an appetite nothing short of colossal? [the gypsy moth, which is immigrating to California with vacationers]." [12]

A story headlined "White House legmen recount cover-up" begins: "Every time John J. Caulfield heard the words 'President of the United States' from one of his superiors, he mentally clicked his heels." [13]

Many of the *Monitor* leads are downright literary—quality prose, not merely the word pulp of much journalism. For example, a story headlined

"Britain pondering morals in high places," begins, "This capital is full of traffic and sunshine, green grass and gay flowers, and visitors laughing together in foreign tongues. But Westminster, at the heart of it, is rather a sad, silent, and reflective place. It weighs scandal in its hand and ponders the cost of it." [14]

An article headed "Anne and Mark plan for November Wedding" begins, "It now seems certain that it will be November when they bring the pumpkin from the palace stables, harness the mice, and send for the magic wand." [15]

Although it may be doubtful that any reader would be likely to follow behind the writer, repeating all his work to check its validity, a careful writer provides everything that *might* be useful. That is the reason for Footnotes 16 and 17.

The *Monitor* uses a relatively high number of descriptive adjectives and adverbs on its front page, at least in relation to the *San Jose Mercury*. In ten front pages the *Monitor* averaged 152 descriptive adverbs and adjectives. The *Mercury* averaged 84.[16]

All of these examples illustrate the interpretative freedom which is given to *Monitor* correspondents. *Monitor* writers do more summarizing, explaining, and emphasizing than almost any others. One indication is the relatively low number of attributed statements which appear on the front page. Five *Monitor* front pages averaged 11 quotations (high 17, low 7). The *Mercury* averaged 16 (high 24, low 19).

Here begins a return to the interview with Holmstrom. The writer used a short quotation from the interview earlier because there it would best fit the structure of his paper. The temptation is usually strong to put *all* interview material in one place because that is the simplest way one can organize research material. But the structure of the research paper, not simplicity for the writer, should dictate placement.

Given the *Monitor's* reliance on vivid, comprehensive stories the role of the individual correspondent is crucial. David Holmstrom is expected to know about everything important happening in or around San Francisco—or at least know who *does* know. One might expect one of the high priests of interpretative journalism to be different from other journalists, but Holmstrom is as unintimidating as the *Monitor's* headlines. His surroundings suit his personal style. The San Fran-

Here the writer includes observations he made while interviewing Holmstrom, most of them designed to show where, how, and by whom the newspaper he analyzes is created.

Again, such information is not available in print; the writer must use interviewing and observation to provide it. Is the information useful? The answer depends on the needs and desires of readers. Some might be so concerned with the analysis of the *Monitor* that they would consider this an irritating interruption. Perhaps most readers would not only appreciate the color and flavor provided by this kind of research but would consider it an important part of the analysis.

cisco office of the *Monitor* is three small rooms, one of which serves as Holmstrom's office. One wall is hidden behind two large filing cabinets, an immense pile of back issues of the San Francisco *Examiner*, the San Francisco *Chronicle*, the Los Angeles *Times*, and the *Monitor*, and a battered swivel chair. Holmstrom's desk is a substantial metal affair littered with papers. One twelve-inch stack of papers represents secondary story ideas, another eight-inch stack contains material for primary stories. The walls are off-white, the carpet a discouraged green. A Smith-Corona portable electric typewriter rests on a marked but cheerful wooden typewriter table.

Holmstrom himself is a tall soft-motioned man with a full grey-spotted beard and an extensive, thinly disguised bald spot. He wears slacks and a sport-coat and tie which seem as informal as coffee and doughnuts. He goes about his work with the unpressured enthusiasm of the self-employed. Some days, he explains, are less exciting than others. On this particular day there is even less pressure than usual because two of his stories are in Boston awaiting publication.

At nine o'clock he drives in his red Volkswagen to a press conference called by a group opposing the expanded use of atomic power plants. At 10:30 he returns, makes several phone calls, scans the morning papers, and opens the mail. Just after 12 he walks two blocks for lunch.

After lunch he makes another flurry of phone calls and receives several. He is working on a story about driver training schools. He has just finished a story about the reduced turnover in university presidencies and another about grade-schoolers' opinions of Watergate. In the late afternoon he wanders over to Blackquake, an exhibition put on by the black community.

This part of the interview-observation findings is obviously central in analyzing the newspaper.

Holmstrom says that about eight per cent of his stories are suggested to him by his editors; the rest are his ideas. The paper prints nearly everything he submits. His days vary considerably, depending on what he's working on. Sometimes he takes work home, but he is usually able to avoid that. The editors, he explains, don't care how or when he works. They just want him to produce good stories.

Note that the writer never refers to himself in these paragraphs (a fact that will be commented upon below).

This freedom is enough to start any cub reporter on another paper shouting for a *Monitor* job application. The extent to which *Monitor* reporters are allowed to call on their own experience to assess events seems to be one of the highest indications of professionalism. The *Monitor* journalist is not merely a recorder of a scene, he is an observer who has the crucial responsibility of making sense of it.

When, if ever, should a writer include himself—his own experiences? Never—if he is merely being self-indulgent. It would have been a sign of self-indulgence for example, had the writer referred to himself in the passages above in which he was interviewing and observing. As the writing of those passages indicates, a writer *can* keep himself out of a scene he is reporting. In most cases, he should so that readers can focus on the scene, not divide their attention between the scene and the writer.

Here, however, the writer's experiences are important because they enable readers to understand interpretative reporting in the *Monitor* by contrasting it with the writer's attempts.

Writing for the *Stanford Daily,* I am often admonished for straying from my source, throwing in unattributed statements, and making generalizations. This is partly due to the cautious rule-orientation of the partially competent, but there is a basic validity in it—as applied to my writing. Colorful and individual as interpretative writing may be, it is by far the most difficult type of news writing. The essential difficulty is that, to interpret events, the writer must understand them. It is not enough to dash out with pencil and notebook and find out who did what to whom. To write in the *Monitor*'s style, the writer must be familiar with the causes, the consequences, the personalities, and the interrelations of events. This is possible only with thought-provoking experiences. In researching the history of the *Monitor,* I found names which now decorate the *Monitor*'s front page cropping up in the *Monitor* of the Thirties. Men who are writing for the *Monitor* have been in and out of newsrooms for many years. A solid block of experience seems to make interpretative news writing possible.

The basic question is, What makes this type of writing so successful in the *Monitor*? The answer, curiously, may be in the paper's sponsorship by a church.

Note that the history of the *Monitor* is traced late in the paper, not at the beginning. In a few cases of historical research, a writer should begin his paper by tracing the beginnings of his subject. But that is usually both the simplest and the dreariest way to begin—and it suggests to readers that the topic the writer will examine *is* history. Instead, most research papers focus on something other than the history of a topic. The writer must *use* history for illumination, as this writer is doing, at an appropriate point.

Mary Baker Eddy, the founder of Christian Science, decided the church should print a daily newspaper. In the early years of the church, Mrs. Eddy was a vigorous and dominant leader. Her leadership was accepted by the membership almost as an article of faith; her status made the *Monitor* a service to God for many of the members and enlisted their enthusiasm. Before 1908, the Church had been publishing various denominational periodicals, often with religiously oriented articles about newsworthy events. Mrs. Eddy did not want the *Monitor* to be a denominational publication but a paper which would stand against the wave of "yellow journalism"—a nonsensational paper which would focus on the positive in human experience and the deeper meanings of events. From its inception the *Monitor* was oriented toward interpretative reporting.[19]

The early staff members of the *Monitor* were staunch Christian Scientists. A surprisingly large number of them were also experienced journalists. They brought a dedication to the Church as well as to journalism.

In the early days, these ideals merged a bit too conspicuously. Often the paper gave front-page prominence to Church events in Boston. And, for a time, the editorial page was well supplied with religion. In 1911, Mrs. Eddy decided this was not in keeping with the goals of the paper and banished religion to an inside section. Now a religious article is published daily on the Home Forum page.[20] On rare occasions the Church slips on to the front page, as it did on June 5, 1973, a story about a major church meeting. This is definitely an exception.

Although most of this paper is devoted to praise of the *Monitor,* the writer wisely indicates that the newspaper has flaws.

Occasionally the *Monitor*'s religious sensitivity has led it astray. The most famous example was the retouching of a photograph of a World War II beach-head to disguise bodies as logs. More mundane are such things as the use of "passed-on" in place of "died." [21] Another convention with a religious origin is never to mention people's ages.

Generally, the combination of professional and religious idealism is an essential factor in the *Monitor*'s high quality. As Holmstrom, who is a Christian Scientist, said of the *Monitor*: "Its inception was during a time of sensational and inaccurate reporting. The *Monitor* stressed the integrity of the individual and the broader meaning of life, and emphasis on what is positive. There was a point when there was a tendency to be too distant and aloof; writers seldom rolled up their sleeves and got into the nitty-gritty of things. But now that's not so true. I think the mission of the *Monitor* makes the *Monitor* an interesting, and an important, thing to do with your life." [22]

Here, again, the writer uses interview material where it fits the structure, not with all the other quotations from the interview. Because this is the section of the paper devoted to history, Holmstrom's reference to *Monitor* history belongs here.

As in an earlier case, the writer cites the quotation in a footnote to give the date of the interview in case the time should ever be a question for other researchers who may refer to his paper.

This dual idealism has provided the paper with eager applicants and basic principles to measure the quality of their work. There is always the ideal to refer to, to determine whether the paper is maintaining the proper emphasis in selecting and explaining the news.

In this the structure of the organization is important. The paper is supervised by the Publishing Society and the Board of Directors of the Church, which are staffed by full-time employees. These officials are in constant contact with the editors of the paper, and their chief concern is its moral base.[23]

The Church has also contributed to the *Monitor*'s success more concretely. The circulation of the paper in 1973 is roughly 185,000. Reader support gives rise to a special advertising policy in which the *Monitor* urges its readers to patronize its advertisers. The *Monitor* will not accept advertisements for medicines, alcoholic beverages, or tobacco, requires advertisers to adhere to certain guidelines on the size and composition of their ads, and often checks their claims. At the local level, committees of Christian Science Churches handle subscriptions and urge church members to patronize *Monitor* advertisers.[24]

Like the earlier indication that the *Monitor* has flaws, this passage on the newspaper's financial problems is important to provide a kind of balance for all the praise. The passage is more important, of course, because it is central to analyzing the *Monitor*—and the news-reading tastes of many Americans.

Considering the editorial and advertising strengths of the *Monitor*, it might seem that the paper would be on a solid financial base. However, there are indications of financial problems. In recent years the size of the paper has been reduced and the writing thinned. About three years ago letters were sent to Christian Scientists appealing for greater support. Ironically, the chief problem springs from the high quality of the *Monitor*. According to a survey, each copy is read by seven people, six of whom do not pay for it.[25] Also, the presence of the words "Christian Science" in the title reduces subscriptions among those of other denominations. And the lack of local news—as an international paper, the *Monitor* has no home base—creates another problem.

But there may be an even more

significant cause for the *Monitor*'s problems. Perhaps too few people *want* to read a high-quality newspaper. Banner headlines sell many other papers. Many readers of other papers are attracted by grisly details which the *Monitor*'s principles exclude from its pages.

This problem may go deeper. One highly intelligent pre-med student said that he disliked the *Monitor* because he simply wanted the hard news from a paper; he wanted to be able to glean the important facts from the first few paragraphs without being obligated to read the entire story.

This attitude is somewhat like that of the boosters of TV situation comedies: "Sure the Advocates is a higher quality program than I Love Lucy, but I watch TV to relax." The danger is that Lucy will drive the Advocates off the air. Few newspapers have the international outlook and the integrity of the *Monitor*. Will America support even a few such papers?

Observe that the writer wisely does not condemn the American people for their lack of attention to a high-quality newspaper. Although his tone makes it evident that he believes that Americans err in failing to read the *Monitor* and the other newspapers that would help them understand public affairs, he ends with a question. Such an ending is likely to provoke thought. Had the writer condemned, many readers of his paper would probably be placed on a bristling defensive.

Because the footnotes and bibliography are written in styles shown previously, it is necessary to indicate only how one cites interviews. Footnote 7 reads:

> [7] Interview with David Holmstrom in his San Francisco office, November 17, 1973.

Another citation of the same interview reads:

> [18] Holmstrom interview.

The writer was correct in deciding that the informal conversation with the pre-med student should not be cited in a footnote. More substantial interviews require citations. If an interviewee asks that his name not be used, the citation can read:

> [26] Interview with student who asked to be anonymous.

Peter Aleshire's interviews with Holmstrom and with the student add an important dimension to the research paper. The interviews and the description of Holmstrom's office and Holmstrom at work provide viewpoints—not to mention color and flavor—that could not be obtained by reading. Aleshire's experience as a college newspaper reporter help readers appreciate the problems in writing the kind of journalism the *Christian Science Monitor* provides.

Although a few topics can be researched thoroughly in the library alone, it should be obvious that most lend themselves to exploration in the living world as well. Everyone who is able to conduct research has abilities that can be employed, improved, and refined in the living world. Why not use them?

Notes

Chapter 1—Pursuing and Interpreting Facts

[1] Frank Maloy Anderson, *The Mystery of A Public Man* (Minneapolis: University of Minnesota Press, 1948).

[2] James Brussell, *Casebook of a Crime Psychiatrist* (New York: Bernard Geis, 1968).

[3] T. S. Eliot, *The Rock* (New York: Harcourt, Brace & Jovanovich, 1934).

[4] Carl L. Becker, "Everyman His Own Historian," *American Historical Review* 37 (January, 1932), 221–36.

[5] A. Kent MacDougall, "Radical Historians Get Growing Following, Dispute 'Myths' of Past," *Wall Street Journal*, 19 October 1971, p. 1.

[6] David Hackett Fisher, *Historians' Fallacies* (New York: Harper & Row, 1970).

[7] Richard D. Altick, *The Scholar Adventurers* (New York: Macmillan, 1950), p. 15.

[8] James B. Conant, *Science and Common Sense* (New Haven, Conn.: Yale University Press, 1950), p. 50.

[9] Quoted in Morris R. Cohen and Ernest Nagel, *An Introduction to Logic and Scientific Method* (New York: Harcourt, Brace & Jovanovich, 1934), pp. 398–9.

[10] Clark L. Hull, "A Primary Social Science Law," *The Scientific Monthly* 71 (October, 1950), 225.

[11] S. M. Lipset, The Psychology of Voting: "An Analysis of Political Behavior," in G. Lindsey, ed., *Handbook of Social Psychology*, vol. 2 (Reading, Mass.: Addison-Wesley, 1954), pp. 1124–75.

[12] Eugene J. Webb, et al., *Unobtrusive Measures: Nonreactive Research in the Social Sciences* (Chicago: Rand McNally, 1966).

[13] Harold D. Lasswell, *The Future of Political Science* (New York: Atherton, 1963), p. 190.

[14] Abraham Kaplan, *The Conduct of Inquiry* (Scranton, Pa.: Chandler, 1964).

Chapter 2—Evaluating Facts

[1] Brit Hume, "Checking out Dita Beard's Memo," *Harper's*, August, 1972, p. 38.

[2] Lester Markel, "Interpretation of Interpretation," *Nieman Reports*, Spring, 1971, p. 10.

[3] Ray Mungo, *Famous Long Ago* (Boston: Beacon Press, 1970), pp. 75–76.

[4] Quoted in Edward P. Thompson, *The Making of the English Working Class* (New York: Pantheon Books, 1964), p. 210.

[5] Robert J. Donovan, "The Rules Have Changed," *Nieman Reports*, March, 1970, p. 10.

[6] Alden Vaughan, *The New England Frontier* (Boston: Little, Brown, 1965), p. 62.

[7] Quoted in *Congressional Record*, 18 July 1972, p. S11111.

[8] Julius Duscha, "Your Friendly Finance Company and Its Friends on Capitol Hill," *Harper's*, October, 1962, p. 76.

[9] Associated Press, "VIPS Meet the GIs—A Muddy Dialogue," *San Francisco Chronicle*, 8 June 1970, p. 1.

[10] Stephen Isaacs, "The Pitfalls of Polling," *Columbia Journalism Review*, May-June, 1972, p. 13.

Chapter 3—Interviewing

[1] David J. Weiss and Rene V. Dawis, "An Objective Validation of Factual Interview Data," *Journal of Applied Psychology* 44 (1960) 381–85.

[2] Kirk Polking, "An Exclusive Tape-Recorded Interview with Irving Wallace," *Writer's Yearbook*, 1966, p. 86.

[3] A summary of many studies may be found in Charles F. Carrel and Robert L. Kahn, "Interviewing," in Gardner Lindzey and Elliot Aronson, eds., *The Handbook of Social Psychology*, vol. 2 (Reading, Mass.: Addison-Wesley), pp. 526–95.

[4] Quoted in Daniel J. Boorstin, *The Image, or What Happened to the American Dream* (New York: Atheneum, 1962), p. 15.

[5] Eugene J. Webb and Jerry R. Salancik, *The Interview, or The Only Wheel in Town,* Journalism Monographs (Austin: University of Texas).

[6] Joseph and Stewart Alsop, *The Reporter's Trade* (New York: Reynal, 1958).

[7] Stewart Alsop, *The Center* (New York: Harper & Row, 1968), p. 201.

[8] Stanley L. Payne, *The Art of Asking Questions* (Princeton: Princeton University Press, 1951), pp. 8–9.

[9] Andrew Collins, "The Interview: An Educational Research Tool," An Occasional Paper Issued by the ERIC Clearinghouse on Educational Media and Technology, p. 3.

[10] Ibid.

[11] Ibid., p. 6.

[12] Although surveying by questionnaire is different from interviewing, the processes in each method as described here are the same.

[13] Personal communication from the author, 22 July 1972.

[14] Eleanor and Nathan Maccoby, "The Interview: A Tool of Social Science," in Gardner Lindzey, ed., *The Handbook of Social Psychology,* Vol. 1, (Reading, Mass.: Addison-Wesley, 1954), p. 453.

[15] Ibid., pp. 476–78.

[16] Herbert H. Hyman, et al., *Interviewing in Social Research* (Chicago: University of Chicago Press, 1954), p. 159.

[17] Saul Pett, "An Interview With An Interviewer," *AP World,* Winter, 1967–68, p. 32.

[18] Payne, *The Art of Asking Questions,* p. 57.

[19] Webb and Salancik, *The Interview, or The Only Wheel in Town,* p. 29.

[20] Alfred C. Kinsey, Wardell Pomeroy, and Clyde Martin, *Sexual Behavior in the Human Male* (Philadelphia: Saunders, 1948), p. 53.

[21] *San Francisco Chronicle,* 2 February 1967, p. 1.

[22] Stuart A. Rice, "Contagious Bias in the Interview: A Methodological Note," *American Journal of Sociology* 35 (1929), pp. 420–23.

[23] Collins, "The Interview: An Educational Research Tool," p. 9.

[24] Transcript of "A Conversation With President Nixon," CBS Television, 2 January 1972, pp. 1–2.

[25] Associated Press, "The Art of the Interview," *AP World,* Summer, 1972, p. 22.

[26] A. J. Liebling, *The Most of A. J. Liebling* (New York: Simon and Schuster, 1963), p. 157.

[27] Transcript of "A Conversation With President Nixon," pp. 13–14.

[28] Alfred Appel, Jr., "Nabokov: A Portrait," *The Atlantic*, November, 1971, p. 91.

[29] Jane Howard, "A Six-Year Literary Vigil," *Life*, 7 January 1966, p. 71.

[30] Associated Press, "The Art of The Interview," p. 19.

Chapter 4—Observing

[1] Annie Dillard, "Sight Into Insight," *Harper's*, February, 1974, p. 44.

[2] Walter Lippmann, *Public Opinion* (New York: Macmillan, 1922), p. 81.

[3] David Krech, Richard Crutchfield, Egerton Ballachey, *Individual in Society* (New York: McGraw-Hill, 1962), p. 31.

[4] Mason Haire and Willa Grunes, "Perceptual Defenses: Our processes protecting an original perception of another personality," *Human Relations* 3 (1950), 403–12.

[5] Gordon Allport and Leo Postman, "The Basic Psychology of Rumor," in Wilbur Schramm, *The Process and Effects of Mass Communication*, 1st ed., (Urbana, University of Illinois Press, 1960), pp. 141–55.

[6] See especially K. Koffka, *Principles of Gestalt Psychology* (New York: Harcourt, Brace & Jovanovich, 1935) and F. C. Bartlett, *Remembering* (Cambridge: Cambridge University Press, 1932).

[7] Quoted in Krech, Crutchfield, and Ballachey, *Individual in Society* (New York: McGraw-Hill, 1962), p. 53.

[8] Maurice Bloch, *The Historian's Craft* (New York: Vintage Books), p. 49.

[9] Karl Wieck, "Systematic Observational Methods," in Gardner Lindzey, ed., *The Handbook of Social Psychology*, Vol. 2, 2nd ed. (Reading, Mass.: Addison-Wesley, 1968), p. 413.

[10] Herbert Jacobs, "How Big WAS the Crowd?" A paper presented at the California Journalism Conference, Sacramento, 24 February 1967.

[11] P. Schoggen, "Environmental Forces in the Everyday Lives of Children with Physical Disabilities." Unpublished manuscript, p. 56.

[12] Aristotle, *Aristotle's Psychology: A Treatise on the Principle of Life*, trans. by William A. Hammond (London: Swan Sonnenschein, 1902), p. 239.

[13] Kurt and Gladys Lang, "The Unique Perspective of Television and Its Effect: A Pilot Study" in Wilbur Schramm, *Mass Communications*, 2nd ed., (Urbana: University of Illinois Press, 1960), pp. 544–60.

[14] Elizabeth Jordan, quoted in S. Nowell-Smith, *The Legend of the Master* (New York: Harper & Row, 1948), p. 16.

[15] William L. Prosser, *Handbook of the Law of Torts* (St. Paul: West Publishing, 1964), p. 216.

[16] Jacobs, "How Big WAS the Crowd?" p. 9.

[17] Eugene J. Webb, Donald T. Campbell, Richard D. Schwartz, and Lee Sechrest, *Unobtrusive Measures* (Chicago: Rand McNally, 1966).

[18] David Riesman and Jeanne Watson, "The Sociability Project: A Chronicle of Frustration and Achievement," in P. E. Hammond, ed., *Sociologists at Work* (New York: Basic Books, 1964), p. 267.

[19] M. Henle and M. B. Hubble, " 'Egocentricity' in Adult Conversation," *Journal of Social Psychology* 9 (1938), 230.

[20] Leon Festinger, H. W. Reichen, and S. Schacter, *When Prophecy Fails* (Minneapolis: University of Minnesota Press, 1956), p. 240.

[21] Gerald Berreman, *Behind Many Masks,* Monograph No. 4 (Ithica, N.Y.: Cornell University Society for Applied Anthropology, 1962), p. 8.

[22] William F. Whyte, *Street Corner Society,* 2nd ed. (Chicago: University of Chicago Press, 1955), p. 304.

[23] Kurt and Gladys Lang, "Decisions for Christ: Billy Graham in New York City." In M. Stein, A. J. Vidich, and D. M. White, *Identity and Anxiety* (Glencoe, Ill.: The Free Press, 1960).

[24] Joyce Brothers, "The President and the Press," *TV Guide,* 23 September 1972, p. 7.

[25] Quoted in Mark L. Knapp, *Nonverbal Communication in Human Interaction,* p. 12.

[26] O. Pfungst, *Clever Hans, The Horse of Mr. Von Osten* (New York: Holt, Rinehart & Winston, 1911).

[27] Knapp, 5–8.

[28] Ibid., 64.

[29] Ibid., 18.

[30] Peter Farb, *Word Play* (Alfred A. Knopf, 1974).

Chapter 5—Using Libraries

[1] Seán O'Faoláin, "Speaking of Books: Facts of Life," *The New York Times Book Review,* 18 April 1965, p. 2.

Chapter 6—Central Sources

[1] Alfred Balk, "The Racial News Gap," *Saturday Review,* 13 August 1966, p. 53.

[2] Israel Shenker, "Oxford Dictionary To Get an Updating, Its First in 39 Years," *The New York Times,* 12 July 1972, p. 35 M.

[3] Tracy Early, "It Takes Only a Moment," *Saturday Review,* 13 September 1969, p. 6.

Chapter 7—Reporting on Research

[1] John P. Marquand, *Book-of-the-Month Club News,* January 1955, p. 1.

[2] Jacques Barzun and Henry F. Graff, *The Modern Researcher* (New York: Harcourt, Brace & World), p. 19.

Index